TOP ACCOUNTING ISSUES FOR 2006 CPE COURSE

D1396922

CCH Editorial Staff Publication

CCH INCORPORATED
Chicago

A WoltersKluwer Company

Contributors

Editor	Perry M. Henderson, CPA, MPA
Contributing Editors	Joseph V. Carcello, Ph.D., CPA CMA, CIA
	Teresa Dimattia, CPA
	Judith Weiss, CPA
	James W. Wetzler, Ph.D.
	Jan R. Williams, Ph.D., CPA
	Scott Taub, CPA
Production Coordinator	Gabriel Santana
Layout	Heather Jonas
	Laila Gaidulis
Production	Lynn J. Brown

This publication is designed to provide accurate and authoritative information in regard to the subject matter covered. It is sold with the understanding that the publisher is not engaged in rendering legal, accounting, or other professional service. If legal advice or other expert assistance is required, the services of a competent professional person should be sought.

ISBN 0-8080-1380-7

Printed in the United States of America

TOP ACCOUNTING ISSUES FOR 2006 CPE COURSE

Introduction

The accounting standards are always changing. Never has this observation more true than now. High profile accounting scandals have resulted in a slew of new standards and projects designed to repair damage and improve financial reporting.

CCH's Top Accounting Issues for 2006 Course helps CPAs stay abreast of the most significant new standards and important projects. It does so by identifying the events of the past year that have developed into hot issues and reviewing the opportunities and pitfalls presented by the changes. The topics reviewed were selected because of their impact on financial reporting and because of the role they play in understanding the accounting landscape in the year ahead. The topics examined in Top Accounting Issues for 2006 are:

- Revenue Recognition
- Business Combinations
- Pension Plans—Employers
- FAS 109: Accounting for Income Taxes
- Financial Instruments

Throughout the course you will find Study Questions to help you test your knowledge. Examples are located throughout to assist you with comprehension of the course material.

This course is divided into two Modules. Take your time and review both course Modules. When you feel confident that you thoroughly understand the material, turn to the CPE Quizzer. Complete one, or both, Module Quizzers for continuing professional education credit. Further information is provided in the Quizzer instructions on page 8.1.

October 2005

COURSE OBJECTIVES

This course was prepared to provide the participant with an overview of important developments affecting accounting. At the completion of the course, you will be able to:

- Differentiate situations in which the Completed Performance model of delivery is applied from those in which the Proportional Performance model is more appropriate.
- Recognize and account for liabilities in a business combination.
- Apply concepts of FAS 87 in recording entries for pension events.
- Analyze how to present temporary differences in financial statements.
- Identify the various types of financial instruments, including derivative instruments.

CCH'S PLEDGE TO QUALITY

Thank you for choosing this CCH Continuing Education product. We will continue to produce high quality products that challenge your intellect and give you the best option for your Continuing Education requirements. Should you have a concern about this or any other CCH CPE product, please call our Customer Service Department at 1-800-248-3248.

NEW ONLINE GRADING gives you immediate 24/7 grading with instant results and no Express Grading Fee.

The **CCH Testing Center** website gives you and others in your firm easy, free access to CCH print courses and allows you to complete your CPE exams online for immediate results. Plus, the **My Courses** feature provides convenient storage for your CPE course certificates and completed exams.

Go to **www.cchtestingcenter.com** to complete your exam online.

One **complimentary copy** of this course is provided with certain CCH Accounting publications. Additional copies of this course may be ordered for $25.00 each by calling 1-800-248-3248 (ask for product 0-0903-200).

TOP ACCOUNTING ISSUES FOR 2006 CPE COURSE

Contents

MODULE 1

MODULE 2

3 Pension Plans—Employers

4 FAS 109: Accounting for Income Taxes

5 **Financial Instruments**

MODULE 1 — CHAPTER 1

Revenue Recognition

LEARNING OBJECTIVES

Revenue recognition is a hot-button issue for users of financial statements, regulators, and standard setters. This has become apparent from a flurry of regulatory enforcement actions, involving improper recording, timing, or valuation of revenue, and from the AICPA's renewed emphasis on revenue recognition issues as a focus of auditing procedures. Getting the revenue into the right period is crucial. But the authoritative literature on this subject is both complex and widely dispersed among many sources. This chapter digests a variety of real-world applications into a single, practical discussion.

Upon completion of this chapter, the professional will be able to:

- Track the changes in accounting literature applied to how and when revenue is recognized.
- Advise clients how the four conditions for considering revenue earned and realizable are fulfilled.
- Differentiate situations in which the Completed Performance model of delivery is applied from those in which the Proportional Performance model is more appropriate.
- Apply the realizability criterion to address the requirement that the fee-generating revenue must be fixed or determinable before revenue is recognized.
- Consider the accounting consequences of the four categories of factors that might cause a fee to be variable.
- Analyze revenue recognition conditions using contractual and noncontractual terms.

OVERVIEW

Revenue. Earning it is the purpose of conducting business. It is the top line in the income statement. Having a lot of it is the key to entry to the Fortune 500 list. Deciding when to recognize it is a question that the accounting industry has wrestled with for a long time. Nevertheless, it is still one of the most difficult numbers in financial statements to get right.

That is where this course figures. It addresses comprehensively the key issues faced in revenue recognition. It describes the appropriate accounting for each issue and explains the reason for that accounting. The chapter also provides examples of key points and includes excerpts from the financial statements of public companies to illustrate major concepts and judgments.

A major reason to explore revenue recognition on a comprehensive basis is that looking at this topic as a whole, instead of issue-by-issue or transaction-by-transaction, makes it easier to understand the underlying principles behind revenue recognition. Given the plethora of accounting literature published, it is surprising that, for the most part, each source follows the same underlying concepts and principles as its counterparts. Looking at the body of revenue recognition guidance all at once, it is easier to see the common threads that run through it. Focusing on the underlying principles also can reveal the basic logic that causes seemingly inconsistent guidance. Although the same principles may be used to account for two or more revenue transactions, the facts and circumstances related to each transaction have a significant effect on the judgments related to applying those principles, and, ultimately, the accounting for those transactions.

WHY A CHAPTER ON REVENUE RECOGNITION?

Revenue Recognition Is Important to Financial Statement Users

Revenue-generating transactions are varied and can be extremely complicated. The way in which revenue is recognized can have a significant effect on the way a company's results of operations look, and the vast array of revenue-generating transactions that companies conduct ensures that this area of accounting will continue to generate new questions and new issues. Because of these realities, understanding how revenue is recognized is essential to understanding the financial statements a company issues.

The importance of revenue recognition to analyzing a company's performance has been in the forefront of the business world in the last several years. In fact, during the late 1990s, revenue was often viewed as the main driver of value of many companies, especially those that were Internet-based. Small changes in revenue often could lead to huge changes in the market value of those companies. Some pundits have attributed the steep stock price declines of so many publicly traded Internet companies, in part, to the fact that their revenue numbers were not repeatable, and, in some cases, misleading.

The Authoritative Literature Does Not Address All of the Issues

Despite the importance of revenue recognition to the financial statements of virtually all companies, the accounting literature addressing revenue recognition is not comprehensive or easy to follow. The literature is often criticized for being incomplete and overly complex, depending upon the transaction. More than 100 pieces of accounting literature address revenue recognition in one way or another. However, most of the guidance is narrow in scope and addresses only a particular issue or type of transaction. Due to a dearth of authoritative literature pertaining to certain issues and industries, industry practice forms the basis of revenue recognition for some transactions.

Revenue Recognition Is a Leading Cause of Financial Reporting Errors

The lack of comprehensive guidance, combined with the variety and complexity of revenue transactions, raised numerous issues in the area of revenue recognition. Although coverage of auditing standards is outside the scope of this course, it is worth noting that the AICPA considers revenue recognition to be so important that it has, in recent years, re-emphasized the necessity for auditors to look closely at it in privately held companies as well as in SEC registrants, particularly in connection with fraudulent financial reporting (SAS 99-*Consideration of Fraud in a Financial Statement Audit* (AU 316.41)).

In the arena of the publicly traded company, the SEC staff issued two reports in early 2003 that highlight revenue recognition as an area prone to problems:

- *Report Pursuant to Section 704 of the Sarbanes-Oxley Act of 2002* (the Section 704 Report); and
- *Summary by the Division of Corporation Finance of Significant Issues Addressed in the Review of the Periodic Reports of the Fortune 500 Companies* (the Fortune 500 Report).

In compiling the information in the Section 704 Report, the SEC staff studied enforcement actions filed during the period July 31, 1997, through July 30, 2002. Improper revenue recognition was the area in which the SEC brought the greatest number of enforcement actions during this period. The nature of the improprieties ranged from the improper timing of revenue recognition (e.g., improper recognition of revenue related to bill-and-hold sales and consignment sales) to fictitious revenue (e.g., falsification of sales documents and failure to consider side letter agreements) to improper valuation of revenue (e.g., failure to appropriately consider rights of return). Other revenue-related areas in which the SEC brought a significant number of actions were disclosure of related-party transactions and the accounting for nonmonetary and round-trip transactions.

The Fortune 500 Report resulted from the review of all annual reports filed by Fortune 500 companies by SEC's Division of Corporation Finance (Corp Fin). This report provides insight into areas commonly questioned by Corp Fin during its reviews of annual reports. Revenue recognition accounting policy disclosures was an area frequently questioned by Corp Fin. In many cases, Corp Fin requested that companies significantly expand their revenue recognition accounting policy disclosures. Industries in which these requests were common included computer software, computer services, computer hardware, communications equipment, capital goods, semiconductors, electronic instruments and controls, energy, pharmaceutical, and retail. The revenue-related topics involved in these requests included accounting for software, multiple-element arrangements, rights of return, price protection features, requirements for installation of equipment, customer acceptance provisions, and various types of sales incentive programs.

In addition, several other recent studies have shown that revenue recognition is the most common accounting issue that causes financial statement restatements. Several high-profile revenue restatements in the past several years have reinforced the focus of the investing public on revenue recognition. Although some of these restatements occurred because fictitious transactions were recorded (i.e., outright fraud), many others related to recording actual transactions incorrectly.

The findings in all of these reports illustrate the complexity of accounting for revenue and highlight the need for an entity to focus more attention on its revenue recognition accounting policy and the processes in place to record revenue.

The Authoritative Literature Is Changing

Largely in response to these problems, the SEC staff issued Staff Accounting Bulletin No. 101, *Revenue Recognition in Financial Statements* (SAB 101), in late 1999. SAB 101 was intended to summarize the SEC staff's views on the application of the existing revenue recognition guidance as well as to summarize that guidance. In addition to causing a number of companies to change their revenue recognition policies, SAB 101 also served to focus the attention of most every public company on revenue recognition. Even companies whose revenue recognition policies did not change as a result of the issuance of SAB 101 generally have paid more attention to their revenue recognition policies and procedures since the bulletin was issued.

This recent attention to revenue recognition has also resulted in a number of new projects being undertaken by various accounting standard-setters, including projects:

- Addressing the accounting and reporting for discounts and rebates.
- Providing guidance for transactions with multiple elements.
- Developing rules for whether certain items should be reported as revenues.

Various standard-setters are working on still more guidance, and, for the first time, the FASB has added a project to its agenda intended to provide comprehensive guidance on revenue recognition.

Tying the Literature Together

As noted earlier, the accounting literature that addresses revenue recognition is incomplete and spread across many different pronouncements. This makes it difficult for companies to identify the appropriate literature that either applies to, or provides analogous guidance for, a transaction. This chapter makes it easier to identify the appropriate literature to follow, or analogize to, by addressing the issues in a topical manner and providing references to the authoritative literature where appropriate.

STUDY QUESTION

---

1. What was the outcome of Staff Accounting Bulletin No. 101?

   a. It caused many companies to change their revenue recognition policies.
   b. Although it was important theoretically, it did not cause many companies to change their actual revenue recognition policies.
   c. Companies whose policies did not change as a result of the bulletin generally have not paid attention to its guidance.
   d. Public companies ignored the bulletin, but private companies have become more focused on revenue recognition issues.

BACKGROUND

The way in which revenue is recognized can have a significant effect on the way a company's results of operations will look. Additionally, the vast array of revenue-generating transactions that companies enter ensures that this area of accounting will continue to generate new questions and issues.

To address these questions and issues as they arise, financial statement preparers, auditors, and accounting standard-setters refer to the general principles and concepts on which accounting for revenue is based. As in other areas of accounting, these principles are set out in the FASB concept statements. For revenue recognition, the underlying concepts indicate that revenue should be recognized when it is both earned and either realized or realizable (CON 5, par. 83).

In many cases, applying the "earned and realizable" concepts is fairly straightforward, and no additional guidance is necessary for determining the appropriate point at which to recognize revenue.

EXAMPLE

The following scenarios represent straightforward applications of the "earned and realizable" concept:

Scenario 1: A restaurant's revenue generally is earned and realizable at the end of the meal, when it has been eaten and paid for by the diner.

Scenario 2: A retail store's revenue generally is earned and realizable when the customer pays for the merchandise at the cash register.

Scenario 3: A manufacturer's revenue generally is earned and realizable upon delivery for COD orders.

Scenario 4: Plumbers, lawn care providers, and many other service providers generally earn their revenue as they perform the related services, and get paid upon completion of those services.

These scenarios are all situations in which revenue is earned and realized at the same, or almost the same, time. In many other common and fairly simple transactions, however, the two events occur at different times. In some cases, revenue is realized before it is earned.

EXAMPLE

The following scenarios show cases in which revenue is realized before it is earned:

Scenario 1: Magazine subscriptions are often paid in advance. In this situation, the publisher realizes the revenue before any magazines are delivered. However, the delivery of the magazines is when the revenue is earned.

Scenario 2: Airlines generally require payment immediately upon the purchase of a ticket, thus realizing the revenue at that time. However, the revenue is not earned until transportation is provided.

In other cases, revenue is earned before it becomes realizable.

EXAMPLE

These scenarios show instances in which revenue is earned before it becomes realizable:

Scenario 1: A manufacturer may sell products on credit. The revenue in that situation is earned when the products are delivered. However, it may not be immediately realizable if the customer's ability to pay is in question.

Scenario 2: Certain retailers provide products to customers on a trial basis, wherein customers have no commitment to pay for the goods unless they keep them for a particular period of time. Although the earnings process may arguably be complete when the product is delivered, the revenue does not become realizable until the trial period lapses.

The common transactions just discussed are all circumstances in which the application of the "earned and realizable" concepts is easy to apply, without any additional guidance or interpretation. Because applying the guidance is so easy in many situations, the FASB and other accounting standard-setters have not provided additional guidance on applying these concepts to most transactions. Instead, guidance has been provided on how to apply the basic concepts to certain transactions in which applying those concepts is difficult, and other guidance has been provided on how certain common issues affect the application of the basic concepts. Thus, the applicability of most of the revenue recognition guidance that exists is limited to a small portion of transactions. Unfortunately, it has recently become clear that there are far more transactions for which these concepts are difficult to apply than the standard-setters have addressed.

SURVEY OF ACCOUNTING LITERATURE

The general principles to be met before revenue is recognized under U.S. GAAP are set forth in the FASB's conceptual framework. The purpose of the conceptual framework is to establish fundamental principles on which authoritative accounting literature will be based. The concept statements therefore are not intended to provide sufficient guidance to allow preparers to determine the proper accounting for a particular transaction. Rather, the concept statements are meant to provide a basis upon which the FASB, AICPA, and other accounting standard-setters can develop necessary guidance. The concept statements provide the goals that the more detailed standards are designed to achieve.

Basis of Revenue Recognition Guidance

For revenue recognition, those goals, as set forth in CON 5, paragraph 83, are that "recognition involves consideration of two factors, (a) being realized or realizable and (b) being earned, with sometimes one and sometimes the other being the more important consideration." This conceptual guidance has been unchanged since it was first issued by the FASB in 1984.

In many areas of accounting, the conceptual guidance is augmented by more specific guidance in the form of one or more Statements on Financial Accounting Standards (abbreviated by FAS and their individual numbers) that provide more detailed guidance on applying the concepts. Although much accounting literature deals with applying the basic concepts for revenue recognition to specific industries or transactions, the only general guidance on applying the basic concepts to transactions in general comes from SAB 101.

Table1.1 summarizes the accounting literature pertaining to revenue recognition.

Table 1.1. Listing of Applicable Literature

Standards Reference	Title
CON 5	Recognition and Measurement in Financial Statements of Business Enterprises
FAS 5	Accounting for Contingencies
FAS 13	Accounting for Leases
FAS 48	Revenue Recognition When Right of Return Exists
FAS 66	Accounting for Sales of Real Estate
FAS 71	Accounting for the Effects of Certain Types of Regulation
FAS 133	Accounting for Derivative Instruments and Hedging Activities
ARB 45	Long-Term Construction-Type Contracts
APB 10	Omnibus Opinion—1966, Installment Method of Accounting
SOP 81-1	Accounting for Performance of Construction-Type and Certain Production-Type Contracts

Standards Reference	Title
SOP 97-2	Software Revenue Recognition
SOP 00-2	Accounting by Producers or Distributors of Films
EITF D-96	Accounting for Management Fees Based on a Formula
EITF 01-8	Determining Whether an Arrangement Contains a Lease
EITF 01-9	Accounting for Consideration Given by a Vendor to a Customer (Including a Reseller of the Vendor's Products)
SAB 101	Revenue Recognition in Financial Statements, as Amended and Codified in SAB Topics 8A and 13
SAB 101 FAQ	Revenue Recognition in Financial Statements— Frequently Asked Questions and Answers

KEY CONCEPTS

The two concepts—earned and realized or realizable—are meant to ensure that (1) the company does not recognize revenue unless and until it has performed under the terms of the arrangement, thereby giving it the right to receive and retain payment as documented in the arrangement, and (2) the company will indeed receive and retain payment in a form that has value to it.

Earned

As stated in CON 5, "revenues are considered to have been earned when the entity has substantially accomplished what it must do to be entitled to the benefits represented by the revenues." This may be delivering goods, performing services, providing information, or any other activity for which one entity would pay another entity. The acts the seller performs to fulfill the earned criteria are termed the **earnings process.**

Thus, to meet the earned criteria, the earnings process must already have been completed, at least in part. In substance, revenue is earned when the seller has fulfilled its end of the bargain. This requirement is basically common sense. Until the company has performed a service, it should not recognize revenue related to amounts it will be paid in return for that performance. In most cases, the point at which revenue is earned is fairly clear from the terms of the transaction.

EXAMPLE

The following scenarios illustrate how transactional terms show the point at which revenue is earned:

Scenario 1: A lawn care service's revenue is earned when it mows the lawn.

Scenario 2: A restaurant's revenue is earned when the customer eats his or her meal.

Scenario 3: An automobile part manufacturer's revenue is earned when it delivers parts to its customers pursuant to orders.

Scenario 4: A car rental agency's revenue is earned via the passage of time as it allows a customer to use one of its cars.

Scenario 5: A grocery store's revenue is earned when the customer proceeds through the checkout line with groceries.

However, in many other transactions it is unclear when revenue has been earned.

EXAMPLE

These scenarios highlight how murky transactions become, making it unclear exactly when revenue has been earned:

Scenario 1: An executive recruiter performs many activities as part of a search, including contacting potential candidates, setting up interviews, and assisting in salary negotiations. However, it is not until the candidate has been hired that the customer sees the benefits of all of these activities.

Scenario 2: A sales agent performs many activities to line up purchasers of its customer's products. However, it is not until products are purchased that its customer sees the benefits of these activities.

In these situations, it is not immediately clear whether revenue is earned over time (e.g., the period over which the search for candidates or purchasers is performed), or only upon successful completion of all necessary activities (e.g., acceptance by an applicant or orders placed by a purchaser).

It is important to note that the completion of the earnings process may have nothing to do with the timing of the payments under the contract. For example, the receipt of a deposit or up-front fee in an arrangement does not indicate that revenue has been earned, even if the deposit or fee is nonrefundable. On the other hand, the fact that payment in an arrangement is not due for some period of time does not necessarily indicate that the revenue has not yet been earned.

STUDY QUESTION

2. In which of the following instances would it be most unclear when revenue has been earned?

    a. A clothing store's sale of a suitcoat
    b. A car rental agency's provision of a rental vehicle
    c. An executive recruiter's conduct of an employment search
    d. A lawn care service's provision of lawn-mowing services

Realized or Realizable

Revenue is considered to be realized or realizable when the seller receives cash from the customer or receives an asset, such as a note receivable, that is readily convertible into cash. In addition, the receipt of nonmonetary assets that are not readily convertible into cash also meets the realizability criterion as long as the fair values of such assets are readily determinable.

Much like the earned criterion, the requirement that revenue be realizable before it is recognized also seems to be common sense. If the company has not received a benefit from the arrangement, it would seem illogical to recognize the revenue. Also similar to the earned criterion, it is often easy to determine whether the realizable criterion has been met. In general, this occurs when either a cash payment is received or the customer becomes legally obligated to make such a payment because the seller has fulfilled its responsibilities under the contract.

However, many provisions can exist in arrangements that raise questions about the realizability of revenue. For example, when payment is received but the customer has a right of return, that right may raise realizability questions. The fee in other arrangements may be variable based on the outcome of one or more events whose outcome will not be known until after delivery or even until after initial payment. Again, this raises questions about the realizability of the arrangement fee.

Four Conditions for Recognition

The accounting literature that has been developed since the conceptual framework guidance was introduced has attempted to provide additional conditions for determining when revenue has been earned and is realizable. As previously mentioned, some of that literature is transaction-specific (e.g., SOP 00-2 on the licensing of motion pictures), and some of it is issue-specific (e.g., FAS 49, *Accounting for Product Financing Arrangements*, on product financing arrangements). In contrast, SAB 101 is more general in nature.

Although different pieces of literature use different terms to get their ideas across, all of the literature generally indicates that revenue is both earned and realizable when each of the following four conditions is met (SAB 101, Topic 13A1; SOP 97-2, par. 8; SOP 00-2, par. 7):

- Persuasive evidence of an arrangement exists.
- The arrangement fee is fixed or determinable.
- Delivery or performance has occurred.
- Collectibility is reasonably assured.

The intent of these four conditions is to provide circumstances that can be consistently evaluated in determining when revenue is both earned and realizable. There is a fair amount of useful guidance in evaluating these conditions in a variety of transactions. Although that guidance is often narrowly scoped, the guidance in each piece of literature follows concepts that are similar enough that general guidance can be developed related to those concepts, which can then be applied to almost all types of transactions.

> ### OBSERVATION
>
> Each of the four conditions must be met by the end of the accounting period during which it is proposed that revenue be recognized. Meeting the conditions after the end of the period—even if earnings have not yet been reported—is not sufficient to recognize revenue in the period in question. Instead, these situations should result in revenue recognition during the period in which the final condition is met.
>
> Meeting the revenue recognition conditions after the end of the period is a *Type II subsequent event*, as discussed in the *AICPA Professional Standards, Volume 1, U.S. Auditing Standards*, AU Section 560.05, "Subsequent Events." Type II subsequent events include "...those events that provide evidence with respect to conditions that did not exist at the date of the balance sheet being reported on but arose subsequent to that date. These events should not result in adjustment of the financial statements."

The analysis of whether collectibility is reasonably assured and persuasive evidence of an arrangement exists generally does not change significantly based on the type of transaction involved. Thus, this discussion of those conditions applies to all transactions.

In contrast, the analysis of the condition regarding the need for a fixed or determinable fee and, especially, the condition regarding delivery or performance, can differ significantly based on the type of transaction involved. This chapter contains a significant amount of guidance on these conditions.

PERSUASIVE EVIDENCE OF AN ARRANGEMENT

To determine whether the "earned" criterion has been met—in other words, to assess whether the seller has substantially completed what it has agreed to do—one must identify what obligations that seller has undertaken.

Functions of Persuasive Evidence

For this reason, revenue cannot be recognized until there is **persuasive evidence** of an arrangement. The existence of persuasive evidence of an arrangement ensures that the seller's obligations are identified. This, in turn, ensures an accurate analysis of whether the seller has fulfilled those obligations and earned the related revenue.

Persuasive evidence of an arrangement also helps to ensure that the realizability criterion is met, as it provides the legal basis on which the seller can demand payment from the customer. If no arrangement exists under which the buyer has agreed to pay the seller for performing under the contract, any revenue the seller believes he or she is owed may not be realizable, because the seller may not have a right to payment under the law.

What Constitutes Persuasive Evidence?

The persuasive evidence of an arrangement condition does not require any specific form of evidence to exist. Rather, the evidence that should exist before revenue is recognized is whatever evidence the company would normally use to document a sales transaction.

Many companies routinely use written contracts to document sales arrangements. For those companies, persuasive evidence of an arrangement generally would not be considered to exist until both parties sign the final contract. Thus, despite the fact that the seller may have delivered the products or services required and billed the customer, no revenue should be recognized if the final contract is still pending.

EXAMPLE

The following scenarios illustrate types of persuasive evidence of an arrangement:

Scenario 1: *Persuasive Evidence of an Arrangement adapted from SAB 101, Topic 13A2, ques. 1.*

FACTS: Company A has product available to ship to customers prior to the end of its current fiscal quarter. Customer Beta places an order for the product, and Company A delivers the product prior to the end of its current fiscal quarter. Company A's normal and customary business practice for this class of customer is to enter into a written sales agreement that requires the signatures of the authorized representatives of the Company and its customer to be binding. Company A prepares a written sales agreement, and its authorized representative signs the agreement before the end of the quarter. However, Customer Beta does not sign the agreement because Customer Beta is awaiting the requisite approval by its legal department. Customer Beta's purchasing department has orally agreed to the sale and stated that the contract will be formally approved the first week of Company A's next fiscal quarter. Company A expects that payment will be made on normal credit terms.

DISCUSSION: In view of Company A's business practice of requiring a written sales agreement for this class of customer, persuasive evidence of an arrangement would require a final agreement that has been executed by the properly authorized personnel of the customer. Customer Beta's execution of the sales agreement after the end of the quarter causes the transaction to be considered a transaction of the subsequent period.

Scenario 2: Persuasive Evidence of an Arrangement—Microstrategy Incorporated Form 10-K—Fiscal Year Ended December 31, 2002.

Product license revenue: The company recognizes revenue from sales of software licenses to end users or resellers upon persuasive evidence of an arrangement (as provided by agreements or contracts executed by both parties), delivery of the software, and determination that collection of a fixed or determinable fee is reasonably assured.

Other companies may use different methods of documenting sales transactions. If a company does not have a standard or customary business practice of using written contracts to document a sales arrangement, there would usually be other forms of written or electronic evidence to document the transaction. Such evidence might be as simple as a restaurant check, a cash register receipt, or a click on the "submit order" button on an Internet site (SAB 101, Topic 13A2, ques. 1).

The methods used to document sales transactions may vary from location to location within a company or based on the type of customer (e.g., corporate versus individual) or transaction (e.g., product versus service). If so, each transaction should be evaluated based upon the documentation that would be expected to exist for that type of transaction.

Scenario 3: *Different Evidence of Arrangement for Different Transactions—8X8, Inc. Form 10-K— Fiscal Year Ended March 31, 2003.*

For all sales, except those completed via the Internet, either a binding purchase order or other signed agreement provides evidence of an arrangement. For sales over the Internet, a credit card authorization serves as evidence of an arrangement.

In some instances, a company may enter into a transaction whose documentation is not consistent with the company's standard documentation for one reason or another. In these cases, judgment must be applied in assessing whether persuasive evidence of an arrangement exists. If a company that normally uses written contracts to document its arrangements delivers its product to a customer, receives payment from the customer, and receives notification of customer acceptance of the product, persuasive evidence of an arrangement may exist even if the formal contract was never signed due to the customer's desire for quick delivery.

DELIVERY

To ensure that the earned criterion is met, delivery or performance must occur before revenue is recognized. This requirement goes to assessing whether the obligations undertaken by the vendor in an arrangement have been completed. Each obligation is generically referred to as an **element** or a **deliverable**. Assessing whether the delivery or performance requirement is met occurs individually for each deliverable in an arrangement. However, when multiple deliverables exist, certain issues must be considered in allocating the arrangement fee to the individual deliverables.

Basic Models

Delivery of an element is considered to have occurred when the seller has fulfilled its obligations related to that element and the customer has realized the value of the element. Delivery of certain elements occurs all at once, whereas delivery of others occurs over a period of time. In fact, although an infinite variety of deliverables can be included in a revenue arrangement, delivery or performance is generally considered to occur for accounting purposes based on one of two models. The decision of which model to use is based on whether the vendor obligations are completed and value is transferred to the customer all at once or over a period of time.

The first model, referred to here as the **Completed Performance model,** is used when a single point in time can be identified at which the vendor performs its obligation. The second model, referred to here as the **Proportional Performance model,** is used when the seller completes the performance obligation and the customer receives value over a period of time. One of the most commonly used examples of the Proportional Performance model is the **Percentage of Completion** method of accounting for long-term construction contracts or other projects that span more than one accounting period, such as ship-building or certain defense contracts.

> **OBSERVATION**
>
> No matter which model is used, the delivery condition is not met until the vendor's obligation to the customer is fulfilled. Therefore, if the vendor hires a third party to fulfill the obligation, revenue cannot be recognized until the third party actually fulfills the obligation. Merely hiring an outside party to provide a deliverable to the customer does not constitute delivery, because hiring a third party does not provide value to the customer. That value is not provided unless and until the customer actually receives the deliverable.

STUDY QUESTION

3. Each obligation in assessing whether delivery of performance has occurred is known as a deliverable or, synonymously:
   a. A pledge
   b. A promise
   c. A stake
   d. An element

Choosing a Model

The choice of which model to use in determining when delivery has occurred is a key step in recognizing revenue. In some cases, identifying an appropriate model is easy because the performance pattern is clear. Other situations require significant judgment. Although some generalizations can be made about what kind of deliverables should be evaluated under each model, it is important to review the substance of each deliverable in determining when delivery occurs for that deliverable.

The following discussion focuses on individual deliverables because it is necessary to separately assess the delivery requirement for each deliverable in an arrangement. However, it is important to note that when an arrangement includes multiple deliverables, delivery of a particular item is generally not considered to have occurred if that deliverable does not have value to the customer on a standalone basis.

Products. Delivery of products is generally evaluated using the Completed Performance model, because the customer realizes all of the value at once—when the product is physically delivered. At that time, the vendor completes its entire obligation with respect to the deliverable. In fact, the Completed Performance model is sometimes referred to as the **product model.**

Although a manufacturer may take a number of actions related to an arrangement before delivery of the product, these actions generally do not provide value to the customer unless and until delivery occurs. Therefore, it is not usually appropriate to recognize revenue on a product sale under the Proportional Performance model as the product is manufactured. Delivery of a product is only evaluated under the Proportional Performance model when the arrangement qualifies for percentage-of-completion accounting. Products may also be evaluated under the Proportional Performance model when the arrangement involves a subscription fulfilled over time.

> **OBSERVATION**
>
> Situations may arise in which arrangements that purport to cover only the sale of products actually contain a lease. EITF 01-8 provides guidance to assist in determining whether an arrangement contains a lease. When an arrangement does contain a lease, the portion of the arrangement that represents a lease must be accounted for as such. This is the case even though the arrangement is not formally characterized as a lease. Given the differences between the models used to account for product sales and leases, determining that an arrangement that on its face is a sale of products but, in fact, contains a lease will likely have significant effects on the timing of revenue recognition. The provisions of EITF 01-8 are discussed later in this chapter.

Services. In many situations delivery of a service is generally evaluated using the Proportional Performance model because the vendor fulfills a portion of its obligations and the customer receives value as each part of the service is performed. As such, revenue is earned as each part of the service is performed as well. For example, a home health service that agrees to visit a patient once a week for a year should recognize a portion of the revenue with each visit (provided the other conditions for revenue recognition have been met). In other situations, when service is provided over a period of time, delivery may be considered to occur ratably throughout that period. For example, the fee in an arrangement to provide high-speed Internet access for one year would be recognized ratably throughout the year (provided the other conditions for revenue recognition have been met).

The correct model to use for some service transactions, however, is not so clear. For example, in certain service transactions, although the service is performed throughout a period of time, the customer realizes value only if and when the final act of the service is performed. This may be true for installation services because the customer may not realize any value from the installation until it is completed. Similarly, a sales agent would generally not be considered to have delivered services until the customer makes a purchase from the supplier. These types of services may be best evaluated under the Completed Performance model.

OBSERVATION

Situations may arise in which arrangements that purport to cover only the sale of services actually contain a lease. EITF 01-8 provides guidance to assist in determining whether an arrangement contains a lease. When an arrangement does contain a lease, the portion of the arrangement that represents a lease must be accounted for as such. This is the case even though the arrangement is not formally characterized as a lease. Given the differences between the models used to account for service transactions and leases, determining that an arrangement that on its face is a sale of services but, in fact, contains a lease will likely have significant effects on the timing of revenue recognition. The provisions of EITF 01-8 are discussed later in this chapter.

EXAMPLE

Scenario 1: *Different Models Applied to Different Contracts in Fixed-Fee Arrangements—Leapnet, Inc. Form 10-K—Year Ended December 31, 2000*

Based on the nature of fixed-fee arrangements, revenue is recognized using the Proportional Performance, Completed Performance, or the Percentage of Completion method. Revenue is recognized using the Proportional Performance method for arrangements that involve several deliverables being provided over time. Proportional performance is determined by relating the actual labor incurred to date to the company's estimate of total labor to be incurred on each contract. Revenue is recognized using the completed performance method for arrangements that are short term in nature and those for which substantial performance of the contract is not achieved until the final deliverable is provided. Revenue is recognized using the Percentage of Completion method for software development arrangements that require significant system customization. The percentage completed is determined by relating the actual labor incurred to date to the company's estimate of total labor to be incurred on each contract. These estimates are reviewed and revised periodically, and adjustments resulting from such revisions are recorded in the period in which the revisions are made.

Scenario 2: Other bases are commonly used in measuring percentages of completion in the construction, shipbuilding and aircraft building industries. These are: (1) engineering estimate, in which revenue is recognized usually at specific performance benchmarks—such as 10 percent complete when site grading passes inspection—that represent the engineers' best estimate of completion; (2) cost-to-cost, in which percentage of completion is measured by the percentage of costs incurred to date to total budgeted or projected costs.

Intellectual Property. Determining when to recognize revenue in licenses of intellectual property is often a matter of pinpointing when delivery has occurred, and, in many cases, whether delivery occurs at a point in time (the Completed Performance model) or over a period of time (the Proportional Performance model). For example, in a transaction involving the right to use copyrighted material for a two-year period, some practitioners would say that delivery occurs as soon as the license to the material begins and the customer has a copy of the material it can use; others would suggest that delivery occurs ratably during the two-year period for which the right to use the material is provided. For certain types of intellectual property transactions, industry- or transaction-specific accounting literature provides guidance on which model to use for assessing delivery. However, little literature addresses the issue for many types of intellectual property.

Leases. For certain transactions, the accounting literature addresses how to determine which model to use for the evaluation of delivery. One major category of transaction for which significant guidance exists is lease transactions. Lease transactions are primarily addressed in FAS 13, which specifies that the lessor should treat certain leases as operating leases and others as sales-type leases. Essentially, an operating lease is evaluated under the Proportional Performance model, with revenue generally being recognized ratably throughout the lease term. Conversely, delivery in a sales-type lease is determined under the Completed Performance model, with performance deemed to be completed upon the physical delivery of the item being leased.

An issue that has received attention recently is the definition of a lease contained in FAS 13. This issue arises when an arrangement that purports to be only a sale of products or services in effect contains a lease. Given the differences between the models used to account for product sales or service transactions and leases, determining that an arrangement that on its face is a sale of products or services, in fact, contains a lease will likely create significant effects on the timing of revenue recognition. To bring some clarity to the definition of a lease and, in turn, to assist in determining whether an arrangement contains a lease, the EITF provided guidance in EITF 01-8. This guidance builds on the principal concepts in the definition of a lease contained in FAS 13 and requires the consideration of the following characteristics in determining whether an arrangement contains a lease.

Only property, plant, or equipment (which includes only land and/or depreciable assets) can be the subject of a lease, and a lease only exists if fulfillment of the arrangement is dependent on the use of specific property, plant, or equipment (the property, plant, or equipment can be either explicitly or implicitly identified) (EITF 01-8, pars. 9–11).

A right to use property, plant, or equipment has been conveyed—and therefore a lease exists—if the purchaser/lessee has the right to control use of the underlying property, plant, or equipment. The right to control the use of the property, plant, or equipment exists if either of the following conditions exists:

- The purchaser/lessee (1) has the right to operate the subject assets (either itself or through directing others) in a manner it determines, or (2) has the ability or right to control physical access to the subject assets, while obtaining or controlling more than a minor amount of the output or other utility of the subject assets.
- The possibility is remote that another party or other parties will take more than a minor amount of the output or other utility of the property, plant, or equipment during the arrangement, and the price the purchaser will pay for the output is neither contractually fixed per unit nor equal to the current market price per unit as of the time of delivery of the output (EITF 01-8, par. 12).

EITF 01-8 also indicates that executory costs should be considered an element that falls within the scope of FAS 13, not as services that fall outside the scope of FAS 13.

If it is determined that an arrangement does contain a lease, the portion of the arrangement that represents a lease must be accounted for as such. This is the case even though the arrangement is not formally characterized as a lease.

Construction and Other Long-Term Contracts. Another type of transaction for which GAAP provides specific guidance on revenue recognition is construction and other long-term contracts. This guidance is included in ARB 45 and SOP 81-1. For arrangements that qualify for long-term contract accounting based upon the guidance in ARB 45 and SOP 81-1, the decision whether to use the Completed Performance or Proportional Performance model should be based on the factors set forth in those documents. For long-term contracts, the two models are referred to as the **Completed Contract** and **Percentage-of-Completion** methods, respectively.

EXAMPLE

The following scenarios illustrate the typical factors that must be taken into account when the practitioner chooses which model to use for assessing delivery of products and services.

Scenario 1: *Completed Performance-Value to Customer On Product Delivery*

FACTS: Company A manufactures and sells furniture. It has a standard product line and a catalog from which customers may choose various colors, fabrics, and finishes. Company A manufactures the furniture only after a customer places an order.

DISCUSSION: Company A performs several activities in fulfilling a customer order, including manufacturing the furniture and physically delivering it to the customer. However, the customer only receives value upon the actual delivery of the furniture. Therefore, delivery or performance is not considered to occur during the manufacturing of the furniture. Company A should evaluate delivery under the Completed Performance model.

Scenario 2: *Proportional Performance-Service Value to Customer Over Time*

FACTS: Company B charges users a fee for nonexclusive access to its website containing proprietary databases. The fee allows access to the website for a one-year period. After the customer is provided a user ID, there are no specific actions Company B must perform related to an individual customer. Rather, Company B must only continue to allow the customer access to the databases.

DISCUSSION: The only specific action Company B performs with respect to a customer is providing the customer a user ID. However, the customer receives value over the course of the year that access to the databases is provided. Therefore, Company B should evaluate delivery under the Proportional Performance model.

Scenario 3: *Mix of Product and Service-Value of Product on Delivery, Service Over Time*

FACTS: Company C provides telecommunications services and enters into an arrangement to sell its business customer a number of generic telephones and to provide basic telephone service for one year.

DISCUSSION: The customer receives some value from the arrangement when the telephones are delivered and also receives additional value throughout the year that service will be provided. Company C should therefore evaluate delivery of the telephones under the Completed Performance model and should evaluate delivery of the telephone service under the Proportional Performance model.

Scenario 4: *Completed Performance-Value of Service to Customer on Delivery*

FACTS: Company D provides training to corporate boards of directors on ways to carry out their responsibilities. When Company D acquires a new client, it spends time learning about the client company, its industry, and its management personnel, and then customizes the training course for that company's board of directors. Company D then delivers the training to the board during a day-long session.

DISCUSSION: Company D performs several services in the course of fulfilling its responsibilities, some of which involve the design of customer-specific content. However, the customer receives value only when the final act—the delivery of the training—occurs. Therefore, Company D should use the Completed Performance model to evaluate delivery for its transactions.

Scenario 5: *Choice of Product and Service/Product or Service-Value of Product on Delivery, Service Over Time*

FACTS: Company E publishes guidance on accounting for various transactions. Company E updates its materials once per year and prints a hard-copy book after each update. Customers may either purchase the most recent hard-copy version of the materials or purchase online access to the information for one year.

DISCUSSION: Customers who buy the hard-copy book receive value from the transaction when the book is delivered, and Company E has no further obligations once the book is delivered. However, online subscribers receive value throughout the year that access is provided, and Company E fulfills a portion of its obligation each day of the year. Therefore, the Completed Performance model is appropriate for sales of books, and the Proportional Performance model is appropriate for sales of online subscriptions.

STUDY QUESTION

4. Which publication provides guidance for determining which model to use for determining delivery in lease transactions?

a. FAS 48
b. FAS 13
c. FAS 71
d. SOP 00-2

Applying the Completed Performance Model

As noted earlier, the Completed Performance model is used when a single point in time can be identified at which the vendor completes its obligation. This point should coincide with the point in time at which the customer has realized value by obtaining an asset, the results of a service, or other benefits. In this model, the delivery criterion with respect to the element is met, in total, at that particular point in time. The Completed Performance model is therefore used when performance takes place all at once, or when it takes place over a period of time but value is not transferred to the customer until the final act is completed. When the Completed Performance model is used, the point in time at which performance is completed must be identified. Because all revenue is recognized at that time, large differences in revenue for a financial reporting period can occur based on whether delivery occurs just before or just after period-end.

In a product sale, performance is generally completed when the product is delivered to the customer. However, determining exactly when that occurs is not always straightforward. For example, when a product is shipped through the mail or by a third-party carrier, delivery may be considered to occur when the product leaves the seller's premises or when it arrives at the buyer's location, depending on the shipping terms. In other situations, although the product is physically delivered, a seller may retain certain risks and rewards that indicate that performance has not actually been completed, despite physical delivery. The resolution of these types of issues and uncertainties is required to appropriately apply the Completed Performance model to a product sale.

When the Completed Performance model is applied to a service transaction, it is generally because the final act of the service is the one that allows the customer to realize the benefits of the service. Therefore, in determining that the Completed Performance model is appropriate for a service, the point at which delivery is deemed to occur will already have been identified. In other transactions, the issues that are likely to be key to determining when to recognize revenue are similar to those in a product sale.

Applying the Proportional Performance Model

In the Proportional Performance model, revenue is recognized as performance occurs, based on the relative value of the performance that has occurred to that point in time. This model is therefore useful when the vendor fulfills its obligation over a period of time and the customer receives value throughout the performance period.

In applying the Proportional Performance model to a service transaction, the key issue is generally the pattern of performance. For example, if a service transaction involves a specified number of similar acts, such as mowing a lawn once a week for an entire summer, an equal amount of revenue should be recognized for each act. When the acts are not similar, however, revenue should be allocated based on their relative values. In other situations, value may be transferred to a customer ratably throughout a period, such as when the service is insurance coverage or access to a health club.

EXAMPLE

**Applying the Proportional Performance Model—
Castle Dental Centers, Inc. Form 10-K—
Year Ended December 31, 2002.**

Patient revenues from orthodontic services are recognized in accordance with the proportional performance method. Under this method, revenue is recognized as services are performed under the terms of contractual agreements with each patient. Approximately 25 percent of the services are performed in the first month, with the remaining services recognized ratably over the remainder of the contract. Billings under each contract, which average approximately 26 months, are made equally throughout the term of the contract, with final payment at the completion of the treatment.

STUDY QUESTION

5. In which of the following service examples would the Completed Performance model best apply?

   a. A monthly service contract to provide lawn maintenance
   b. A home health agency that agrees to provide weekly services to a patient throughout the course of a year
   c. An arrangement to provide online services and Internet access for one year
   d. An installation service

FIXED OR DETERMINABLE FEE

The requirement that the fee be fixed or determinable before revenue is recognized directly addresses the realizability criterion. For example, if the fee is dependent upon future events, it is not certain that it will indeed be paid. Therefore, a question arises whether the fee is realizable. However, a fee that is not fixed or determinable may also indicate that the revenue has not yet been earned, if the reason the fee is not fixed or determinable is that the seller is still required to perform in some manner.

Meaning of Fixed or Determinable

Although several pieces of accounting literature—including SOP 97-2, SOP 00-2, and SAB 101—refer to the need for the fee to be fixed or determinable before revenue is recognized, none of them provides a clear definition of what it means for a fee to be fixed or determinable. Instead, they use examples to illustrate certain concepts regarding a fixed or determinable fee.

Many arrangement terms raise questions about whether the fee is fixed or determinable. For example, customer rights of return or cancellation introduce uncertainty into the arrangement. Similarly, fees subject to change based upon the future success or failure of the work performed may indicate that a fee is not fixed or determinable. In addition, arrangements may have penalty or bonus clauses that introduce potential variability into the arrangements.

The answer as to whether a fee is fixed or determinable is not always an "all or nothing." In many arrangements, a portion of the fee is not subject to change for any reason, but another portion of the fee varies based on one or more factors. In these instances, the portion of the fee not subject to change should be considered fixed or determinable, even if the rest of the fee is not.

OBSERVATION

The requirement that a fee be fixed or determinable refers to whether the fee can vary based upon future events. In certain situations, although a fee cannot change based upon future events, it cannot be calculated until certain information related to past events is collated and evaluated. For example, consider an arrangement in which a company provides transaction-processing services and prices those services based on the number of transactions processed for a particular customer each month. At month-end, the fee cannot change based on future events, but the company may not yet have calculated the fee owed by every customer, because it may need to review monthly activity reports from its various locations to make such calculations.

In these situations, the fact that information about past events must be gathered and analyzed does not preclude a conclusion that the fee is fixed or determinable. Instead, the company should record its best estimate of the revenue at period-end and adjust that estimate when information is completely analyzed, allowing a precise determination of the fee. If this analysis is completed before the financial statements are released, its results should be incorporated into those financial statements.

> The analysis of information about events that occurred before the end of the accounting period is a *Type I subsequent event,* as discussed in *AICPA Professional Standards Volume 1, U.S. Auditing Standards,* AU Section 560.03, "Subsequent Events." Type I subsequent events include "...those events that provide additional evidence with respect to conditions that existed at the date of the balance sheet and affect the estimates inherent in the process of preparing financial statements....The financial statements should be adjusted for any changes in estimates resulting from the use of such evidence."

Evaluating Terms That Allow for Variable Fees

Some arrangements contain provisions that can cause the fees to change. These arrangements should be analyzed to determine whether all or part of the fee is fixed and determinable. The accounting literature provides little guidance on conducting such an analysis. However, by extrapolating from the guidance that does exist and applying some concepts that are prevalent in the accounting for various issues, it is possible to develop general provisions regarding the accounting consequences of various factors that might cause a fee to be variable.

To frame this discussion, the factors can be grouped into the following categories:

- **Factors in the customer's control.** These include general return rights and incentive fees based on the customer's usage of a product.
- **Factors in the seller's control.** These include certain forms of price protection and bonuses relating to cumulative performance over the term of a contract.
- **Factors in control of a specified third party.** For example, an agent's fee might be partially refundable based on whether the end customer exercises a right of return, or a lease agreement may require additional lease payments if the lessee exceeds certain sales levels (in this situation, the additional lease payments are in control of the lessee's customers).
- **Factors based on an index or other underlying variables.** These include fees based on investment return as compared to an index, fees that change with changes in the Consumer Price Index (CPI) or the inflation rate, and contingencies based on the weather.

Factors in the Customer's Control

General Rule. If an arrangement fee can be increased by future customer actions, the increase is not fixed or determinable until the customer takes such action. This would be the case if a vendor could receive a bonus based on the usage of a delivered product or a licensor of intellectual property were due a fee for each sale of a product incorporating the licensed technology. Thus, even if most customers do use the product in the manner specified, revenue could not be recognized until that usage occurs.

OBSERVATION

Arrangements like this may be specified in various ways to achieve the same result. For example, an arrangement could entitle the seller to a $20,000 bonus if the customer uses the product more than 20 times in the first year after the sale. Alternatively, the same economics could be created if the arrangement started with a $20,000 higher fee, and specified that a penalty of $20,000 would occur if the customer did not use the product more than 20 times in the first year after sale. Either of these arrangements should be accounted for as if the $20,000 at risk is not fixed or determinable unless and until the customer uses the product 20 times.

There are other situations in which a customer may be able to take actions or exercise rights that would reduce the amount of revenue ultimately realized by the seller. Volume or other rebates and rights of return are some examples. When a customer can take an action that would reduce an arrangement fee, the portion of the fee at risk should generally not be considered fixed or determinable. In other words, revenue in this type of situation should generally be recognized as if the customer will exercise the right or take the action that would reduce the arrangement fee. However, once the customer's right to take the action that would reduce the arrangement fee has expired, the additional revenue should be considered fixed or determinable.

Exception—Ability to Estimate Breakage. Although the general rule is that fees subject to change based on customer actions are not fixed or determinable, the fact is that there are many situations in which customers' actions with respect to certain rights can be predicted. In many cases, customers do not take advantage of the rights they have in an arrangement. This is called **breakage.** FAS 48, which addresses rights to return products, established that, in certain circumstances, it is appropriate to record revenue based on estimated breakage, as long as that estimate of breakage is a reasonable and reliable one. Using FAS 48 as an analogy, accounting standard-setters have expanded the ability to recognize revenue based on breakage estimates to other types of rights as well. Importantly, this exception applies only when the customer's future action would reduce the fee. That is, recognition of revenue based on anticipated breakage is only appropriate when the customer must affirmatively take some action to reduce the fee, and the fee will be higher if the customer takes no action.

Rights of Return. When a customer holds the right to receive a full refund by returning a product, a fixed or determinable fee would appear to be lacking. Indeed, some might also suggest that there is no persuasive evidence of an arrangement when the customer retains such optionality. Nevertheless, despite the existence of such rights, revenue can often be recognized before the right of return expires. These rights have been specifically addressed in FAS 48, which concludes that revenue may be recognized upon delivery in a sale with a right of return as long as a reliable estimate of returns can be made and certain other conditions are met. In general, if a company enters into a large number of homogeneous transactions, it will be capable of making such an estimate based on its historical experience. In that situation, the only revenue that must be deferred is the amount expected to be refunded.

Rights to Cancel Service Transactions. In some service transactions, a customer has a right similar to a product return right—that being the **right to cancel the remainder of the service and receive a full refund** (i.e., not just a refund based on the remaining service to be performed). This is common in the sale of certain memberships (such as warehouse club memberships), and may exist for a limited time in the sales of insurance policies, warranties, and similar items. Cancellation rights in service transactions are not covered in FAS 48, which is limited to product returns. However, the application of similar concepts to those in FAS 48 may allow a company to make reliable estimates of refunds or cancellations. If this is true, recognition of revenue with deferral of the amount expected to be refunded is acceptable, although not required.

> ### SEC REGISTRANT ALERT
>
> **Revenue Deferral in Breakage Situations**
>
> In Question 7 of SAB 101, the SEC staff expressed its views that, although recognition of revenue based on a reliable estimate of breakage may be acceptable, deferral of all revenue until the refund period ends is preferable in breakage situations.

Other service transactions may include a right to cancel the remainder of the service for a pro-rata refund (a refund of only a portion of the fee) based on the proportion of the service remaining to be provided. In these situations, the fee becomes fixed or determinable ratably throughout the service period, as the amount of the refund the customer could receive decreases. Because the service is also generally considered to be delivered on a proportional basis throughout the period, these types of cancellation rights generally do not cause further delays in revenue recognition.

STUDY QUESTION

6. Which of the following applies to FAS 48?

   a. Cancellation rights in service transactions are covered.

   b. Cancellation rights in service transactions are not covered.

   c. Service companies cannot apply concepts similar to those in FAS 48 to make reliable estimates.

   d. None of the above applies.

Coupons and Rebates. Certain revenue arrangements give the customer the ability to send in a form or other documentation of their purchase to obtain a full or partial rebate of the purchase price (for example, a $20 mail-in rebate packaged with a computer printer). In other arrangements, a vendor may sell products to a retailer and also issue coupons (for example, a newspaper coupon for 50 cents off a box of cereal) to the retailers' customers. In both of these instances, a portion of the fee from the sale can change after the seller has performed under the arrangement. In general, the existence of a coupon or rebate indicates that the portion of the purchase price subject to potential rebate or refund is not fixed or determinable.

Of course, redemption rates on coupons and rebates are much lower than 100 percent of the potential redemptions. In fact, newspaper coupon redemption rates rarely, if ever, exceed single-digit percentages. Therefore, in EITF 01-9, the EITF concluded that revenue potentially subject to rebate or refund may be recognized as long as a reliable estimate of breakage can be made. The following factors may impair a company's ability to make a reasonable estimate of coupon or rebate redemptions (EITF 01-9, par. 23):

- The offer period is long.
- Relevant historical experience is absent.
- There is no large volume of relatively homogeneous transactions.

Other sales incentives involve an offer to rebate or refund a specified amount of cash only if the customer completes a specified cumulative level of purchases or remains a customer for a specified time period. Similar to rebates that are exercisable based on a single purchase, revenue potentially subject to rebate may be recognized based upon estimates of breakage, if reliable estimates can be made.

In the case of either a rebate available based on a single purchase or a volume rebate, if a reliable estimate cannot be made, none of the revenue that is potentially subject to rebate is considered fixed or determinable. Thus, the revenue cannot be recognized until the rebate right lapses.

EXAMPLE

Estimate of Rebate Liability—*Symantec, Inc.*
Form 10-K—*Fiscal Year Ended March 28, 2003*

We estimate and record reserves as an offset to revenue for channel and end-user rebates, related primarily to products within our Enterprise Security, Enterprise Administration, and Consumer segments. Our estimated reserves for channel volume incentive rebates are based on distributors' and resellers' actual performance against the terms and conditions of volume incentive rebate programs, which are typically entered into quarterly. Our reserves for end-user rebates are estimated on the terms and conditions of the promotional program, actual sales during the promotion, amount of actual redemptions received, historical redemption trends by product and by type of promotional program, and the value of the rebate. We also consider current market conditions and economic trends when estimating our reserve for rebates. If we made different judgments or used different estimates, material differences might result in the amount and timing of our net revenues for any period presented.

Other Situations. The concept of reliably estimating breakage in order to overcome a situation that initially causes a fee to appear to not be fixed or determinable has only been addressed in the specific situations discussed above. Analogy to FAS 48, Question 7 of SAB 101, or EITF 01-9 may be appropriate in certain other limited situations.

However, no amount of evidence is sufficient to allow the recognition of revenue that will not be received unless customers take actions in the future. For example, if a fee in a license arrangement is $100 for a three-month license and the customer has an option to extend the license to one year for an additional $50, the $50 extension fee cannot be considered fixed or determinable until the option is exercised, no matter how strong the seller's evidence is that such extension will be exercised. In these situations, any additional revenue should not be considered fixed or determinable, and thus should not be recognized until the customer takes the specified actions.

Factors in the Seller's Control

In some cases, the fee in an arrangement may be variable based upon the seller's performance. For example, the fee in an arrangement to deliver a large amount of equipment may have fixed fees for the equipment, plus a bonus payment if the seller completes all deliveries (or a penalty if the seller does not complete all deliveries) within a particular period. In other situations, a seller may offer price protection to the buyer, agreeing to rebate a portion of the arrangement fee in the event that it subsequently sells the same product or service to another customer at a lower price.

General Rule. Much like factors in the customer's control, the fact that an arrangement fee is subject to change based on the seller's future actions often results in a conclusion that the fee is not fixed or determinable. For example, if a seller can earn a bonus by completing a service ahead of schedule, that bonus should typically not be recognized until the service is completed ahead of schedule and the bonus is earned.

> **OBSERVATION**
>
> Such performance-based arrangements may be specified in various ways to achieve the same result. For example, an arrangement could entitle the seller to a $20,000 bonus if the service is completed by a particular date. Alternatively, the same economics could be created if the arrangement started with a $20,000 higher fee, and specified that the seller would be penalized $20,000 if it did not finish by the same date. Either of these arrangements should be accounted for as if the $20,000 at risk is not fixed or determinable unless and until the project is completed by the specified date.

Exception—Ability to Predict or Control Actions. Because FAS 48 and the other literature discussed above provide exceptions that allow revenue to be recognized even though it is at risk due to future customer actions, it stands to reason that similar exceptions might exist for actions in the seller's control. In fact, it should generally require a lower threshold of evidence for a seller to conclude it can predict the results of its own actions, as opposed to those of its customers. Thus, if a vendor can reliably predict the results of its actions, it should recognize revenue based on those predictions. However, if a reliable estimate cannot be made—for example, because the arrangement in question is unique or contains different performance criteria than are typically included in the vendor's arrangements—revenue should be recognized assuming that the vendor's future actions will result in only the minimum potential revenue. The accounting literature provides specific guidance on this topic in certain situations.

Conditional Rights of Return. Revenue attributable to delivered items in an arrangement may be potentially refundable based upon whether the seller delivers all of the other items in the arrangement. In these cases, the customer right of return is conditional and will only exist if the seller fails to perform. As such, whether the customer obtains a right of return is in the seller's control.

Price Protection Based Solely on Seller's Prices. A seller may agree to refund a portion of the purchase price to its customers in the event of a decrease in the seller's standard selling prices. In these situations, the seller may be able to estimate the effects of that agreement, as it is in control of whether those prices are lowered. If that is the case, the vendor may conclude that the fee is fixed in whole or in part, due to its ability to determine whether prices are reduced and a refund triggered. However, if the vendor has shown an inability to predict price decreases or an inability to keep its prices at preferred levels, perhaps due to aggressive competition, the fee should not be considered fixed or determinable (SOP 97-2, par. 30).

Exception—Recognition Based on Current Measurements. In some cases, a service provider may agree to a fee calculated based upon a formula applied to a particular period of time. For example, a hotel manager may agree to a fee based partially on the operating income of the hotel for a calendar year, or a sales agent may be entitled to a bonus if he or she increases sales by a certain percentage compared to the prior year. In these situations, a question arises whether any portion of the incentive fee is fixed or determinable before the end of the measurement period. The SEC staff commented on this situation in the EITF Staff Announcement entitled "Accounting for Management Fees Based on a Formula" (EITF Abstracts Topic D-96), noting that it would accept a conclusion that such fees are determinable at any point in time based on the formula and contract terms as they would be calculated at that date, whether the vendor can predict the results of its future actions. However, the SEC staff also indicated that it preferred a conclusion that none of the incentive fee is fixed or determinable until the end of the measurement period.

> **OBSERVATION**
>
> In an arrangement in which a bonus or additional fee is earned only if a particular threshold is met, no part of the bonus or additional fee is fixed or determinable until the threshold is met, even if the progress to date indicates that the threshold will be met. Recognition at interim dates would be acceptable only if termination provisions exist calling for a final measurement based on progress to date (SAB 101, Topic 13A4, ques. 8).

> **EXAMPLE**
>
> **Accounting for Fees Based on a Formula**
>
> **FACTS:** Investment Advisor A manages Fund B and is paid a flat fee per month, plus 20 percent of Fund B's returns in excess of 12 percent annually. The contract is terminable by either party with reasonable notice at the end of each quarter. In the event of a termination, the amount due for the incentive fee will be calculated at the termination date based on the fund returns to date compared to a 12 percent annual return pro-rated for the portion of the year that has passed.

Assume that Fund B's returns exceed 3 percent (one-quarter of the 12 percent annual target) by $120,000 in the first quarter, $60,000 in the second quarter, and $50,000 in the fourth quarter, and that the return on the fund is $80,000 less than the 3 percent target in the third quarter. Thus, the total return of Fund B for the year exceeds the 12 percent target return by $150,000. Advisor A's share of the $150,000 is $30,000.

DISCUSSION: Advisor A may choose from two accounting policies. The first would be to recognize no incentive fee revenue until the end of the one-year measurement period, under the theory that none of the incentive fee is fixed or determinable until then, as future poor performance in a subsequent interim period could cause the loss of incentive fee revenue earned in a prior interim period. This method, which is preferred by the SEC staff, would result in the recognition of $30,000 in incentive fee income on the last day of the year.

The second method would record as incentive fee revenue the amount that would be due under the formula at any point in time as if the contract was terminated at that date. Accordingly, Advisor A would record $24,000 of incentive fee revenue in the first quarter and $12,000 in the second quarter. In the third quarter, however, $16,000 of the previously recognized revenue would be reversed. Finally, $10,000 of incentive fee revenue would be recognized in the fourth quarter.

STUDY QUESTION

> **7.** Which of the following is an example of a factor that might cause a fee to be variable, which is in the seller's control?
>
> **a.** Changes in the inflation rate
> **b.** Incentive fees based on customer usage
> **c.** An agent's fee that is partially refundable based on the end customer exercising the right of return
> **d.** Price protection and bonuses relating to cumulative performance during the term of the contract

Factors in Control of a Third Party

Certain contracts include clauses that provide for a variable fee based on actions of a party other than the buyer or seller. Agency arrangements often include these clauses. For example, a sales agent may agree to refund its commission if the end customer returns the product. Alternatively, the agent may receive a bonus if a customer that the agent introduces to the supplier makes additional purchases from the supplier or renews his or her subscription. Another common situation in which third-party actions may affect a company's revenue arises in leases that have contingent rentals based on the lessee's sales. Other arrangements, particularly if they are long-term in nature, may contain pricing terms that change if there are changes in tax law or industry regulations.

General Rule. Third-party actions are likely to be even more difficult to predict than customer actions. As such, it is not appropriate to assume that third parties will take actions resulting in additional payments from the customer to the vendor in an arrangement. Furthermore, if a third party can take an action that reduces a company's revenue, it is generally appropriate to assume the third party will take such action.

For example, the lessor in an operating lease that includes additional rent if sales exceed a certain level should not recognize that additional rent until the specified level of sales is reached, even if sales trends indicate that such level will be reached. Similarly, an agent whose fee is at risk if the end customer cancels its arrangement with the seller should generally not recognize the fee as revenue until the end customer's cancellation right lapses.

Exception—Ability to Estimate Breakage, Cancellation, and Return Rights. As much as it is often possible to estimate breakage with respect to customer rights, it may be possible to estimate breakage with respect to certain third-party return or cancellation rights. And like the accounting when breakage of customer return and cancellation rights can be reliably estimated, revenue can be recognized despite the existence of third-party cancellation and return rights, as long as the amount of refunds can be reliably estimated. The same characteristics that make reliable estimates possible in these situations also make estimating breakage with respect to potential cancellations of other service transactions possible.

Price-Matching. Certain retailers, such as electronics stores, routinely offer a form of price protection based on their competitors' prices. These stores may offer to refund the difference between the price paid by a customer and a lower price on the same product offered by a competitor within the next 30 days. Unlike price protection based only on the particular vendor's future prices, estimating the effects of a price-matching offer is likely to be difficult. However, if a sufficient history exists and the competitive environment is stable, it may be possible to estimate the effects of a price-matching policy. If reliable estimates can be made, revenue may be recognized net of expected price-matching payments. If a reliable estimate cannot be made, as is likely to be the case, no revenue should be recognized until the price-matching period ends.

EXAMPLE

Third-Party Actions and Fixed or Determinable Fees—
(Adapted from SAB 101 FAQ, ques. 18)

Scenario 1: A leasing broker's commission from the lessor upon a commercial tenant's signing of a lease agreement is refundable under lessor cancellation privileges if the tenant fails to move into the leased premises by a specified date.

Scenario 2: A talent agent's fee receivable from its principal (a celebrity) for arranging an endorsement for a five-year term is cancelable by the celebrity if the customer breaches the endorsement contract with the celebrity.

Scenario 3: An insurance agent's commission received from the insurer upon selling an insurance policy is entirely refundable for the 30-day period required by state law and then refundable on a declining pro-rata basis until the consumer has made six monthly payments.

DISCUSSION: In all of these cases, there is the potential for the arrangement fee to vary based upon the actions of a third party named in the contract. Thus, absent a large volume of homogeneous transactions sufficient to allow a reliable estimate of the effects of these rights to be made, the fee in question should only be recognized as the third party takes actions or its right to take actions that affect the arrangement fee lapses.

In Scenarios 1 and 2, it is highly unlikely that such a large volume of homogeneous transactions would exist to allow a reliable estimate of cancellations, because the nature of the transactions would generally cause each one to be unique.

However, in Scenario 3, it may be possible that such a history exists. The company should therefore evaluate whether it has sufficient evidence to make a reliable estimate of cancellations, thereby allowing the recognition of revenue net of expected cancellations. If sufficient history does not exist, no revenue should be recognized until the 30-day full-refund period has lapsed. The revenue will then become fixed or determinable on a ratable basis until the customer has made six payments.

Exception—Regulators' Approval of Rate Increases. In some cases, a regulated company such as a utility is permitted to bill requested rate increases before the regulator has ruled on the request. The fact that the regulator has the power to deny the request raises a question about whether the increased rates are fixed or determinable. The FASB addressed this question in the context of regulated businesses that are within the scope of FAS 71. The FASB concluded that, in these situations, contingent refundability should be treated as a collectibility issue, rather than a fixed or determinable issue. Thus, the criteria in paragraph 8 of FAS 5 would determine whether a provision for estimated refunds should be recognized.

Exception—Fees at Risk Due to Changes in Law or Regulation. When the third-party action that could change the arrangement fee is a change in a law or regulation, it is generally appropriate to predict no such changes. Thus, revenue would be recognized as if the current laws and regulations would continue. For example, FAS 109, *Accounting for Income Taxes,* in providing guidance on the effects of potential changes in tax law on income tax calculations, specifically prohibits the assumption of any changes until those changes are enacted into law. Similar analysis would generally be appropriate with respect to other changes in laws or regulations. However, if changes that would result in a reduced fee are considered probable, a reserve for refunds might be required under FAS 5.

Other Exceptions. Other exceptions to the general conclusion that the portion of a fee subject to change based on third-party actions is not fixed or determinable would be rare. However, if the unique circumstances of the arrangement make it remote that the portion of the fee at risk will actually be lost, it may be possible to conclude that the fee is fixed or determinable despite the existence of the contingency. Each situation should be addressed individually to determine whether this is the case.

EXAMPLE

Fee May Vary Based on Third-Party Actions

FACTS: Company X acts as a sales representative for Company Y. Company X's commission is earned on a sliding scale such that its commission on the first 10,000 units of Company Y's products sold in a year is $5 per unit, and the commission for each unit beyond that is $7 per unit. Company X has been selling Company Y's products for several years and has always sold at least 20,000 units. At the end of the first quarter, Company X has sold 5,000 units of Company Y's product, and collected $25,000 from Company Y. Company X believes that it will sell approximately 5,000 units per quarter for the rest of the year.

DISCUSSION: Company X believes that it will eventually realize $120,000 in commissions during the year (10,000 units at $5, plus another 10,000 units at $7), an average of $6 per unit, and has historical experience that supports this estimate. Therefore, Company X may believe that it should record a receivable of $5,000 at the end of the first quarter, in addition to the revenue it has already collected. However, whether Company X meets its estimated sales is at least partially in control of third parties, that is, the customers who purchase Company Y's product. As such, the additional revenue is not fixed or determinable. Company X should therefore recognize only the $25,000 it has collected as revenue in the first quarter. Revenue attributable to additional sales should be recorded only when those sales occur.

STUDY QUESTIONS

8. Which of the following statements is correct regarding factors under the control of a third party?
   a. Third-party transactions are more difficult to predict than customer actions.
   b. It is generally inappropriate to assume that a third party will take an action to reduce a company's revenue if it is able to do so.
   c. An agent whose fee is at risk if the end customer cancels its arrangement with the seller should recognize the fee as revenue before the end customer's cancellation right ends.
   d. Third-party actions are easier to predict than customer actions.

9. Which of the following standards specifically prohibits the assumption of any potential changes in tax law or income tax calculations until those changes are enacted into law?
   a. FAS 66
   b. FAS 109
   c. FAS 133
   d. FAS 5

Factors Based on an Index

Many leases have **rent escalation clauses** tied to the inflation rate or Consumer Price Index. Certain arrangements to deliver commodities include fees that are based on the market price of the commodity at some particular point in time. These are just two illustrations of factors that are not related to particular actions that may cause an arrangement fee to be variable. In general, these factors are characterized by being outside of any party's direct control.

OBSERVATION

Indexed arrangements should be evaluated to determine whether a derivative is embedded in the sales arrangement. Some arrangements that are not derivatives in their entirety are embedded with features that have all three defining characteristics of a derivative. Depending on their nature and their relationship to the economics of the remainder of the arrangement, such embedded features may have to be accounted for separately, similar to a freestanding derivative. If that circumstance exists in a sales arrangement, the separated derivative is subject to all of the accounting requirements for a freestanding derivative, and the remaining host arrangement is accounted for based on the applicable revenue recognition principles. To the extent a sales arrangement contains fees that are affected by factors based on an index, FAS 133 should be consulted to determine whether the arrangement contains an embedded derivative and, if so, how that derivative should be accounted for.

Much like fees that vary based upon future actions of the vendor, the customer, or a third party, fees that vary based upon future changes in an index or other underlying factor may not be fixed or determinable, because it is not appropriate to recognize revenue based on predictions of future events. As discussed previously, there are cases in which it is permissible to recognize revenue based on predictions of future customer, seller, or third-party actions if a sufficient body of evidence exists such that reliable estimates can be made. It is generally not possible to have such evidence related to future changes in an index or other underlying factor.

Therefore, revenue should be recognized in these situations based on the then-current measurement, assuming no future increases or decreases. The effects of changes in the index or underlying should be recognized as soon as such changes occur (FAS 13, par. 5n).

Fees Affected by Multiple Factors

Many arrangements have fees that can vary based on multiple factors, each of which may be in control of a different party or tied to a different index. In general, each factor should be evaluated separately, with revenue being recognized only if it is concluded that none of the factors preclude the fee from being considered fixed or determinable.

COLLECTIBILITY

The final condition that must be met before revenue is recognized is that collection of the fee must be reasonably assured. This condition gets to the heart of whether the fee in the arrangement is indeed realizable. Clearly, if a fee is not collectible, no revenue should be recognized, as the company does not actually expect to benefit from the arrangement.

The accounting literature does not specify any particular criteria to use in evaluating whether collection is probable. However, the same factors that are evaluated when one records a bad debt reserve on accounts receivable should be useful as one determines whether collection of an arrangement fee is reasonably assured. This evaluation should be performed as soon as the other three conditions for revenue recognition are met.

Accounting If Collectibility Is Not Reasonably Assured

If collectibility is not reasonably assured at the time the other three revenue recognition conditions are met, revenue should not be recognized until collection becomes reasonably assured or occurs. In general, the direct costs of the transaction should be expensed as if revenue had been recognized. Because collection has been deemed less than probable, such costs generally would not meet the definition of an asset. Therefore, they should not be capitalized or remain on the balance sheet.

In rare circumstances, recognition of revenue and costs under the installment or cost recovery method may be appropriate (APB 10, par. 12)—for example, if recovery of the value of the goods sold in a product sale is reasonably assured even though collectibility of the arrangement fee is not. However, the use of these methods is usually limited to sales of real estate (FAS 66, par. 22).

EXAMPLE

Collectibility Not Reasonably Assured—*Covad Communications Group, Inc.* Form 10-K—*Fiscal Year Ended December 31, 2002*

Some of the company's ISP and telecommunications carrier customers are experiencing financial difficulties. During the years ended December 31, 2002, 2001, and 2000, certain of these customers either (1) were not current in their payments for the company's services or (2) were essentially current in their payments but, subsequent to the end of the reporting period, the financial condition of such customers deteriorated significantly and certain of them have filed for bankruptcy protection. Based on this information, the company determined that (1) the collectibility of revenues from these customers was not reasonably assured or (2) its ability to retain some or all of the payments received from certain of these customers that had filed for bankruptcy protection was not reasonably assured. Accordingly, the company classified this group of customers as "financially distressed" for revenue recognition purposes. Revenues from financially distressed customers that have not filed for bankruptcy protection are recognized when cash for those services is collected—assuming all other criteria for revenue recognition have been met—but only after the collection of all previous outstanding accounts receivable balances. Payments received from financially distressed customers during a defined period prior to their filing of petitions for bankruptcy protection are recorded in the consolidated balance sheet caption "unearned revenues" if the company's ability to retain these payments is not reasonably assured.

Uncollectible Amounts and Bad Debts

It is important that collectibility be evaluated before revenue is initially recognized so that collectibility problems that existed before revenue recognition can be separated from similar problems that arise later. If collection is reasonably assured initially, allowing revenue to be recognized, and later events necessitate an accounts receivable reserve or write-off, the related expense should be reported as bad debt expense, which may be classified in various places in the income statement.

EVALUATING THE REVENUE RECOGNITION CONDITIONS

Arrangement-by-Arrangement Analysis

In evaluating whether the four conditions discussed in this chapter are met, it is important to consider all aspects of the arrangement. The contracts underlying the arrangement should be reviewed in full to ensure that all contractual terms are properly considered.

For most companies, this review should begin with the company's standard sales contracts. However, any modifications to the standard contract must also be evaluated for their effects on revenue recognition. Modifications from the standard contract could require a company to recognize revenue differently for different contracts. For example, if a company sells products with different FOB terms, revenue on those shipped FOB Shipping Point may generally be recognized upon shipment, whereas revenue on those shipped FOB Destination may not be recognized until the customer receives the products. Similarly, different customer acceptance provisions or cancellation rights in various contracts may cause otherwise similar contracts to be accounted for differently.

> **OBSERVATION**
>
> Many provisions can affect the timing of revenue recognition. Companies should therefore have controls in place to limit the types of provisions that sales personnel agree to add to the standard contract. In addition, controls should be in place to ensure that all sales contracts are reviewed by accounting personnel who can appropriately evaluate whether any nonstandard terms in the contract should affect revenue recognition.

All Contractual Terms Must Be Considered

Some companies may use contracts that contain terms generally ignored in practice, despite their inclusion in the contract. For example, a contract may provide a customer with the right to have an equipment vendor's engineering staff on-site for a limited period of time after installation of the equipment. However, as long as installation goes smoothly, customers typically do not take advantage of this right. In other situations, an arrangement may provide the customer with the right to a certain amount of service, but history may show that customers, on average, do not use the maximum amount of service to which they are entitled. This is the case in wireless telephone plans that include a basket of monthly minutes.

In most situations, delivery should be evaluated under the assumption that the vendor will have to fulfill all of its obligations under the arrangement, including those that are only to be performed if requested by the customer. However, if the company has significant historical experience with a large volume of homogeneous contracts that include similar terms, and that experience allows the company to reliably estimate breakage, it is acceptable to recognize revenue assuming that such breakage will occur. It is important to note that there must be significant objective evidence available to support a conclusion that obligations will not have to be fulfilled. Rarely does a company have such evidence.

SEC REGISTRANT ALERT

Breakage in Nonrefundable Prepaid Arrangements

In a December 2002 speech, the SEC staff discussed the issue of breakage as it arises in situations where customers prepay, on a nonrefundable basis, for services or goods that they ultimately do not demand. The SEC staff observed that FAS 140, *Accounting for Transfers and Servicing of Financial Assets and Extinguishments of Liabilities—a Replacement of FASB Statement No. 125,* requires either performance or legal release to extinguish a liability. The prepayment for future delivery of services or goods creates a liability. Following a FAS 140 approach would result in no recognition of income for products or services paid for, but not demanded by the customer, until the end (or expiration) of the performance period. Alternatively, the SEC staff indicated that they will not object to revenue recognition prior to the expiration of the performance period provided the following conditions exist:

- Management can demonstrate that the demand for future performance is remote based on a large population of homogeneous transactions.

- There is objective reliable historical evidence supporting the estimate of breakage.

The SEC staff also indicated that (a) it would be skeptical of an accounting model that results in immediate income for breakage and (b) whether breakage represents revenue or a gain (i.e., other income) depends on the facts and circumstances.

Even if sufficient evidence exists to estimate breakage, it should be an extremely rare occurrence that consideration of breakage results in immediate income recognition. Instead, the arrangement fee should be recognized based on the products or services expected to be delivered to the customer throughout the performance period.

For example, consider a situation in which a customer prepays $10,000 for 100 hours of professional services to be provided over the course of one year, but the professional services provider has sufficient history and experience demonstrating that the customer will ultimately demand only 80 hours of professional services during the performance period. In this situation, the professional services provider may adopt an accounting policy that would result in recognizing the $10,000 of revenue throughout the 80 hours of services expected to be provided as they are rendered—$125 per hour of service rendered. Alternatively, the professional services provider may adopt an accounting policy that would result in recognizing $8,000 of revenue throughout the 80 hours of services expected to be provided as they are rendered and recognizing $2,000 of breakage income upon expiration of the arrangement. However, the professional services provider may not adopt an accounting policy that would result in recognizing $2,000 of breakage income upon initiation of the arrangement and $8,000 of revenue throughout the 80 hours of services expected to be provided as they are rendered. To do so would be to recognize revenue before performance has occurred.

EXAMPLE

Reliable Estimate of Breakage—*Learning Tree International, Inc.* *Form 10-K—Fiscal Year Ended September 30, 2002*

The company offers its customers a multiple-course sales discount referred to as a "Training Passport," which allows an individual passport holder to attend up to a specified number of the company's courses during a one-year period for a fixed price. For a Training Passport, the amount of revenue recognized for each attendance in one of the company's courses is based upon the selling price of the Training Passport, the list price of the course taken and the estimated average number of courses passport holders will actually attend. Upon expiration of a Training Passport, the company records the difference, if any, between the revenues previously recognized and the Training Passport's selling price. The estimated attendance rate is based upon the historical experience of the average actual number of course events that Training Passport holders have been attending. The average actual attendance rate for all expired Training Passports has closely approximated the estimated rate used by the company. If the Training Passport attendance rates change, the revenue recognition rate for all active Training Passports and for all Training Passports sold thereafter is adjusted.

The company believes it is appropriate to recognize revenues on this basis in order to more closely match revenue and related costs, as the substantial majority of its Passport holders do not attend the maximum number of course events permitted. The company believes that the use of historical data is reasonable and appropriate because of the relative stability of the average actual number of course events attended by the tens of thousands of Passport holders since the inception of the program in fiscal 1993. Although the company has seen no material changes in the historical rates as the number of course titles has increased, it monitors such potential effects.

In general, determining the estimated average number of course events that will be attended by a Training Passport holder is based on historical trends that may not continue in the future. These estimates could differ in the near term from amounts used in arriving at the reported revenue.

Multiple Contracts and Side Letters

Most of the time, the boundaries of an arrangement are clear and are defined by the contract between the parties. However, to ensure that all appropriate terms are considered in recognition of revenue for an arrangement or deliverable, it may be necessary to consider multiple contracts as part of a single arrangement. For example, a contract for the sale of products may not lay out any rights of return. However, a master supply agreement with the same customer may grant that customer significant return rights on all purchases.

In other situations, a company may enter into a side letter arrangement with the customer that effectively amends the contract between the parties by granting the customer additional rights, requiring the seller to provide additional products or services, or altering the payment terms. Obviously, any revenue accounting that does not consider such a side letter would likely reflect incorrect conclusions.

SEC REGISTRANT ALERT

Side Agreements

In early 2003, the SEC staff issued the *Report Pursuant to Section 704 of the Sarbanes-Oxley Act of 2002* (the Section 704 Report). In compiling the information in the Section 704 Report, the SEC staff studied enforcement actions filed during the period July 31, 1997, through July 30, 2002. The greatest number of enforcement actions brought by the SEC related to improper revenue recognition. A common theme in these enforcement actions related to the existence of side letters that were not considered, or inappropriately considered, in recognizing revenue. This is a strong indication that more attention should be given to uncovering the existence and understanding the terms of side agreements and the effects they have on revenue recognition.

Noncontractual Terms

Although all of the rights and obligations of both parties to a revenue arrangement are often contractually documented, there are other situations in which rights and obligations are established by common business practice, local law, or custom. For example, rights of return are often not specifically documented in a sales arrangement, but are often accepted for a limited time if the customer is not satisfied. Similarly, even products that are not covered by a written warranty will often be replaced or repaired by the seller if they do not function properly. All such rights and obligations should be considered in the recognition of revenue.

STUDY QUESTION

10. Rights and obligations that are established by common business practice, local law, or customer are most accurately defined by the term:

  a. Assumed terms
  b. Customary terms
  c. Noncontractual terms
  d. Nondefinable terms

CONCLUSION

The proper recognition of revenue in financial statements is coming under increasing scrutiny by the investing public, and by regulators and standards-setting bodies. This is evidenced by the ever-expanding body of regulatory pronouncements, accounting standards, and auditing standards that touch upon this area. As this chapter's discussion shows, the timing and valuation of revenue can be subtly nuanced and subject to estimates that involve high degrees of professional judgment. For these reasons, accountants who prepare financial statements—whether for publicly traded or privately held enterprises—and their auditors, should revisit this body of literature periodically and carefully consider its application in current practice.

MODULE 1 — CHAPTER 2

Business Combinations

LEARNING OBJECTIVES

Business combinations present accounting challenges. This is especially true in recent years because of the numerous mergers and acquisitions that have occurred. This chapter provides advanced in-depth coverage of the many specialized situations covered in Levels B and C GAAP for business combinations. FAS 141, *Business Combinations*, the primary source of Level A GAAP, is summarized in the Overview. Readers should have familiarity with its content in order to place the remaining portions of this chapter in context.

Upon completion of this chapter, the professional will be able to:

▣ Recognize and account for liabilities in a business combination.

▣ Account for deferred taxes on in-process research and development activities.

▣ Perform valuation of debt assumed in a business combination.

▣ Understand new basis accounting.

▣ Understand accounting issues for business combinations of entities under common control.

OVERVIEW

A **business combination** occurs when two or more entities combine to form a single entity. An **asset combination** results when one company acquires the assets of one or more other companies, or when a new company is formed to acquire the assets of two or more existing companies. In an asset combination, the target companies cease to exist as operating entities and may be liquidated or become investment companies. An **acquisition** or **stock combination** occurs when one company acquires more than 50 percent of the outstanding voting common stock of one or more target companies, or when a new company is formed to acquire controlling interest in the outstanding voting common stock of two or more target companies.

Until 2001, two basic methods of accounting existed for business combinations: (1) the purchase method and (2) the pooling-of-interests method. In 2001, the FASB issued FAS 141, *Business Combinations,* which eliminated the pooling-of-interests method.

In a purchase method combination, the combined entity reports the assets and liabilities of the target company at fair market value on the date of acquisition. Any excess of the fair market value of the consideration given over the fair market value of the net assets acquired is reported as goodwill. If the fair market value of the consideration given is less than the fair market value of the net assets acquired, the resulting negative goodwill is immediately written off against identifiable long-term assets before a deferred credit for negative goodwill is recorded. The operating statements for purchase method combinations report combined results only for the period subsequent to the combination.

The following pronouncements are the sources of GAAP for business combinations that are included in the highest level of authority in the SAS 69 hierarchy:

FAS 72   *Accounting for Certain Acquisitions of Banking or Thrift Institutions*

FAS 141   *Business Combinations*

FAS 147   *Acquisitions of Certain Financial Institutions*

FIN 9   *Applying APB Opinions No. 16 and 17: When a Savings and Loan Association or a Similar Institution Is Acquired in a Business Combination Accounted for by the Purchase Method*

A technical bulletin (FTB 85-5) and numerous Emerging Issues Task Force (EITF) consensus positions that are discussed in this chapter are additional sources of GAAP that are in lower levels of the SAS 69 GAAP hierarchy.

FASB TECHNICAL BULLETINS: FTB 85-5, *Issues Relating to Accounting for Business Combinations*

Background

FTB 85-5 responds to questions in specific areas related to business combinations in accordance with FAS 141, *Business Combinations*.

Standards

The costs incurred to close duplicate facilities of an acquiring company are not recognized as part of the costs of acquisition in a business combination. Only the direct costs of an acquisition are included in the cost of a purchased company. Expenses of closing duplicate facilities should be charged to expense in determining net income.

The proper accounting by a parent company account for minority interest in an exchange of stock between two of its subsidiaries if one or both of the subsidiaries are partially owned depends on whether the minority shareholders are party to the exchange of shares. If shares owned by minority shareholders are exchanged for shares of ownership in another subsidiary of the parent, or in a new subsidiary that is formed by combining multiple subsidiaries of the parent, the transaction is accounted for by the parent as the acquisition of shares from the minority interest and is based on fair value. This accounting is based on the fact that the previous minority interest is purchased and a new minority interest is established in a different subsidiary. If the minority interest does not change, however, the transaction is not a purchase and should be accounted for based on existing carrying amounts rather than fair value.

EITF ISSUES: ISSUE 93, *Recognition of Liabilities in Connection with a Purchase Business Combination*

Overview

In a purchase business combination, the acquirer frequently incurs costs to exit activities at both companies as a result of the acquisition. To combine the operations of the two companies, the acquirer also incurs integration costs related to such actions as training the acquiree's personnel, upgrading the acquiree's computer system, and consolidating and restructuring certain functions. In addition, the acquirer may incur costs for severance pay and other expenses related to the termination of personnel in one company whose functions are duplicated by personnel in the other company.

Accounting Issue

What types of direct, integration, or exit costs should be accrued as liabilities that are assumed and included in the allocation of the acquisition cost in a business combination accounted for as a purchase under the provisions of APB 16, *Business Combinations*, and when should those costs be recognized?

> **OBSERVATION**
>
> FAS 141, which supersedes APB 16, retains the guidance in APB 16 related to determining the cost of an acquired entity.

EITF Consensus

Costs to Exit an Activity. The Emerging Issues Task Force's consensus on whether a cost to exit an acquiree's activity should be recognized as a liability that is assumed and included in the allocation of the acquisition cost follows the two-step approach used in the consensus on exit costs in Issue 94-3: (1) an exit plan must exist and (2) certain criteria for recognition must be met.

If the following conditions are met, an acquirer is said to have formulated a plan to exit an acquiree's activity:

- As of the date the acquisition is completed, management with the appropriate authority begins making plans to exit an acquiree's activity.
- As soon as possible after completing the acquisition, management with the appropriate authority completes its evaluation of which of the acquiree's activities to exit and completes a plan to exit that activity.

- The plan identifies:
  - Significant actions to implement it.
  - Acquired activities that will not be continued.
  - The method of disposition of the activities to be exited, and their locations.
  - The expected completion date of all actions.
- Required actions to exit an activity should be taken as soon as possible after completing the plan, and the period of time in which it will be implemented indicates that the plan is unlikely to change significantly.

An exit cost resulting from a plan to exit an acquiree's activity should be recognized as a liability assumed in an acquisition if it meets one of the following criteria:

- The combined company will not realize a future benefit from the cost, the cost is incremental to costs incurred by the acquiree or acquirer before the business combination, and the cost will be incurred directly as a result of the plan to exit the acquiree's activity. **Incremental cost,** as used in this criterion, means that the cost would not have been incurred by **either** company before the acquisition.
- The combined company will incur the cost as a result of a contractual obligation entered into by the acquiree before the acquisition. The combined company either will continue incurring the cost after the plan is completed without realizing an economic benefit, or will incur a penalty to cancel the contractual obligation.

Examples of such exit costs include the following:

- A penalty to be paid for terminating a lease on an acquiree's idled facility.
- The remaining cost of a noncancelable lease on an acquiree's facility after operations have ceased.
- Other costs, such as real estate taxes, related to an acquiree's leased facility that will be idle after operations have ceased.
- Salaries and benefits to an acquiree's employees and other costs incurred in connection with the closing of an acquiree's plant after operations have ceased.

STUDY QUESTIONS

1. All of the following are conditions indicative of a plan to exit an acquiree's business combination activity by an acquirer *except:*
   a. Identification of significant actions to implement the plan as well as acquired activities that will not be continued
   b. The expected start date of each action
   c. The location of the activities
   d. The method of disposition

> **2.** As a criterion for an exit cost, *incremental cost* means that the cost would not have been incurred by the acquirer before the acquisition. *True or False?*

Involuntary Employee Termination Benefits and Relocation Costs. If all of the following conditions are met, an acquirer should recognize as liabilities costs to involuntarily terminate or relocate an acquiree's employees and should include those costs in the allocation of the acquisition cost in a purchase business combination accounted for in accordance with the provisions of APB 16:

As of the date the acquisition is completed, management with the appropriate authority begins making plans to involuntarily terminate or relocate an acquiree's employees.

As soon as possible after completing the acquisition, management with the appropriate authority:

1. Completes its evaluation of which of the acquiree's employees to terminate or relocate.
2. Approves and commits the company to the plan.
3. Informs the acquiree's employees about the termination or relocation plan, which includes sufficient details to enable affected employees to determine the type and amount of benefits they will receive on termination or relocation.

The plan must be completed and communicated to employees within one year of the date of the acquisition.

The plan identifies the number of the acquiree's employees to be terminated or relocated, their job classifications or functions, and their locations.

Required actions to involuntarily terminate or relocate employees will begin as soon as possible after completing the plan, and the period of time in which the plan will be completed indicates that the plan is unlikely to change significantly.

Costs Not Meeting the Above Conditions. Costs to exit an acquiree's activity or to involuntarily terminate or relocate an acquiree's employees that do not meet the required conditions to exit an activity or involuntarily terminate or relocate an acquiree's employees should be accounted for the same as indirect and general expenses of an acquisition, as discussed in paragraph 76 of APB 16. In addition, if a plan's actions as initially determined or later revised result from events that occur after the acquisition date, related costs should not be recognized as part of the acquisition. Such costs should be recognized as expenses or capitalized when incurred based on the nature of the expenditure and the combined entity's capitalization policy, not as costs of the purchased entity.

Costs related to the acquirer's activities or employees are not included in the purchase price allocation because, as discussed in FTB 85-5, *Issues Relating to Accounting for Business Combinations,* the cost of an acquisition is not allocated to an acquiring company's assets and liabilities.

If an actual cost incurred is less than the amount recognized as a liability assumed in a purchase business combination as a result of the above consensus positions, the acquisition cost should be reduced by the difference between the accrued amount and the actual cost. If the cost exceeds the amount accrued as a liability assumed in the purchase business combination, the acquisition cost should be increased if the adjustment to the original estimate occurs within one year of the acquisition date. Adjustments that occur after one year of the acquisition date should be included in the determination of net income of the period in which they occur. The Task Force also noted that the costs discussed in this Issue, which are recorded as part of the acquisition cost of the purchased entity, are not preacquisition costs accounted for under the provisions of FAS 38, *Accounting for Preacquisition Contingencies of Purchased Enterprises—An Amendment of APB Opinion No. 16.*

> **OBSERVATION**
>
> Paragraph 24 of FAS 141 provides guidance on accounting for costs of a business combination.

Disclosure. In addition to the disclosure requirements in paragraphs 95 and 96 of APB 16, a combined company should disclose the following information. However, the disclosures are required only if the activities to be exited are significant to the combined company's revenues or operating results or if the costs under these consensus positions are material to the combined company as of the date the acquisition is completed.

The combined company should disclose the following information in the notes to the financial statements of the period in which the business combination occurs:

- Unresolved issues, the types of additional liabilities that may result in an adjustment of the allocation of the acquisition cost, and how that adjustment will be reported, if a plan to exit an activity or involuntarily terminate or relocate an acquiree's employees has not been completed as of the balance sheet date.
- The type and amount of liabilities assumed and included in the acquisition cost allocation for costs to exit an activity or to involuntarily terminate or relocate an acquiree's employees.
- Major actions of a plan to exit an activity or to involuntarily terminate or relocate an acquiree's employees, an acquiree's activities that will be

discontinued, the method of disposition, the anticipated date of completion of major actions, and a description of employee groups that will be terminated or relocated.

The combined company should disclose the following information in the notes to the financial statements for all periods presented after the acquisition date through and including the period in which all of the plan's actions have been fully executed:

- The type and amount of exit costs, involuntary employee termination costs, and relocation costs paid and charged against the liability.
- Adjustments to the liability account and whether a corresponding amount was used to adjust the allocation of the acquisition cost or included in determining net income for the period.

> **OBSERVATION**
>
> Paragraphs 51–58 of FAS 141 provide guidance on required disclosures for a business combination.

SEC Staff Comment

The SEC Observer stated that registrants should follow the provisions of SEC SAB 92, *Accounting and Disclosures Relating to Loss Contingencies,* in accounting for unresolved preacquisition contingencies related to a business combination. Those disclosures and disclosures about the types of costs discussed in this Issue will be closely monitored by the SEC staff.

> **OBSERVATION**
>
> Paragraphs 40 and 41 of FAS 141 provide guidance on accounting for preacquisition contingencies.

Discussion

This Issue was raised by the SEC staff as a result of the EITF's consensus in Issue 94-3 because companies often incur similar costs in connection with a purchase business combination.

The Task Force adopted a consensus that is modeled on the consensus in Issue 94-3, with certain modifications, and that also applies to costs of relocating an acquiree's employees. The rationale for this approach was that costs included in the purchase price allocation should be limited to incremental costs; that is, costs that neither company would have incurred without entering into the business combination.

Although not stated explicitly in the consensus, integration costs other than relocation costs should be accounted for as indirect and general expenses related to the acquisition. They may, however, be considered in determining the value of individual assets acquired.

STUDY QUESTION

---

3. Which of the following is *not* a required disclosure by the combined company under APB 16?

   a. Plan actions to involuntarily terminate or relocate the acquiree's employees

   b. The amount of liabilities assumed and included in the cost allocation for exit costs

   c. Types of additional liabilities that may result in an adjustment of the allocation of the acquisition cost

   d. All of the above are required disclosures

ISSUE 95-8, *Accounting for Contingent Consideration Paid to the Shareholders of an Acquired Enterprise in a Purchase Business Combination*

Overview

Company A acquires Company B, a nonpublic company, in a purchase business combination. Company A pays $15,000,000 at closing and agrees to pay the selling shareholders 50 percent of the acquired company's earnings exceeding $1,500,000 during each of the subsequent three years. Several of the selling shareholders will be employed by Company A in key positions that could affect Company B's operating results.

Accounting Issue

What criteria should an entity use to determine whether contingent consideration based on earnings should be accounted for as (1) an adjustment of the purchase price of an acquired entity, in accordance with paragraph 80 of APB 16, or (2) compensation for services or use of property or profit sharing, as required in paragraph 86 of APB 16?

EITF Consensus

The decision whether to recognize contingent consideration based on earnings in a business combination as (1) an adjustment of the acquisition cost, in accordance with paragraph 80 of APB 16, or (2) compensation for services, use of property, or profit sharing, in accordance with paragraph 86 of APB 16, is subject to judgment and should be based on the relevant facts and circumstances.

The factors in the table titled Contingent Consideration—Issue 95-8, which are not all-inclusive, should be considered when assessing whether contingent consideration based on earnings (or other measures of performance) in a business combination is, in substance, additional acquisition cost or compensation for services, use of property, or profit sharing.

As stated in the list of factors in the table titled Contingent Consideration—Issue 95-8, if contingent payments are forfeited on termination of employment, there is a strong indication that the substance of the arrangement is compensation for services after the combination, not additional acquisition cost.

ISSUE 96-5, *Recognition of Liabilities for Contractual Termination Benefits or Changing Benefit Plan Assumptions in Anticipation of a Business Combination*

Overview

This Issue is related to EITF Issue 94-3 and Issue 95-14, which discuss the timing of liability recognition for termination benefits paid to involuntarily terminated employees. However, neither Issue addresses the timing of liability recognition for termination benefits for a plan that is governed by an existing contractual agreement that will be implemented only if the business combination occurs.

The Issue applies, but is not limited to, the following types of agreements, which are referred to here as **contractual termination benefits:**

- Golden parachute employment agreements that require payment if control changes in a business combination;
- Union agreements requiring payment of termination benefits for involuntary terminations when a plant closes as a result of a business combination; and
- Postemployment plans requiring payments for involuntary terminations due to a business combination.

Curtailment losses also may be incurred as a result of the write-off of unrecognized prior service costs and a change in the projected benefit obligation from a significant reduction in the expected years of future service of current employees. This Issue refers to payments under the above-mentioned agreements.

Guidance on loss recognition for curtailments and liabilities is found in the following:

FAS 5	*Accounting for Contingencies.*
FAS 88	*Employers' Accounting for Settlements and Curtailments of Defined Benefit Pension Plans and for Termination Benefits.*
FAS 106	*Employers' Accounting for Postretirement Benefits Other Than Pensions.*
FAS 112	*Employers' Accounting for Postemployment Benefits.*

To recognize a loss under FAS 5, which is the primary guidance on loss accruals, it must be probable before the financial statements are issued that an asset has been impaired or a liability has been incurred at the date of the financial statements and the amount of the loss is reasonably estimable. FAS 88 states that a loss and a liability should be recognized for a pension plan curtailment and for contractual termination benefits when it is probable that the curtailment will occur or that employees will be entitled to the contractual benefits and the amount can be reasonably estimated. FAS 106 provides comparable guidance for other postretirement curtailment losses. Under the guidance in FAS 112, costs related to the termination of employees under a postemployment benefit plan may result in curtailment losses or accruals for contractual termination benefits.

This Issue addresses a transaction in which a company has agreed to a business combination. The company believes the combination is probable and has developed a plan under which certain employees will be terminated if the combination is consummated. Termination benefits will be paid under a preexisting plan or contractual relationship.

Accounting Issue

Should a liability for contractual termination benefits and curtailment losses under employee benefit plans that will be triggered when a business combination is consummated be recognized when it is probable that the business combination will occur or when the business combination is consummated?

EITF Consensus

The EITF reached a consensus that an entity should recognize a liability for contractual termination benefits and curtailment losses under employee benefit plans triggered by a business combination only when the business combination is consummated.

Discussion

The EITF's consensus is based on the view that a business combination is not merely a confirming event—it is the event necessary to trigger a contractual obligation to pay termination benefits when an entity undergoes a business combination. Proponents argued that the company can avoid the liability until the business combination has been consummated. In addition, the FASB staff believes that if a business combination is considered a discrete event, a liability for contractual termination benefits should be recognized only when the business combination has been consummated, because the effects of a business combination should not be recognized until it has occurred. Because the effects of a business combination cannot be recognized until it has been consummated, and because all those effects should be recognized in the same accounting period, the treatment of the liability for contractual termination benefits should be consistent with that for restructuring costs under the consensus in Issue 95-14, which prohibits recognition of such costs before the business combination has been consummated. In effect, a business combination is an example of the second type of subsequent event discussed in AU Section 560 of the codification of Statements on Auditing Standards—an event that occurs after the year-end but before the issuance of financial statements that should be disclosed but for which a liability need not be accrued.

STUDY QUESTION

> **4.** The primary guidance on loss accruals for curtailments and liabilities is:
>
> **a.** FAS 88, Employers' Accounting for Settlements and Curtailments of Defined Benefit Pension Plans and for Termination Benefits
> **b.** FAS 112, Employers' Accounting for Postemployment Benefits
> **c.** FAS 5, Accounting for Contingencies
> **d.** FAS 106, Employers' Accounting for Postretirement Benefits Other Than Pensions

ISSUE 96-7, *Accounting for Deferred Taxes on In-Process Research and Development Activities Acquired in a Purchase Business Combination*

Overview

FAS 2, *Accounting for Research and Development Costs,* provides that costs resulting from or used in research and development (R&D) activities may be capitalized if they are deemed to have a future use. Examples of such identifiable tangible and intangible assets are patents received or applied for, designs for new products or processes, materials and supplies, equipment and facilities, and R&D projects in process. Under FIN 4, *Applicability of FASB Statement No. 2 to Business Combinations Accounted for by the Purchase Method,* if identifiable tangible and intangible assets resulting from R&D activities performed by a company that is acquired in a business combination have no alternative future use (such R&D activities are referred to in this Issue as in-process R&D), they should be written off on the date the business combination is consummated.

Amounts assigned to identifiable assets and liabilities of an acquired company are determined based on the guidance in APB 16. This Issue assumes that R&D is allocated in accordance with paragraph 87 of APB 16 as amended by paragraph 288d of FAS 109, *Accounting for Income Taxes,* which states that the tax basis of an asset or liability should not be considered in determining fair value.

The Issue has arisen because under FAS 109, deferred tax assets and liabilities generally are recognized for differences between the assigned values of assets and liabilities acquired in a business combination and their tax bases. The Statement does not, however, discuss whether to record deferred taxes for in-process R&D

before those amounts are written off for financial reporting purposes. It is assumed here that the in-process R&D has no underlying tax basis.

Accounting Issue

Should an acquiring entity in a business combination recognize a deferred tax liability for the difference between amounts assigned for financial reporting purposes to in-process R&D, which will be written off based on the guidance in FIN 4, and their underlying tax basis?

EITF Consensus

The EITF reached a consensus that amounts assigned to in-process R&D for financial reporting purposes should be written off before deferred taxes are measured on the initial basis differences in a purchase business combination. Therefore, the gross amount of in-process R&D is charged to expense at acquisition, and no deferred taxes are provided on those differences.

Discussion

The consensus is based on the notion that there is no recordable temporary difference, because in-process R&D acquired in a business combination is written off as part of the accounting for the business combination and thus never appears on the combined entity's balance sheet.

STUDY QUESTION

> **5.** The EITF consensus regarding financial reporting on amounts assigned to in-process R&D in business combinations was that:
>
> **a.** The amounts are eligible for deferred taxation.
> **b.** The amounts should be written off before deferred taxes are measured on the initial basis differences.
> **c.** The amounts may be capitalized because they have no future use.
> **d.** None of the above was the EITF consensus.

ISSUE 97-8, *Accounting for Contingent Consideration Issued in a Purchase Business Combination*

Overview

Certain business combinations provide for the payment of contingent consideration if certain conditions are met at a future date. Such consideration may be paid in cash or some other form of consideration, or it may be embedded in a security or it may be in the form of a separate financial instrument. The securities or financial instruments may be publicly traded and freely traded by the seller receiving them as contingent consideration.

Paragraphs 78 and 79 of APB 16 provide guidance on how to determine the cost of an entity acquired in a purchase business combination. Paragraph 78 states that securities issued *unconditionally* and amounts of contingent consideration that can be determined at the date of acquisition should be included in the cost of the acquisition and recognized on that date. Under paragraph 79, *contingent* consideration is usually recognized at a future date when the contingency is resolved and the consideration is issued or becomes issuable. Generally, an additional cost of the acquisition is recognized for the issuance of securities or distribution of other consideration when resolving contingencies based on earnings. Amounts paid in the form of additional securities or other consideration to resolve contingencies based on security prices are not added to the acquisition cost.

OBSERVATION

The guidance on contingent consideration in paragraphs 78–83 of APB 16 has been carried forward unchanged to paragraphs 26–31 of FAS 141, which supersedes APB 16.

Accounting Issue

Should an issuer of contingent consideration embedded in a security or issued as a separate financial instrument in a purchase business combination recognize the security or financial instrument at its fair value and include that amount in the acquisition cost at the acquisition date (based on the guidance in paragraph 78 of APB 16) or recognize it when the contingency is resolved (based on the guidance in paragraphs 79–83 of APB 16)?

EITF Consensus

The issuer should recognize contingent consideration embedded in a security or issued as a separate financial instrument that is publicly traded or indexed to a security that is publicly traded at the fair value of the security or financial instrument on the acquisition date, based on the guidance in paragraph 78 of APB 16, and include it in the acquisition cost. The cost of the acquisition would not be affected by subsequent changes in the value of the security.

Contingent consideration not in the form of a publicly traded security or a form that is indexed to a security or separate financial instrument that is publicly traded should be accounted for based on the guidance in paragraphs 79–83 of APB 16, which require recognition when the contingency is resolved.

The guidance in this consensus is effective for purchase business combinations consummated after July 24, 1997.

The Task Force observed that Issue 96-13 and Issue 86-28 provide guidance on subsequent accounting for financial instruments recognized at fair value at the date of the acquisition under this consensus.

Under FIN 45, *Guarantor's Accounting and Disclosure Requirements for Guarantees, Including Indirect Guarantees of Indebtedness of Others,* guarantors are required to recognize a liability when a guarantee is issued. Entities that have entered into business combinations that include an obligation to pay contingent consideration are exempted under paragraph 7(c) from the initial recognition and initial measurement requirements. However, such obligations should be disclosed in accordance with the interpretation's requirements.

> **OBSERVATION**
>
> FAS 150, *Accounting for Certain Financial Instruments with Characteristics of Both Liabilities and Equity,* provides guidance to issuers on the classification and measurement of financial instruments with characteristics of both liabilities and equity, except for mandatorily redeemable financial instruments of nonpublic entities. Financial instruments under the scope of FAS 150 issued as consideration in a business combination should be recognized as a liability or as an asset under some circumstances. FAS 150 changes the guidance for the subsequent measurement of consideration issued in a business combination in the form of freestanding financial instruments that are publicly traded or indexed to a publicly traded security. Those financial instruments now are measured at fair value under the guidance in paragraph 23 of FAS 150 rather than under the provisions of EITF Issue 96-13, as codified in Issue 00-19. The guidance in FAS 150 does not apply to hybrid instruments with embedded derivative features.

Effect of FAS 133

FAS 133, *Accounting for Derivative Instruments and Hedging Activities,* does not apply to an issuer's accounting of a contract for contingent consideration in this Issue, because if a contract is issued in connection with a business combination, it is not considered a derivative according to paragraph 11(c) of FAS 133. However, the Statement may apply to a holder's accounting if the contingent consideration is a derivative under that Statement. The consensus in this Issue applies if a contract for contingent consideration does not qualify as a derivative under FAS 133.

> **OBSERVATION**
>
> EITF Issue 99-12, which incorporates the guidance in Issue 95-19, provides measurement guidance for securities issued to consummate a business combination accounted for under the purchase method.

Discussion

The distinction made by the Task Force in reaching its consensus is based on the ability to value the securities. A security that is traded on a public market or one that is indexed to a publicly traded security can be readily valued. Because its value is known on the date of issuance, it is more similar to securities issued unconditionally, and thus should be recognized as part of the purchase price on the acquisition date under the guidance in paragraph 78 of APB 16. Proponents also believed that recognition of the value of the securities at acquisition enables a purchaser to recognize the entire cost of the acquisition based on the fair value of all securities issued.

STUDY QUESTION

> **6.** If issuers require guidance on most instruments having characteristics of both liabilities and equity, guidance is provided in:
>
> **a.** FAS 150
> **b.** FAS 133
> **c.** APB 16
> **d.** FAS 141

ISSUE 97-15, *Accounting for Contingency Arrangements Based on Security Prices in a Purchase Business Combination*

Overview

Paragraphs 78 and 79 of APB 16 provide guidance on how to determine the cost of an entity acquired in a purchase business combination, as described above in Issue 97-8. This guidance, and that in paragraphs 81 and 82, is carried forward by FAS 141.

Paragraphs 81 and 82 provide guidance on accounting for additional consideration paid for an acquisition that is contingent on future security prices when a security's value is the same or higher than its value on the date of combination. Because that guidance provides that unconditional consideration issued at the combination date should be recognized at the guaranteed amount, it does not apply to situations in which a purchaser agrees to issue additional consideration in the form of additional shares on a specified future date:

- If the security's price on that date is less than a guaranteed specified price (a **below-market guarantee**) which is also below the price used to calculate the unconditional consideration on the date of the combination.
- If the total value of the number of shares issued on the combination date is less than a specified target value.

In the first situation, the purchaser provides a safety net for the seller by guaranteeing that if the price of the security on a future date is less than a certain amount, the purchaser will issue additional shares (illustrated by Scenario 1 in the example below). If the acquisition were recorded based on the guidance in paragraphs 81 and 82, the amount recognized would be less than the fair value of the unconditional consideration issued on the date of the combination, which would result in reduced goodwill and higher future earnings. In Scenario 2, the total value of all shares to be issued cannot be determined on the date of the combination, because the agreement provides for the issuance of a limited number of additional shares based on the per share price on a future date. Although there is a target amount in this situation, it is not guaranteed. If the price falls below a minimum price, additional shares would be issued, but the total consideration may be less than the target amount (illustrated by Scenarios 2 to 4).

EXAMPLE

The Task Force discussed the issues in the context of the following scenarios:

Scenario 1. On 2/1/X7, Company X purchases a subsidiary of Company Y for 500,000 shares of its stock, which has a fair value of $25 a share on the acquisition date. Company X guarantees Company Y that its shares will have a fair value of at least $20 per share on 2/1/X8, that is, the total consideration will equal at least $10 million. If the fair value of Company X's shares is less than $20 per share, Company X will issue additional shares to Company Y so the total consideration will equal $10 million. Thus, if the per share price is $18 on 2/1/X8, the Company would issue to the seller an additional 55,556 shares.

Scenario 2. On 2/1/X7, Company X purchases a subsidiary of Company Y for 500,000 shares of its stock, which has a fair value of $20 a share on the acquisition date. Company X has agreed to issue a maximum of 166,667 additional shares if the value of the original shares issued to the seller is less than an unguaranteed target value of $20 million on 2/1/Y2. Thus, the Company would issue the maximum number of additional shares if the security's price per share is $30 or less on that date; the number of additional securities issued would decrease ratably to zero as the price per share increases from $30 to $40.

Scenario 3. On 2/1/X7, Company X purchases a subsidiary of Company Y for 400,000 shares of its stock, which has a fair value of $10 per share on the acquisition date. Because Company X has agreed to issue a maximum of 1.2 million additional shares if the value of the original shares issued to the seller is less than an unguaranteed target value of $8 million on 2/1/Y2, the Company would issue the maximum number of additional shares if the security's fair value is $5 or less on that date. Thus, the number of additional shares issued would decrease ratably to zero as the security's price increases from $5 to $20.

Scenario 4. On 2/1/X7, Company X purchases a subsidiary of Company Y for 500,000 shares of its stock, which has a value of $10 a share on the combination date. Because Company X has agreed to issue a maximum of 500,000 additional shares if the value of the original shares issued to the seller is less than an unguaranteed target value of $5 million on 2/1/Y2 based on the price per share on that date and the number of shares issued on the combination date, the Company would issue the maximum number of additional shares if the security's value is $5 or less on that date. The number of additional securities issued would range between a maximum of 500,000 shares and zero as the security's price increases from $5 to $10.

Accounting Issues

At what amount should a purchaser recognize the cost of an acquisition on the date of a business combination if the agreement provides for a below-market guarantee under which the purchaser will issue contingent consideration at a future date to make up for a deficiency between the fair value of the security on that date (e.g., $6) and a guaranteed minimum future price of the security ($7) stated in the agreement?

At what amount should a purchaser recognize the cost of an acquisition on the date of a business combination under an agreement that requires the purchaser to issue additional shares of stock if the value of the shares originally issued is less than a target value on a future date, but the target value does not represent a guaranteed minimum amount of consideration?

EITF Consensus

A purchaser that has given a stated or implied below-market value guarantee in a business combination should recognize the cost of an acquisition at the fair value of the unconditional consideration issued at the date of the combination. (Issue 99-12 provides guidance to determine the date used to value marketable equity securities in a purchase business combination.) The amount recognized as the cost of the acquisition should not be affected by contingent consideration, if any, that is paid or issued at a future date as a result of a below-market value guarantee.

On the combination date, the cost of the acquisition in Scenario 1 above would be recognized at $12,500,000 (500,000 shares at $25 per share), the amount of unconditional consideration issued on the date of the combination.

A purchaser that has agreed to issue contingent consideration based on a security's price that is higher at a specified future date than the fair value on the combination date, but has not guaranteed a minimum value of the total consideration issued, should recognize as the cost of the acquisition an amount equal to the maximum total number of shares that could be issued multiplied by the fair value per share of the security on the combination date. (Issue 99-12 provides guidance to determine the date used to value marketable equity securities in a purchase business combination.) However, if a stated or implied target value is limited, the amount recognized should be the lower of the target value at which no additional consideration would be issued and the maximum total number of shares that could be issued multiplied by the fair value per share on the date of the combination. The recognized cost of the acquisition should not be affected by additional consideration, if any, that is issued as a result of the contingency.

EXAMPLE

The cost of the acquisitions in previous scenarios above would be as follows:

Scenario 2: On the date of the combination, the cost of the acquisition would be recognized at $13,333,340 (a total of 666,667 shares issued at $20 per share), which is less than the target value of $20 million.

Scenario 3: On the date of the combination, the cost of the acquisition would be recognized at the target amount of $8 million, which is less than $16 million, an amount based on the maximum total shares that could be issued multiplied by the price per share on the combination date (1.6 million shares at $10 per share).

Scenario 4: On the date of the combination, the cost of the acquisition would be recognized at the target amount of $5,000,000, which is less than $10 million, an amount based on the maximum total shares that could be issued multiplied by the price per share on the combination date (1 million shares at $10 per share).

Under FIN 45, *Guarantor's Accounting and Disclosure Requirements for Guarantees, Including Indirect Guarantees of Indebtedness of Others,* guarantors are required to recognize a liability when a guarantee is issued. Entities that have entered into business combinations that include an obligation to pay contingent consideration are exempted from the initial recognition and initial measurement requirements under paragraph 7(c), and under paragraph 7(d), which applies to obligations reported as equity under GAAP. However, information about such obligations should be disclosed in accordance with the interpretation's requirements.

OBSERVATION

FAS 150, *Accounting for Certain Financial Instruments with Characteristics of Both Liabilities and Equity,* provides guidance to issuers on the classification and measurement of financial instruments with characteristics of both liabilities and equity. Financial instruments under the scope of FAS 150 that are issued as consideration in a business combination should be recognized as a liability or as an asset under some circumstances. Financial instruments under the scope of FAS 150 that are issued in a business combination as contingent or noncontingent consideration should be classified in accordance with the guidance in the Statement. FAS 150 applies to certain freestanding financial instruments that are settled by issuing a variable number of the issuer's equity shares in a business combination and may include certain instruments discussed in this Issue. The guidance in FAS 150 does not apply to hybrid instruments with embedded derivative features.

Effect of FAS 133

The provisions of paragraph 12 of FAS 133 may apply to a holder's accounting for instruments discussed in this Issue that are hybrid instruments, which contain an embedded derivative and a host contract. An option that is indexed to the issuer's stock is clearly and closely related to the host contract, and, according to paragraph 12(a), would not be accounted for separately by an issuer or a holder. Issuers that meet the conditions in paragraphs 11(a) and 11(c) of the Statement are exempted from applying its provisions. The EITF's consensus in this Issue continues to apply to contingent consideration that does not qualify for the accounting in FAS 133.

Discussion

Proponents of the consensus on the first issue argued that the transaction should be recognized at the amount of consideration issued unconditionally on the acquisition date, because a below market guarantee is not substantive and should be ignored when recognizing the cost of an acquisition. They also believed that the measurement of a transaction that has already occurred should not be changed subsequently.

When the consensus was initially reached, proponents believed that it is appropriate to recognize the acquisition at the maximum number of shares to be issued multiplied by the price at the combination date, which may exceed the unconditional consideration issued. The proponents reasoned that that amount provides a reasonable estimate of the fair value of the total consideration for the acquisition, including additional consideration, if any, that may be issued. At a subsequent meeting, the Task Force revised the initial consensus, because when it was applied to situations in which the total target value is limited (such as in Scenarios 3 and 4 above), the total consideration based on the number of total shares issued at the price of the shares at acquisition exceeded the target amount. To address that anomaly, the Task Force decided to cap the cost of the acquisition at the target value.

ISSUE 98-1, *Valuation of Debt Assumed in a Purchase Business Combination*

Overview

Paragraphs 87 and 88 of APB 16 provide guidance on the allocation of the purchase price of a purchase business combination to assets acquired and liabilities assumed, but it is unclear how the purchase price should be allocated to debt assumed in a business combination. Paragraph 87 states that debt assumed would normally be allocated at an amount equal to the fair value of the debt at the date of acquisition. However, paragraph 88 states that accounts payable, long-term debt, and other claims payable should be valued at present values of amounts to be paid using current interest rates.

Although the present value of the debt at current interest rates may frequently be equal to fair value computed based on the guidance in FAS 107, *Disclosures about Fair Value of Financial Instruments,* the amounts may differ if the views about the objective of the allocation differ. For example, if the objective of a present value computation is not to compute fair value, the resulting amount may differ significantly from fair value. If an issuer has agreed to pay a specified call premium for an option to prepay the debt before maturity, the prepayment option would be included in computing the fair value of the debt. In contrast, some would ignore the issuer's right to prepay the debt when they discount the contractual cash flows to determine the present value of the debt.

Accounting Issues

Should the amount assigned to debt assumed in a purchase business combination be equal to its fair value at the acquisition date?

Should other features of the debt instrument, such as call provisions and prepayment penalties, be considered if the amount assigned to debt assumed in a purchase business combination is based on the present value of future cash flows discounted at the appropriate current interest rate?

EITF Consensus

Debt assumed in a purchase business combination should be recognized at its fair value on the date of acquisition. If quoted market prices—which would provide the best evidence of the fair value of the debt—are unavailable, management can estimate the amount based on quoted market prices for debt with similar characteristics or on valuation techniques, such as the present value of estimated future cash flows using an appropriate discount rate, option pricing, or matrix pricing models.

If the debt is valued using present value techniques, the estimated cash flows should consider the provisions of the debt agreement, such as the issuer's right to prepay.

> **OBSERVATION**
>
> FAS 141, which supersedes APB 16, carries forward the guidance in paragraphs 87 and 88 of the Opinion to paragraphs 36–38 of the Statement. FAS 141 does not affect the consensus in this Issue.

Discussion

Proponents of the first consensus issue argued that paragraph 87 of APB 16 articulates the general rule for the valuation of debt assumed in a purchase business combination. In fact, paragraph 87 refers back to the principles in paragraph 68, which requires the cost of a group of assets acquired to be allocated to the individual assets in the group based on the fair value of the asset. They note that as stated in paragraph 88, the information contained in that paragraph is intended to provide only "general guides for assigning amounts to individual assets acquired and liabilities assumed."

Proponents of using fair value also argued that present value is one of several methods used to estimate fair value and that at the time APB 16 was written, calculations of the present value of cash flows were considered the best method of determining fair value as indicated by the statement in paragraph 72 of APB 16 that "the present value of a debt security represents the fair value of the liability."

Proponents of the consensus believe that there is a direct relationship between fair value and present value calculations. They supported that view with the following statements from the authoritative literature. Paragraph 40 of FAS 107 states that "[f]air values of financial instruments depict the market's assessment of the present value of net future cash flows directly or indirectly embodied in them, discounted to reflect both current interest rates and the market's assessment of the risk that the cash flows will not occur." The same concept is repeated in paragraph 40 of FAS 115, *Accounting for Certain Investments in Debt and Equity Securities.* Therefore, they argued that present value calculations used to estimate the fair value of debt acquired in a business combination should not be based on the original contractual cash flows of the debt, but on the future cash flows required to extinguish the debt, which should include all factors considered by the market, including the debtor's right to call the debt.

STUDY QUESTION

---

7. The apparent conflicting treatment of debt assumed in a business combination between APB 16 paragraphs 87 and 88 was addressed in the EITF consensus that:

   a. The purchase price should be allocated to the debt should be valued at present values of amounts to be paid using current interest rates.
   b. Fair value of debt at the acquisition date should prevail.
   c. There is a direct relationship between fair value and present value calculations.
   d. None of the above was the EITF consensus for assumed debt.

ISSUE 99-12, *Determination of the Measurement Date for the Market Price of Acquirer Securities Issued in a Purchase Business Combination*

Overview

The guidance in APB 16 is unclear as to the date that should be used to value equity securities issued in a purchase business combination. Paragraph 74 states that "the market price for a reasonable period before and after the date the terms of the acquisition are agreed to and announced should be considered in determining the fair value of the securities issued." In contrast, paragraph 94 states that "[t]he cost of an acquired company should be determined as of the date of the acquisition," which is defined in paragraph 93 as "the date assets are received and other assets are given or securities are issued."

For example, two companies agree to a business combination that will be consummated by the issuance of the acquirer's securities and accounted for by the purchase method. Although the combining entities agree to and announce the terms of the combination at the initiation date, the transaction may not be consummated for an extended period of time because of the need for shareholder ratification, approval by regulatory authorities or lenders, and the resolution of other contingencies. Because the price of the securities may fluctuate during the period between the initiation date and consummation of the transaction, the measurement date used to determine the market price of the securities issued affects the cost of the acquisition. The EITF reached a consensus on this transaction in Issue 95-19, which has been incorporated into this Issue as the first issue discussed below.

Since the EITF reached its consensus in Issue 95-19, there has been some diversity in practice in determining the new measurement date, or date of change, for arrangements requiring that the number of shares of the acquiring entity's common stock issued in the acquisition be adjusted based on a formula prescribed in the agreement. For example, the number of shares exchanged for a target's shares might be based on a fixed value per share or a fixed ratio (e.g., 1 for 2 =.5) that may be adjusted using a formula specified in the original agreement if the price of the acquirer's shares is not within a specified price range.

Accounting Issues

What date should an acquiring company use to value marketable equity securities issued to effect a purchase business combination?

If the number of shares or the amount of other consideration issued under a formula arrangement in the original agreement of a purchase business combination could change, what date should be used as the measurement date on which the value of the shares to be issued would be determined?

EITF Consensus

Securities issued to consummate a purchase business combination should be valued according to the guidance in paragraph 74 of APB 16 by using the market price of the securities over a reasonable period of time before and after the combining entities agree on the purchase price and announce the proposed transaction. The measurement date should not be affected by the need to get shareholder or regulatory approvals.

Task Force members observed that the **reasonable period of time** referred to in paragraph 74 should be only the few days between the date the parties enter into an agreement and the announcement date. In addition, the Task Force observed that the measurement date for valuing equity securities in a hostile tender offer is when the transaction is announced and enough shares have been tendered to make the offer binding or when the target agrees to the purchase price.

The Task Force observed that sometimes the number of shares or other consideration comprising the purchase price may change after the original measurement date because of additional negotiations or changes in the market price of the securities. This could result in a change in the security's exchange ratio or in a cash component of the purchase price. Under those circumstances, a new measurement date should be established as of the date of the change.

The measurement guidance in this Issue should also be applied to the acquirer's equity securities in Issue 97-8, which are issued to consummate a purchase business combination, including instruments that meet the criteria in Issue 97-8 for recognition as part of the cost of the acquisition.

For purchase business combinations that include a formula under which the number of shares or amount of other consideration may change, the measurement date for valuing an acquirer's equity securities to be issued in a combination is the first date since the date of the agreement and announcement of the terms of the acquisition on which the number of shares and amount of other consideration become fixed and will not be revised in subsequent applications of the formula.

> **EXAMPLE**
>
> An acquisition announced on February 1, 2005, includes a formula stating that the number of shares will be adjusted if the average closing price of the security during the 10 days ending on July 31, 2005, is less than $25. July 6, 2005, is the measurement date if the 10-day average closing price falls below $25 for the first time on that date and does not recover to $25 or more by July 31, 2005. However, the initial date on which the parties agreed to the terms of the purchase transaction is the measurement date, if the number or shares or other consideration stated in the original announcement does not change by the date of the final application of the formula.

The value of the securities should be based on market prices a few days before and a few days after the measurement date established in Issue 1, but the measurement period should not extend beyond the date on which the business combination is consummated.

STUDY QUESTION

> **8.** The EITF consensus regarding the measurement date for valuing acquirer securities in a business combination should follow the guidance of paragraph 94 of APB 16 as "the date assets are received and other assets are given or securities are issued." *True or False?*

ISSUE 04-1, *Accounting for Preexisting Relationships between the Parties to a Purchase Business Combination*

Overview

This Issue addresses situations in which two parties that enter into a business combination have had a previous relationship.

Accounting Issues

Should consummation of a business combination between two parties that have had a relationship before entering into this transaction be evaluated to determine whether that contractual relationship should be settled and accounted for separately from the business combination?

How should the amount of a settlement be measured if separate accounting is required to settle a relationship between two parties that existed before the business combination?

Should assets of the acquired entity related to a relationship between the two parties that existed before the business combination be recognized in the business combination as intangible assets separate from goodwill?

EITF Consensus

The EITF has reached the following consensus positions.

If a business combination is consummated between two entities that had a relationship before the combination, the combination should be evaluated to determine whether the preexisting relationship still exists. Under those circumstances, a **combination** is a transaction with multiple elements that consist of (a) the business combination, and (b) settlement of the preexisting relationship.

Settlement in a business combination of an executory contract that existed before the combination should be measured based on (a) the amount by which the contract is favorable or unfavorable to the acquirer in comparison to prices in current market transactions for the same or similar item, or (b) stated settlement provisions in the contract, if any, available to the counterparty to which the contract would be unfavorable, whichever is less. If the stated settlement amount is less than the off-market component of the contract, the difference should be included in the business combination.

An unfavorable contract may not necessarily result in a loss contract for the acquirer. The EITF noted that the amount an acquirer may recognize in its consolidated income statement as a gain or loss from the settlement may differ from the amount an acquirer would measure if it previously had recognized in its financial statements an amount related to the preexisting relationship. For example, if as a result of a previous business combination, an acquirer recognized an $8 liability related to a supply contract with the supplier it has acquired, and the measured loss on the contract is $10 based on the consensus, the acquirer's income statement would show a $2 loss.

Acquisition of a right that an acquirer previously had granted to a acquiree to use the acquirer's recognized or unrecognized intangible assets, such as a trade name under a franchise agreement or rights to the acquirer's technology under a licensing agreement, should be considered a reacquired right that should be included in the business combination transaction. The EITF noted that if a contract related to a reacquired right includes terms that are favorable or unfavorable compared to the pricing of current market transactions for similar items, a gain or loss on settlement should be measured based on (a) the amount by which the contract is favorable or unfavorable to the acquirer in comparison to market terms, or (b) stated settlement provisions in the contract, if any, available to the counterparty to which the contract would be unfavorable, whichever is less. The consensus on Issue 2 provided additional measurement guidance.

A reacquired right, excluding the amount recognized as a settlement gain or loss under the consensus for Issue 3, should be recognized as an intangible asset that is separate from goodwill. The EITF noted that under FAS 142, *Goodwill and Other Intangible Assets,* the fair value of all identifiable intangible assets, including those related to trade names and technology assets, must be valued separately when implied goodwill is determined. For example, an entity that reacquires a right to its trade name in a certain geographical area should recognize the value of the reacquired trade name as a separate intangible asset or as part of its recognized trade name. Allocation of cash flows related to its trade name to separate assets that represent other geographic locations in Step 2 of the goodwill impairment test is not required.

An acquirer should recognize a gain or loss on settlement in connection with the effective settlement of a lawsuit, including threatened litigation, or an executory contract in a business combination, unless the existing authoritative literature requires another treatment. The EITF noted that the amount an acquirer may recognize as a gain or loss from settlement in its consolidated income statement may differ from the amount the acquirer would measure if it previously had recognized an amount in its financial statements related to the preexisting relationship. Also, the EITF noted that the effective settlement of a lawsuit in a business combination should be measured at fair value.

An acquirer should make the following disclosures if the parties to a business combination have a preexisting relationship:

- The nature of the preexisting relationship.
- The measurement of the settlement amount of the preexisting relationship, if any.
- The valuation method used to determine the settlement amount.
- The amount of any settlement gain or loss recognized.
- The classification in the statement of operations of any settlement gain or loss recognized.

ISSUE 04-3, *Mining Assets:*
Impairment and Business Combinations

Overview

Some mining entities have been excluding estimated cash flows associated with a mining asset's economic value beyond its proven probable (VBPP) reserves and the effects of anticipated fluctuations in the minerals' future market prices over the period of cash flows when testing such assets for impairment in accordance with the guidance in FAS 144, *Accounting for the Impairment or Disposal of Long-Lived Assets,* and in making the purchase price allocation of business combinations. Both VBPP and an estimate of the future market price of the minerals are generally included in a mining asset's fair value.

VBPP is defined in the SEC's Industry Guide 7, *Using Cash Flow Information and Present Value in Accounting Measurements,* as (1) **proven reserves,** for which quantity is computed from certain dimensions, such as workings or drill holes; for which quality is determined from detailed samplings; and the geologic character of which is well defined because of the close proximity of the sites for inspection, sampling, and measurement, and (2) **probable reserves,** the quantity, grade, and quality of which is computed based on information similar to that used for proven reserves, but the sites for inspection, sampling, and measurement are farther apart. The degree of assurance is lower than that of proven reserves, but is high enough that continuity can be assumed between the points observed. Proven and probable reserves are distinguished based on the level of geological evidence and the subsequent confidence in the estimated reserves. In addition to information about VBPP, the SEC also requires registrants to complete a feasibility study before accepting a registrant's statement that mining assets are proven and probable reserves.

The scope of this Issue applies to mining entities—which include entities that find and remove wasting natural resources—other than oil- and gas-producing entities under the scope of FAS 19, *Financial Accounting and Reporting by Oil and Gas Producing Companies.*

Accounting Issues

Should VBPP be considered when an entity allocates the purchase price of a business combination to mining assets?

Should the effects of anticipated fluctuation in the future market price of minerals be considered when an entity allocates the purchase price of a business combination to mining assets?

EITF Consensus

The EITF reached the following consensus positions:

- VBPP should be included in the value allocated to mining assets in the purchase price allocation of a business combination in the same manner that a market participant would include VBPP in determining the asset's fair value.
- The effects of anticipated fluctuations in the future market price of minerals should be included when the fair value of the mining assets is determined in a purchase price allocation. Estimates of those effects should be consistent with the expectations of marketplace participants—that is, available information, such as current prices, historical averages, and forward pricing curves should be considered. The assumptions should be consistent with the acquirer's operating plans for developing and producing minerals and should be based on more than one factor.
- The cash flows associated with VBPP estimates of future discounted and undiscounted cash flows should be included in the evaluation of mining assets for impairment under FAS 144. In addition, estimated cash flows used to determine impairment should include estimated cash outflows necessary to develop and extract the VBPP.
- The effects of anticipated fluctuations in the future market price of minerals should be included when one estimates discounted and undiscounted cash flows used to determine impairment under FAS 144. Estimates of those effects should be consistent with the expectations of marketplace participants—that is, available information, such as current prices, his-

torical averages, and forward pricing curves should be considered. The assumptions should be consistent with the acquirer's operating plans for developing and producing minerals and should be based on more than one factor.

Transition. The first and second consensus positions should be applied prospectively to business combinations completed and goodwill impairment tests performed in reporting periods that begin after March 31, 2004. The consensus positions may be applied early if financial statements have not been issued. On initial application, an impairment charge, if any, should be reported in income from continuing operations. The third and fourth consensus positions should be applied prospectively to asset impairment tests performed in reporting periods that begin after March 31, 2004. They may be applied early if financial statements have not been issued.

STUDY QUESTION

9. Which of the following should **not** be included in estimating discounted and undiscounted cash flows used to determine impairment of mining assets under FAS 144?

   a. Effects of anticipated fluctuations in the future market price of minerals
   b. Estimated cash outflows necessary to develop and extract the VBPP
   c. Effects of anticipated fluctuations in the future market price of minerals
   d. All of the above should be included in estimating these discounted and undiscounted cash flows

ISSUE 85-21, *Changes of Ownership Resulting in a New Basis of Accounting*

Overview

Company A has acquired the voting common stock of Company B in a business combination accounted for as a purchase transaction. APB 16 requires Company A to account for the assets and liabilities acquired in the transactions at their fair values. However, the accounting literature provides no guidance as to whether Company B should report its assets and liabilities on the same basis as Company A, thus adopting a "new basis of accounting."

Accounting Issues

At what level of change in ownership should a company adopt a new basis of accounting to report its assets and liabilities?
How should the new basis of accounting be computed?
At what amount should minority interests be reported?

EITF Consensus

The EITF did not reach a consensus on this Issue.

SEC Observer Comment

The SEC Observer stated that SEC registrants are required to adopt new-basis accounting only if virtually 100 percent of the stock has been acquired and there is no outstanding publicly held debt or preferred stock. The SEC Observer stated further that net assets (in a business combination) or long-lived assets transferred between companies under common control or between a parent and subsidiary should be reported at their historical cost in the subsidiary's separate financial statements.

Discussion

Although the authoritative accounting literature does not provide guidance on this Issue, SEC SAB 54, *Application of Push-Down Basis of Accounting in Financial Statements of Subsidiaries Acquired by Purchase,* provides guidance to SEC registrants. It requires the parent company's cost of acquiring a subsidiary to be "pushed down" to the subsidiary's separate financial statements if "substantially all" of the subsidiary's voting common stock has been acquired and the parent can control the form of ownership. SAB 54 encourages but does not require new-basis accounting if less than "substantially all" of a company's stock has been acquired or there is outstanding publicly held debt or preferred stock.

EITF members noted that the application of SAB 54 is inconsistent when less than 100 percent of a company is acquired or when there is a step acquisition. The Task Force's views also differed about whether private companies should apply new-basis accounting.

OBSERVATION

New-basis accounting is a component of the FASB's project on the reporting entity and consolidation. The FASB issued a Discussion Memorandum, *New Basis Accounting,* in December 1991.

STUDY QUESTION

10. According to the SEC Observer, public companies (SEC registrants) are required to adopt new-basis accounting if:

a. There is no outstanding common stock

b. All of the stock has been acquired

c. Less than 10 percent of the registrants' outstanding debt is publicly held

d. Any of the above circumstances requires new-basis accounting

ISSUE 87-21, *Change of Accounting Basis in Master Limited Partnership Transactions*

Overview

The enactment of the Tax Reform Act of 1986 resulted in the formation of an increasing number of master limited partnerships (MLPs), which are partnerships whose interests are traded publicly. MLPs may be formed to:

- Realize the value of undervalued assets.
- Pass income and deductible losses through to its shareholders.
- Raise capital.
- Enable companies to sell, spin-off, or liquidate operations.
- Combine partnerships.

MLPs are generally formed from assets in existing businesses operated in the form of limited partnerships and in connection with a business in which the general partner is also involved.

The following are different methods of creating an MLP:

- In a **roll-up,** two or more legally separate limited partnerships are combined into one MLP.
- In a **drop-down,** units of a limited partnership that was formed with a sponsor's assets (usually a corporate entity) are sold to the public.
- In a **roll-out,** a sponsor places certain assets into a limited partnership and distributes its units to shareholders.
- In a **reorganization,** an entity is liquidated by transferring all of its assets to an MLP.

Effect of FAS 141

FAS 141, which supersedes APB 16, applies to transactions in which all entities transfer net assets, or the owners of those entities transfer their equity interests to a newly formed entity in a transaction that is referred to as roll up. Its scope excludes, however, transfers of net assets or exchanges of equity interests between entities under common control. All the facts and circumstances should be analyzed to determine the nature of the transaction and the appropriate method of accounting for it.

Accounting Issues

Can new-basis accounting ever be used for the assets and liabilities of an MLP? How should an MLP account for transaction costs in a roll-up?

EITF Consensus

A new basis is not appropriate in the following circumstances:

- The MLP's general partner in a roll-up was also the general partner of the predecessor limited partnerships, and no cash has been exchanged in the transaction.

- A sponsor in a drop-down receives 1 percent of the units of the MLP as its general partner and 24 percent of the units as a limited partner, with the remaining 75 percent of the units sold to the public. The general partner can be replaced by a two-thirds vote of the limited partners.
- An MLP is created as a roll-out.
- An MLP is created as a reorganization.

In addition, the conclusion on a roll-up would not change even if the general partner was the general partner of only some of the predecessor limited partnerships. Task Force members noted that if a general partner of predecessor limited partnerships who will not be a general partner of the MLP receives MLP units in settlement of management contracts or for other services that will not carry over to the MLP, those units have the characteristics of compensation rather than equity, and should be accounted for as such by the MLP. The Task Force did not reach a consensus on situations in which new-basis accounting would be appropriate, but did not preclude the possibility.

STUDY QUESTION

---

11. The method used to create an MLP when a sponsor places assets into a limited partnership and distributes the partnership units to shareholders is the:

    a. Roll-up

    b. Drop-down

    c. Roll-out

    d. Reorganization

SEC Observer Comment

The SEC Observer announced that the SEC would not object to new-basis accounting in an MLP created as a drop-down to the extent of the percentage of change in ownership if both of the following occur:

- 80 percent or more of the MLP is sold to the public.
- The limited partners can replace the general partner by a "reasonable" vote.

Discussion

Issue of New-Basis Accounting. The issues of change of control and voting interest would normally be the primary concerns in determining whether there should be new-basis accounting. However, the EITF found it difficult to resolve the issue of control in an MLP. Some argued that there is no change in control in a roll-up of existing limited partnerships because the general partner of the MLP was also the general partner of the limited partnerships that have been combined. Under those circumstances, the transaction would not qualify for accounting as a business combination because APB 16 does not apply to transactions in which there were no outsiders. Others argued that accounting for business combinations may apply if one party's voting control is close to a majority. However, a majority of a working group formed to discuss the issues recommended combining the limited partnerships at carryover basis.

Determining who has control in an MLP is also difficult because control may not be based on a majority ownership of the voting shares. For example, although a general partner may own less than a majority of the voting interest, the limited partners may be able to exercise control only in limited situations, such as the removal of the general partner. ARB 51 discusses situations in which majority ownership may not be indicative of control, but it does not discuss situations in which there may be control without a majority ownership.

Some analogized an MLP created as a drop-down to push-down accounting. However, here again the primary issue was whether there is a new control group. An AICPA Issues Paper on push-down accounting had recommended that a change in basis be "pushed down" to the subsidiary's financial statements in a business combination accounted for as a purchase if there was at least a 90 percent change in ownership.

A roll-out was considered to be a spin-off, which was being accounted for in practice at carryover basis. A reorganization did not involve a change of owners because it was merely a change in legal entity. In practice, reorganizations were also being accounted for at carryover basis.

Issue of Roll-up Transaction Costs. The issue was whether transaction costs, such as professional fees, in a roll-up should be accounted for as an expense, as part of the purchase price, or as a reduction of the partners' equity accounts. Treating those costs as part of the purchase would be appropriate under purchase accounting, while reducing the proceeds would be consistent with offerings that are not business combinations.

ISSUE 88-16, *Basis in Leveraged Buyout Transactions*

Overview

Newco, a holding company with no substantial operations, is formed to acquire Oldco, an operating company, in a leveraged buyout (LBO) transaction that may occur either as a single, highly leveraged transaction or in several transactions in which Newco acquires all of Oldco's outstanding voting equity interests. Although Newco is controlled by a new group of investors, one or more shareholders who had a voting interest in Oldco may have an interest in Newco and may be considered part of Newco's control group. Some of those shareholders have a lesser voting equity interest in Newco than they had in Oldco.

This scenario raises the question whether Newco's investment in Oldco shares should be accounted for at fair value, predecessor basis, book value, or a combination of these values. The different alternatives of accounting for such transactions is the result of different views as to whether such a transaction is, in substance, a purchase of a new business (evidenced by a change in control), a recapitalization or reorganization of an existing business (evidenced by no change in control), or a step acquisition in which there is a partial change of control.

The EITF reached a consensus in Issue 86-16 that a combination of predecessor basis, book value, and fair value would be appropriate for LBOs discussed in that Issue. That Issue primarily focused on transactions in which a shareholder that was part of the Oldco control group continued as part of the Newco control group with a greater interest in Newco voting stock than that shareholder's interest in Oldco voting stock.

The consensus reached in Issue 86-16 did not, however, provide guidance for transactions in which a shareholder has a lesser interest in Newco voting stock than in Oldco voting stock. Therefore, some have questioned whether the accounting guidance in that Issue applies to cases in which a shareholder's interest declines.

Because the purpose of Issue 88-16 is to provide accounting guidance for **all** LBO transactions, regardless of whether a shareholder's interest in Newco voting stock is greater than or less than that shareholder's interest in Oldco voting stock, this consensus supersedes the consensus in Issue 86-16.

Accounting Issue

Under what circumstances should Newco recognize the acquisition of Oldco shares at a new basis rather than at predecessor cost, and how should Newco value its investment in Oldco?

EITF Consensus

Note: The format of the EITF's consensus positions in this Issue follows the format established in Issue 86-16, which differs from that used for other Issues. The consensus positions are presented in three sections. Section 1 states conditions for a change of control in LBO transactions, and Sections 2 and 3 provide guidance for Newco's valuation of its investment in Oldco shares. Although this Issue supersedes the consensus positions in Issue 86-16, some portions of those consensus positions are carried forward to the consensus positions in this Issue.

> **OBSERVATION**
>
> FAS 141, *Business Combinations*, supersedes the guidance in APB 16, *Business Combinations.* FAS 142, *Goodwill and Other Intangible Assets*, supersedes the guidance in APB 17, *Intangible Assets.* FAS 142 provides guidance on subsequent accounting for goodwill and intangible assets acquired in a purchase business combination. That guidance should be used to account for goodwill and other intangible assets recognized in LBO transactions under the scope of this Issue.

The EITF reached the following consensus positions on the issues:

- A partial or complete change in accounting basis is appropriate only if control of voting interests is held by a new controlling shareholder or group of shareholders.
- Control changes if one of the following conditions is met:
  - One shareholder, who may or may not be a member of management, or management as a group, and who did not control Oldco, gains control of Newco by owning a majority (more than 50 percent) voting interest.
  - A group of new shareholders (not shareholders in Oldco) that meets the criteria for inclusion in the Newco control group gains control of Newco.
  - The Newco control group (regardless of whether it consists of new or continuing shareholders) gains control of Newco, and no subset of that group had control of Oldco. (A Newco **control group subset** is any one shareholder or any combination of shareholders in that group.)

Divisions of Shareholders. Newco's shareholders, including continuing shareholders, are divided into management, shareholders whose percentage of equity interest in Newco is greater than in Oldco, and shareholders whose percentage of equity interest in Newco is equal to or less than in Oldco.

They are treated as follows:

- Management shareholders are presumed to be part of the Newco control group. That presumption may be overcome in rare instances; for example, if management did not participate in promoting the LBO. However, even if the presumption is overcome, management would still be considered part of the Newco control group if it meets the same conditions, discussed below, that any individual shareholder would have to meet to be considered part of the Newco control group.
- An individual shareholder with a greater interest in Newco than in Oldco is automatically considered part of the Newco control group if the shareholder has at least a 5 percent equity interest in Newco. If not, the shareholder is automatically excluded from the control group.

Inclusion in the Control Group. Whether the control group should include or exclude an individual shareholder having an equity interest in Newco that is equal to or less than that shareholder's equity interest in Oldco is determined by the outcome of the voting-interest and capital-at-risk tests (see Discussion below). A shareholder is automatically included in the control group if that shareholder's voting interest in Newco is either of the following:

- At least 20 percent of the total voting interests of Newco.
- At least 20 percent of the fair value of the cumulative capital at risk in Newco, at any risk level, based on either the shareholder's ownership of Newco equity and debt securities or indirect guarantees made by the shareholder on Newco's or its shareholders' behalf, such as commitments to provide cash under certain conditions.

A change in control should be substantive, genuine, and not temporary.

- A new controlling shareholder or group of shareholders should be able to make operating and financial decisions, such as the refinancing of debt and sale and acquisition of assets.
- It must be probable at the transaction date that Oldco shareholders will not regain their controlling voting interest.
- The conditions for control would not be met if the controlling shareholder group has a plan or intends to either (1) sell a portion of its interest within one year of consummating the transaction or (2) issue additional voting Newco shares. This requirement would not apply, however, if a shareholder commits to transfer its investment to another member of the control group, or if the voting rights of securities held by controlling shareholders enable other members of the control group to maintain control even if the voting interest is sold.
- In evaluating whether control has changed, it is necessary to consider the effect of Newco dilutive securities other than options or warrants that are substantially equivalent to Newco's voting interests, and that have been issued to or are held by investors that are not members of the controlling shareholder group. Voting rights, duration until exercise or conversion, probability that exercise or conversion will be triggered by certain events, and the relationship between fair value and the exercise or conversion price are a few of the factors that should be considered in determining whether dilutive securities are substantially equivalent to Newco's voting interests.
- It is presumed that Newco warrants and options to acquire voting interests issued to or held by investors that are not members of the controlling shareholder group are equivalent to voting interests. That presumption may be overcome, however, if the securities can be exercised only after

an extended time period, only after providing future service over a period of years, or if the securities are exercised only in order to sell the voting securities obtained, such as in a public offering. The relationship between the exercise price of Newco's warrants or options and the fair value of the Newco voting interest should also be considered, but this factor would not be persuasive by itself, because of the volatility of new, highly leveraged securities.

Basis of Accounting. If control has not changed, the transaction should be accounted for as a recapitalization or restructuring that would not result in a change in accounting basis.

The accounting should not be based on the form of the transaction by which an investor gains an interest in Newco. In general, the interest of an investor in Newco who owned an equity interest in Oldco should be carried over at the investor's predecessor basis in its equity interest in Oldco or in its equity interest in Newco, whichever is less.

The controlling factor in determining basis is whether an investor held an equity interest before and after the transaction.

The EITF agreed that the total carrying amount of Newco's investment in Oldco should be the sum of the amounts assigned to each of the following components, which are computed as discussed below:

- The Newco control group: Their equity interest in Newco or Oldco, whichever is less, is based on predecessor basis, and any increase in equity interest is based on fair value. For example, if management had a 20 percent equity interest in Oldco and now has a 52 percent equity interest in Newco, 20 percent of this equity interest would be recognized at predecessor basis and 32 percent at fair value.

- Shareholders, whether new or continuing, not considered part of the Newco control group with less than a 5 percent individual equity interest in Newco: Recognize at fair value.

- Individual continuing shareholders with an equity interest in Newco equal to or less than their equity interest in Oldco that (a) have at least a 5 percent equity interest in Newco, and (b) collectively have less than a 20 percent equity interest in Newco: Recognize at fair value (subject to the monetary test). (See Discussion, below, regarding the monetary test.)

- Newco's remaining investment in Oldco: At fair value, subject to the monetary test.

Applying the Monetary Test. The fair value of securities issued by Newco to acquire Oldco should be objectively determinable. Fair value should only be used if at least 80 percent of the fair value of consideration paid to acquire Oldco equity interests consisted of monetary consideration (the monetary test).

The monetary test should be applied as follows:

- Securities acquired from Oldco shareholders may be recognized at fair value if 80 percent or more of the consideration, net of consideration used to acquire shares in Newco, consists of cash, debt, and debt-type instruments such as mandatorily redeemable preferred stock. When applying the 80 percent test, equity securities in Newco received at formation in exchange for shares in Oldco should be included in the denominator at the amount that would have been paid in monetary consideration.

- New equity must be obtained independently of Oldco. Consequently, proceeds of a loan from Oldco used by Newco controlling shareholders to acquire an equity interest in Newco do not qualify as monetary consideration and should be presented as a reduction of equity in Newco's financial statements until paid. The same rule applies to Newco shares acquired with proceeds from an unusual bonus or other unusual payment from Oldco.

- If the 80 percent test is not met, Newco equity securities issued to acquire an interest in Oldco should be valued at predecessor basis, because the portion of Newco's investment in Oldco recognized at fair value should not exceed the percentage of total monetary consideration.

STUDY QUESTIONS

12. The EITF consensus is that a shareholder is automatically included in the control group of the holding company formed to acquire the old company if the shareholder's voting interest in the old company is at least:

   a. More than 50 percent
   b. 30 percent
   c. 25 percent
   d. 20 percent

13. To be recognized at fair value under the monetary test, the securities acquired from the old company shareholders must have _____ or more of the consideration (other than that used to acquire Newco shares) consisting of cash, debt, and debt-type instruments.

   a. Half
   b. 51 percent
   c. 75 percent
   d. 80 percent

14. If the minimum percentage is not met for the monetary test, Newco equity securities issued to acquire an interest in Oldco should be valued at the predecessor basis. *True or False?*

SEC Observer Comment

The SEC Observer announced that although SEC registrants are encouraged to apply the EITF's consensus positions in Issue 88-16 for LBOs completed or substantially completed at May 18, 1989 (the date the EITF reached its consensus), they would be permitted to continue applying the guidance in Issue 86-16 for those transactions. However, registrants are expected to apply the guidance in Issue 88-16 for LBOs not completed or substantially completed at May 18, 1989. All registrants with LBOs are expected to disclose the accounting policy used to determine the carrying amount of Newco's investment in Oldco and the rationale for that determination.

Discussion

Because the consensus positions in Issue 86-16 did not provide useful guidance when the fact patterns changed, the EITF reconsidered some of its consensus positions in that Issue and reached consensus positions that apply to all LBO transactions. The Issue 88-16 consensus positions provide guidance on some of the following problems, among others, in determining the basis of Newco shares:

- The effect on change in control if a **controlling** Oldco shareholder becomes part of the Newco control group
- Determining whether an Oldco shareholder is a member of the Newco control group
- Valuing the interests of Oldco shareholders who have a lesser interest in Newco than they had in Oldco
- Accounting for Newco nonvoting equity securities issued to Oldco shareholders who are members of Newco's control group

The Task Force agreed on the following as a basis for their consensus positions:

- Management and related parties are each considered to be one shareholder.
- All outstanding Oldco options, warrants, and convertible securities held by continuing shareholders should be reviewed to determine whether and to what extent their exercise or conversion should be assumed at the time of an LBO.
- The consensus positions apply to all transactions in which an Oldco shareholder has an equity interest in Newco, and not only to transactions in which Oldco shareholders exchange Oldco shares for Newco shares. For example, the consensus positions apply to situations in which Newco purchases Oldco shares and Oldco shareholders buy shares of Newco.

As in Issue 86-16, this consensus also requires a new control group to have a controlling interest and the change in control to be genuine as prerequisites for new basis accounting. Section 1 of Issue 88-16 specifies four conditions related to the change in control. Control changes if both of the following apply:

- One of the conditions has been met; that is, unilateral control of Newco has been obtained by an individual or group that did not have unilateral control of Oldco.
- The change in control is genuine and not temporary (subject to certain requirements).

Because a change in control is a prerequisite for new basis accounting, an important factor in that determination is who should be included in the Newco control group. To broaden the scope of the consensus in Issue 86-16, the Task Force established three groups of shareholders with equity interests in Newco to which the consensus positions apply:

- Management.
- Shareholders holding a greater percentage of equity in Newco than they held in Oldco.
- Shareholders with the **same or lower** percentage of equity in Newco than they held in Oldco.

The consensus establishes new guidelines to evaluate the equity interests of each of those groups. Specifically, the Task Force devised special tests—the voting-interest test and the capital-at-risk test—to determine whether Oldco share-holders with decreasing interests should be included in the control group.

Generally, under the Task Force's consensus concerning the valuation of Newco's investment in Oldco, the equity interests of new shareholders are recognized at fair value, whereas those of Oldco shareholders who are included in the Newco control group, as well as certain Oldco shareholders who are not in the Newco control group, are recognized at predecessor cost. However, new basis is limited to less than 80 percent unless monetary consideration for Newco's interest in Oldco comprised at least 80 percent of the total consideration.

Definitions and Illustrations in EITF Issue 88-16

- **Continuing Shareholder.** A shareholder with equity interest in Newco that also had an equity interest in Oldco.
- **Management.** Oldco employees and management that have management positions and residual interests in Newco. Item 401 of SEC Regulation S-K should be considered in determining the individuals to be included in management.
- **Monetary Consideration.** Cash, debt, and debt-type instruments such as mandatorily redeemable preferred stock.

Illustration of the Monetary Test

$$\frac{\text{Consideration composed of debt and cash}}{\text{Total consideration}} = \frac{\$87,000}{\$97,000} = 89.7\%$$

The preceding transaction passes the monetary test, because monetary consideration is greater than 80 percent.

- **Predecessor Basis.** The basis of a continuing shareholder's investment in a business, measured as the original cost of the investment plus or minus the shareholder's share of the change in the equity of the business (earnings or losses less dividends and any other distributions) since the investment was acquired.
- **Residual Interest.** A shareholder's proportionate share of the equity of a business after equity securities with redemption or liquidation features has been redeemed.

Illustration of Residual Interest

Type of security	Number of Shares
Voting common stock (no par)	100
Nonvoting common stock (no par)	100
Redeemable prefered stock	100

A shareholder owns the following:

Type of security	Number of shares
Voting common stock	20
Nonvoting common stock	40
Redeemable preferred stock	30

The shareholder's residual interest in the business is therefore 30 percent (20 shares voting common stock plus 40 shares nonvoting common stock divided by 200 common shares).

- **Unilateral Control.** Ownership of more than 50 percent of a business's voting interest, unless voting rights are restricted legally or otherwise to preclude shareholders from exercising their normal voting rights and privileges.

- **Voting Interest.** A shareholder's proportionate share of all securities that gives the shareholder voting rights.

Illustration of Voting-Interest Test

	OLDCO Investor	Total NEWCO	Percentage of Total
Voting common shares	10	100	
Voting preferred stock shares	5	30	
Voting shares obtainable through options and warrants	3	20	
	18	150	12%

Capital at risk includes all Newco equity, short-term and long-term debt, notes payable, capital-lease obligations and guarantees made by Newco shareholders. The capital-at-risk test is applied as follows:

1. Each component of capital, or risk level, is ranked from the lowest to the highest level of priority in liquidation.
2. A percentage of a continuing shareholder's capital at risk is calculated on a cumulative basis.

The following two examples illustrate the capital-at-risk test. In each illustration, Newco capital consists of common stock, preferred stock, and debt, in that order of descending risk.

Illustration 1

NEWCO Capital		
	Continuing Shareholder's Portion	Total	Cumulative Capital at Risk
Common Stock	$8	$100	8% (a)
Preferred Stock	0	50	5.33% (b)
Debt	20	50	14% (c)
	$28	$200	

(a) $8/$100 = 8%
(b) ($8 + $0) / ($100 + $50) = 5.33%
(c) ($8 + $0 + $20) / ($100 + $50 + $50) = 14%

Based on the capital-at-risk test, the continuing shareholder in the above illustration would not be part of the Newco control group, because that shareholder's capital at risk is less than 20 percent at any cumulative risk level.

Illustration 2

NEWCO Capital

	Continuing Shareholder's Portion	Total	Cumulative Capital at Risk
Common Stock	$19	$100	19% (a)
Preferred Stock	14	50	22% (b)
Debt	0	50	16.5% (c)
	$28	$200	

(a) $19/$100 = 19%
(b) ($19 + $14) / ($100 + $50) = 22%
(c) ($19 + $14 + $0) / ($100 + $50 + $50) = 16.5%

The continuing shareholder in this illustration meets the capital-at-risk test at the preferred stock risk level. The fact that the shareholder's total capital at risk is less than 20 percent is irrelevant.

Newco's Basis of Accounting in Oldco

For purposes of computing fair value, the total amount of the investment that can be based on fair value is limited to the percentage derived when monetary consideration paid to all Oldco shareholders is divided by the total consideration paid to all Oldco shareholders. Excluded from monetary consideration, however, are amounts paid to Oldco shareholders that were subsequently reinvested in Newco equity securities.

This limitation does not apply, however, if the ratio of monetary consideration to the total consideration to Oldco shareholders is 80 percent or more. The following illustrations clarify the application of that limitation:

	Illustration 1	Illustration 2
Monetary consideration paid to all OLDCO shareholders	$50,000	$90,000
Total consideration paid to all OLDCO shareholders	$100,000	$100,000
Percentage derived	50%	90%
Does limitation apply?	yes, 50% is less than 80%	No, 90% is greater than 80%
Maximum amount of the investment that can be based on fair value	$50,000 ($100,000 X .5)	$100,000 (Because no limitiation applies)

If control does not change in a leveraged buyout (LBO), the carrying amount of Newco's investment in Oldco would be based entirely on the book value of Oldco's net assets, and any debt or preferred stock issued in connection with the LBO would be treated as a reduction of the shareholders' equity of Newco.

ISSUE 90-12, *Allocating Basis to Individual Assets and Liabilities for Transactions within the Scope of Issue No. 88-16*

Overview

This Issue addresses how to allocate basis to individual assets and liabilities when a company (Newco) acquires 100 percent of the assets of another company (Oldco) in a leveraged buyout (LBO) transaction. As a result of the accounting required under the consensus in EITF Issue 88-16, Newco's purchase price of Oldco, which is the value assigned to Newco's investment in Oldco, may be accounted for partly at fair value and partly at predecessor cost; that is, at the residual equity interest of Newco shareholders who were also Oldco shareholders. EITF Issue 88-16 does not, however, address how to allocate the purchase price to Oldco's individual assets in consolidation.

Accounting Issue

How should Newco allocate its investment in Oldco to Oldco's individual assets and liabilities if Oldco was acquired in an LBO transaction in which a portion of Newco's Oldco investment is valued at predecessor basis?

EITF Consensus

The EITF reached a consensus that Newco's investment in Oldco should be allocated to its individual assets and liabilities based on the partial purchase method, which is similar to a step acquisition.

The EITF recognized that, generally, all retained earnings and accumulated depreciation are eliminated in LBO transactions accounted for under the consensus in Issue 88-16 as a result of the allocation used in measuring the investment. Although that practice is inconsistent with the partial purchase method, which would require carrying over Oldco's retained earnings and accumulated depreciation for the portion of the investment valued at predecessor basis, this consensus does not require or change that practice.

SEC Staff Comment

One of the problems that result from using the partial purchase method to allocate Oldco's assets and liabilities is that Newco's realization of tax benefits from Oldco's net operating loss (NOL) carryforwards is split into an acquired NOL carryforward and a carryforward from losses in the prior year (not acquired). The SEC staff would object to the allocation of NOL carryforwards in that manner, even though a strict application of the partial purchase method would require that treatment. The SEC staff believes that the entire NOL carryforward should be considered an acquired carryforward.

Discussion

Generally, in an acquisition of a 100 percent interest in a company, the purchase price is allocated to assets and liabilities based on their fair values. However, in an LBO transaction accounted for under the consensus in Issue 88-16, in which part of the investment is valued at predecessor basis, the allocation of fair value to each asset and liability will not be equal to Newco's investment in Oldco.

Newco's investment in Oldco can be equal to Oldco's net assets in one of two ways. Under the full purchase method, the amount assigned to goodwill is adjusted so that Oldco's net assets equal Newco's investment. Under the partial purchase method, one portion of the amount allocated to each asset is based on its fair value and another portion is based on predecessor basis. The proportion of fair value and predecessor basis is the same as the proportion used to determine the amount of Newco's investment in Oldco. For example, if 70 percent of the investment in an LBO transaction is based on the fair value of the net assets and 30 percent is based on predecessor basis in the net assets acquired, Oldco's assets and liabilities would be allocated in the same manner. (This treatment is similar to the one used in consolidation, if only 70 percent of an entity's net assets had been acquired.)

The EITF reached its consensus based on the same rationale used to reach the consensus in Issue 88-16. That is, LBO transactions are similar to step acquisitions, under which assets and liabilities are revalued in proportion to a change in ownership. Proponents of this method argued that Oldco's assets and liabilities should be allocated in consolidation in the same manner used to measure Newco's investment in Oldco. Similarly, companies that acquire a majority interest in a subsidiary, but not a 100 percent interest, do not present a minority interest in consolidated financial statements at fair value.

STUDY QUESTION

15. For basis allocations discussed in Issue 90-12 that use the partial purchase method:

   a. One portion of the amount allocated to each asset is based on its fair value and another portion is based on the predecessor basis.

   b. The proportion of fair value and predecessor basis is the inverse of the proportion used to determine the amount of Newco's investment in Oldco.

   c. The treatment is the opposite of that used in consolidation.

   d. None of the above

Illustration Using EITF Issue 90-12 Consensus

The following illustration shows the book and fair values of Oldco's assets and liabilities, and the amount that would be allocated to each asset and liability under the partial purchase method, assuming that new shareholders acquire 70 percent of Newco at fair value and Oldco shareholders acquire 30 percent of Newco at predecessor basis or book value.

	Allocation of Basis		
	Book Value	**Fair Value**	**Partial Purchase Method**
Cash	$10,000	$10,000	$10,000 (a)
Accounts recievable	$40,000	$40,000	$40,000
Inventory	100,000	110,000	107,000 (a)
Fixed Assets	250,000	300,000	285,000 (a)
Goodwill	—	140,000	98,000
Accounts payable	(100,000)	(100,000)	(100,000) (a)
Pension liabilities	—	(100,000)	(70,000) (a)
Net assets	$300,000	$400,000	$370,000

(a) Calculation based on 70% fair value and 30% book value
(b) The amount required for assets less liabilities to equal the purchase price

ISSUE 91-5, *Nonmonetary Exchange of Cost-Method Investments*

Overview

A cost-method investor has an investment in the common stock of a company, which is involved in a business combination. The investor will receive either new stock that represents an ownership interest in the combined entity, or the shares currently held by the investor will represent an ownership interest in the combined entity. According to the provisions of paragraph 70 of APB 16, the company that will hold a majority interest in the combined entity is considered to be the acquirer. The combined company will continue to be publicly traded.

> **OBSERVATION**
>
> FAS 141 (paragraphs 15-19) requires that the acquiring entity be identified in all business combinations. It provides, generally, that the acquiring entity is the one that distributes cash or other assets or incurs liabilities, in a combination that is effected solely by those means. In combinations effected through an exchange of equity interests, the entity that issues the equity interests is usually the acquiring entity. In combinations involving more than two entities, consideration should be given to which entity initiated the combination and whether the assets, revenues, and earnings of one entity are significantly greater than those of the others.

Accounting Issues

Should an investor that uses the cost method to account for an investment in shares of Company B (the acquiree) account for an exchange of those shares in a business combination at fair value, thus recognizing a new accounting basis in the investment and a realized gain or loss to the extent fair value differs from the investor's cost basis?

Should an investor in Company A, which is considered the acquirer in a business combination, account for a cost-method investment in the same manner as the investor in the previous situation?

Would the consensus on both of the preceding issues change if before the business combination, an investor in either company also held an investment in the other company that was a party to the transaction?

EITF Consensus

A cost-method investor in a company considered to be the acquiree should recognize the investment at fair value.

> **OBSERVATION**
>
> FAS 115 requires entities to report investments in marketable equity securities at fair value. *Realized* gains on securities available for sale (not trading securities) are reported in the financial statements in income. *Unrealized* holding gains and losses are reported in the financial statements in other comprehensive income in accordance with the guidance in FAS 130, which amends FAS 115, but the total amount of accumulated unrealized gains and losses should continue to be reported in a separate component of shareholders' equity until those amounts are realized. Accordingly, under the consensus in Issue 1, an investor would recognize a new cost basis in the securities of Company B exchanged for securities in the combined entity and report a realized gain or loss in income.

A cost-method investor in a company considered to be the acquirer should continue to carry the investment at historical cost.

> ### OBSERVATION
>
> Although the investor would continue carrying the investment at its historical cost, under the provisions of FAS 115, as amended (see the Observation above), the investor is required to report the fair value of the investment in its financial statements and to report *unrealized* holding gains or losses in comprehensive income.

The conclusion in Issues 1 and 2 would not change if an investor in either company also held an investment in the other company before the merger.

> ### OBSERVATION
>
> Paragraphs 15–19 of FAS 141 provide guidance for determining which company is the acquirer.

Illustration Using EITF Issue 91-5 Consensus

Company Z has an investment in 1,000 shares of Company T, which it carries at cost ($35,000), and an investment in 1,000 shares of Company A, which it also carries at cost ($50,000). Company T enters into a business combination with Company A. Shareholders of Company T receive 0.5 shares of stock in Company A for each share of Company T. After the combination, 1,000,000 shares of the combined entity are outstanding, of which 550,000 (or 55 percent) are owned by former shareholders in Company A and 450,000 shares are owned by former shareholders in Company T. The fair value of a share in the combined entity is $80.

As a result of the transaction, Company Z would own 1,500 shares of the combined entity (1,000 × .5 shares of Company T plus 1,000 shares of Company A). Based on the consensus in the issue of a new accounting basis, Company Z would change its basis in the 500 shares of Company A received for its stake in Company T to $40,000 (500 × $80) and would realize a gain of $5,000. Under the consensus in Issue 2, Company Z would continue carrying its investment in the combined entity at $50,000, which is the cost basis of its investment in Company A.

Discussion

The underlying question in EITF Issue 91-5 is whether the investor's exchange of shares of one entity for shares in the combined entity is an event that culminates the earnings process. That depends on whether the original investment is in the company whose shareholders receive the greater interest in the shares of the combined entity (the acquirer) or in the company whose shareholders receive the lesser interest (the acquiree). The EITF's consensus positions reflect the view that the exchange of shares by the acquiree's shareholders results in the culmination of the earnings process. Those shareholders actually disposed of their investment in Company T (in the illustration immediately preceding) in exchange for shares in the combined entity in which they will not have a controlling interest.

ISSUE 90-5, *Exchange of Ownership Interests Between Entities under Common Control*

Overview

A parent company plans to combine its two subsidiaries, Sub A and Sub B, both of which have minority interests outstanding. The transaction could be effected by having Sub A issue stock or pay cash to the parent for the parent's interest in Sub B. In addition, Sub A could acquire the minority interest in Sub B.

AICPA Accounting Interpretation (AIN) 39, *Transfers and Exchanges between Companies Under Common Control,* of APB 16 and FTB 85-5 require a transfer of net assets or an exchange of shares between companies under common control to be recorded at historical cost, similar to a pooling. Accordingly, Sub A would record its investment in Sub B at historical cost.

Applying AIN 39 of APB 16 and FTB 85-5 becomes more complicated if the parent company had originally acquired Sub B in a purchase transaction in which the purchase price differed from the parent's share in the historical cost of Sub B's assets and liabilities. (The parent did not use push-down accounting to revalue the subsidiary's assets and liabilities because of the existence of a minority interest in Sub B.) As a result, the recorded cost of the parent's investment in Sub B and the historical cost of Sub B's net assets in the parent's consolidated financial statements differ from the historical cost of the parent's share of net assets in Sub B's financial statements.

EXAMPLE

A parent company acquired a 70 percent interest in Sub B for $125 million while the carrying amount of Sub B's assets and liabilities was $100 million at the date of acquisition. If the parent does not push down its basis to the subsidiary's financial statements, the parent's investment in Sub B is $125 million while its share of Sub B's assets and liabilities is $70 million (70 percent of $100 million). Further, Sub B's assets and liabilities will be shown at $155 million in the parent's consolidated financial statements ($125 million for the parent company's share of 70 percent of the subsidiary's net assets and $30 million for the 30 percent minority interest).

Neither Accounting Interpretation (FIN) 39 of APB 16 nor FTB 85-5 provides guidance as to whether a subsidiary should be presented in the parent's consolidated financial statements at the historical cost of the parent company's investment in a subsidiary, or at the historical cost of the parent's share of the subsidiary's assets and liabilities as shown in the subsidiary's financial statements.

OBSERVATION

FAS 141 supersedes FIN 39, but FAS 141 carries its guidance forward and unchanged in paragraphs D11–D13. The consensus in this Issue continues to apply to transactions initiated after June 30, 2001.

Accounting Issues

Should the acquiring subsidiary's consolidated financial statements reflect the acquired subsidiary's assets and liabilities at the historical cost in the financial statements of the acquiree or at the historical cost in the consolidated financial statements of the parent?

If a subsidiary that acquires the net assets of another subsidiary under common control also acquires a minority interest in that subsidiary in a transfer of assets or an exchange of shares, does the amount at which the acquisition is recognized depend on whether the consideration to the minority shareholders is in cash or stock?

EITF Consensus

The acquiring subsidiary's consolidated financial statements should reflect the acquired subsidiary's assets and liabilities at their historical cost in the parent company's consolidated financial statements. The Task Force noted that because the parent company is transferring its interest in one controlled subsidiary to another controlled subsidiary, the transfer is at the historical cost of the subsidiary's assets and liabilities in the parent's consolidated financial statements as required by Accounting Interpretation 39 of APB 16. In addition, the acquiring subsidiary must be a substantive entity with its own operations.

Regardless of the method of payment, the acquisition of one subsidiary's minority interest by another subsidiary under common control should be recognized in the acquiring subsidiary's consolidated financial statements at fair value under the purchase method using an objective and reliable basis to value the shares, such as a quoted market price.

Discussion

As stated previously, Accounting Interpretation 39 of APB 16 requires a transfer of net assets or an exchange of shares between companies under common control to be recorded at historical cost, similar to a pooling. This issue revolved around an interpretation of the term **historical cost** as used in the Interpretation. Some believed that the APB was referring to the recorded amounts of the assets and liabilities in the acquired subsidiary's financial statements. However, the EITF's consensus is based on the view that the APB was referring to the parent company's basis in the subsidiary's assets and liabilities when they used the term historical cost. To support their position, proponents of this view compared the transfer of a parent's investment in Sub B to Sub A to a transfer of another asset, such as a building, which would be transferred at the parent's basis.

The EITF's consensus on the second Issue follows the guidance in paragraph 6 of FTB 85-5, which states that:

> [i]f some or all of the shares owned by minority shareholders are ex- changed for shares of ownership in another subsidiary of the parent (or a new subsidiary formed by combining two or more subsidiaries of the parent), then the transaction is recognized by the parent company as the acquisition of shares from the minority interest, which accord- ing to paragraph 43 of Opinion 16 should be accounted for by the purchase method, that is, based on fair value.

The EITF noted, however, that FTB 85-5 requires the exchange to be sub- stantive; that is, a change of ownership has to occur. Otherwise, the exchange should be accounted for at historical cost.

STUDY QUESTIONS

16. Under Issue 90-5, the acquisition of one subsidiary's minority interest by another subsidiary under common control should be recognized in the acquiring subsidiary's consolidated financial statements at fair value under the purchase method. *True or False?*

17. The AICPA's Accounting Interpretation 39 of APB 16 uses the term *historical cost* to mean:

   a. Recorded amounts of assets and liabilities in the acquired subsidiary's financial statements

   b. Recorded amounts of assets and liabilities in the acquiring subsidiary's consolidated financial statements

   c. The parent company's basis in the subsidiary's assets and liabilities

   d. None of the above is the meaning

ISSUE 90-13, *Accounting for Simultaneous Common Control Mergers*

Overview

Parent Company enters into two transactions with Newsub. First, Parent obtains a controlling interest in Newsub in a cash transaction. Second, Parent transfers its subsidiary, Oldsub, to Newsub for additional shares in Newsub. The two transactions are negotiated almost simultaneously.

A company engaged in several lines of business may structure a transaction in this manner to enable it to combine the operations of one of its subsidiaries in a specific line of business with a publicly traded company in that business and also retain control of the subsidiary. As a result of the transaction, Parent has a publicly held subsidiary operating in an identifiable line of business that enables Parent and Newsub's shareholders to assess Newsub's operations and value based on the price-earnings ratio in that separate line of business.

Some believe this transaction is a transfer between two entities under common control and should be accounted for under the provisions of AICPA Accounting Interpretation 39 of APB 16, which would require accounting for the transaction at historical cost. Others believe that Parent is exchanging its subsidiary for an interest in an independent entity and would therefore account for the transaction as a purchase business combination at fair value.

Accounting Issues

In a two-step acquisition in which Parent transfers its ownership in Oldsub to Newsub (in which Parent has just acquired a majority interest), should Parent's transfer of its interest in Oldsub be accounted for as a purchase of an additional interest in Newsub or as a transfer between two entities under common control under the provisions of Accounting Interpretation 39 of APB 16?

If Accounting Interpretation 39 of APB 16 does not apply and the transfer is recorded at fair value:

- Should Parent recognize a gain on the transfer of Oldsub?
- How should Parent determine the values to be assigned to the assets and liabilities of Newsub, Oldsub, and the minority interest for presentation in its consolidated financial statements?
- How should Newsub account for the transaction?

EITF Consensus

If Parent's acquisition of a controlling interest in Newsub and the transfer of Oldsub to Newsub were negotiated at the same time, the two transactions cannot be separated and should be viewed as a simultaneous common control merger. Accordingly, Interpretation 39 of APB 16 would not apply and the transfer should be recognized at fair value.

OBSERVATION

FAS 141 supersedes FIN 39 but carries its guidance forward and unchanged in paragraphs D11–D13.

In accordance with the consensus in EITF Issue 86-29, Parent should recognize the transaction as a partial sale of Oldsub to the minority shareholders of Newsub and as a partial acquisition of Newsub.

To determine the values to be assigned to the assets and liabilities of Newsub, Oldsub, and the minority interest for presentation in its consolidated financial statements, Parent should:

- Revalue Newsub's assets and liabilities based on the percentage of the interest in the company that the Parent acquired.
- Revalue Oldsub's assets and liabilities based on the percentage of the subsidiary that it sold.

> **OBSERVATION**
>
> The guidance in Issue 2c has been superseded by paragraphs 15–19 of FAS 141, which supersede the guidance in APB 16, paragraph 70, on how to identify the acquiring entity in a business combination.

EITF members noted that the revaluation of Oldsub's assets and liabilities is consistent with the consensus on Issue 2a—that the Parent should record a gain or loss based on the percentage of its interest in Oldsub that it sold.

Discussion

Under the provisions of APB 16, an acquiring entity records an acquiree's assets and liabilities in a purchase business combination at fair value unless the acquirer and the acquiree are under the common control of another entity. If both entities are under the common control of another entity, the acquirer records an acquiree's assets and liabilities at historical cost, similar to a pooling of interests, in accordance with Accounting Interpretation 39 of APB 16.

If one entity (Parent) exchanges shares of a subsidiary (Oldsub) for shares of Newsub, the relationship after the transaction would be depicted as shown in Figure 1.

The accounting for the transaction differs depending on the relationship of Parent, Oldsub, and New-

Figure 1

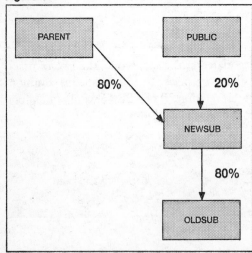

sub before the transaction. **Figure 2**
If Parent did not con-
trol Newsub before the
transaction (as in the next
diagram), Parent would
record its investment in
Newsub at the fair value of
the shares received and record a gain on the partial
sale of Oldsub to New-
sub's minority sharehold-
ers in accordance with the
consensus in EITF Issue
86-29 (Figure 2).

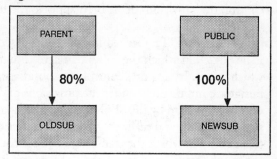

If, however, Parent **Figure 3**
controlled Newsub before
the transaction (as in the
following diagram), Par-
ent would recognize its
increased investment in
Newsub at the historical
cost of Oldsub's assets and
liabilities (Figure 3).

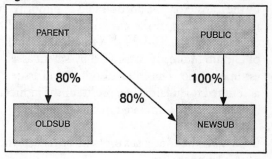

The transaction discussed in this Issue was made in two steps:
1. Parent acquired control of Newsub.
2. Parent transferred Oldsub to Newsub.

If the transaction is viewed as two independent transactions, the shares in Newsub that Parent obtained in Step 1 would be valued at fair value, and the shares obtained in Step 2 would be valued at historical cost. However, if the transaction is viewed as one simultaneous transaction, all the shares would be valued at fair value.

Issue 1. The underlying issue here was whether Parent should recognize a gain or loss on the transfer of its interest in Oldsub to Newsub. Under Accounting Interpretation 39 of APB 16, no gain or loss is recognized if a transaction does not involve outsiders. This type of transaction is not considered a business combination under APB 16 and would therefore be accounted for at historical cost. Thus, if the EITF had determined that Parent acquired its interest in Newsub in one transaction and later transferred Oldsub to Newsub in exchange for an additional interest, the transaction would have been accounted for under the Interpretation. However, because the EITF determined that the two transactions—obtaining control and the merger—were negotiated before Oldsub and Newsub were under common control, the provisions of APB 16 apply to the transfer of Oldsub.

Issue 2a. The EITF reached its consensus based on the guidance in EITF Issue 86-29, in which the EITF had agreed that exchanges of securities in which one entity acquires control of a subsidiary should be accounted for as business combinations under the provisions of APB 16. However, because of concerns raised by the SEC staff that a company could get a 100 percent step-up in basis and realize a gain on a transfer of similar productive assets to an entity in which the transferor acquires control and thus continues to control the transferred assets, the EITF agreed in Issue 86-29 that gain recognition should be limited to that portion of the assets no longer controlled by the transferor (the portion sold to minority shareholders). Consequently, in its consensus in the current Issue, the EITF agreed by analogy to the consensus in Issue 86-29 that no gain should be recognized on the portion of Oldsub indirectly controlled by Parent as a result of its controlling interest in Newsub. The EITF also noted in Issue 86-29 that if an exchange is accounted for at fair value, profit for the indirectly controlled portion of the asset should be eliminated in consolidation.

Issue 2b. The consensus on Issue 2c reflects the view that Newsub consists of two components:

- Newsub, in which Parent has a majority interest.
- Oldsub, in which Parent also has retained a majority interest as a result of its majority interest in Newsub.

That is, the EITF agreed that Newsub's and Oldsub's assets and liabilities should be valued at fair value or historical cost in proportion to the interests acquired, sold, or retained. Therefore, Parent would value the percentage of Newsub's assets and liabilities acquired at fair value and the percentage of Oldsub's assets and liabilities retained at historical cost. The minority interest in Newsub's assets and liabilities retained by its former shareholders would be valued at historical cost, but the minority interest in Oldsub's assets and liabilities acquired by Newsub's minority shareholders would be valued at fair value.

ISSUE 01-3, *Accounting in a Purchase Business Combination for Deferred Revenue of an Acquiree*

Overview
Under the purchase accounting guidance in FAS 141, *Business Combinations,* an acquirer allocates the cost of an acquiree to identifiable assets acquired and liabilities assumed based on their fair values, so that assumed liabilities are accounted for as part of the purchase price. If an assumed liability is

associated with deferred revenue on an acquiree's balance sheet before an acquisition is consummated, the fair value of the assumed liability after the acquisition date may differ from the amount previously recognized on the acquiree's balance sheet as deferred revenue.

Accounting Issues

When a liability for deferred revenue appears on an acquiree balance sheet before the acquisition, how should an acquirer determine whether the liability should be recognized in a purchase business combination? If the liability is recognized, how should it be measured?

How should recognized liabilities be presented in an acquiree's balance sheet after an acquisition?

Should an acquirer recognize an expense or reduce revenue for an exclusivity arrangement acquired and recognized as an intangible asset in a business combination?

EITF Consensus

The EITF reached the following consensus positions:

- An acquirer should recognize a liability for an acquiree's deferred revenue arrangement only if it has assumed a legal obligation to provide goods, services, or other consideration to customers (legal performance obligation). If an acquiree recognized deferred revenue because it was obligated to grant a customer future concessions—for example, due to an inability to make reasonable estimates of returns under FAS 48, *Revenue Recognition When Right of Return Exists*, for price protection provisions under the terms of a revenue arrangement, or as a result of extended payment terms—the acquirer has assumed a legal performance obligation.

- An acquirer that has no legal performance obligation should not recognize a liability in a business combination if, for example, an acquiree had recognized deferred revenue, for example, because:
  - Collectibility of a receivable was not reasonably assured.
  - An acquiree received a note subject to subordination for a real estate sale and accounted for that sale under the cost recovery method by recognizing the deferred gain as revenue on the cash basis after the cost of the property has been recovered.
  - An acquiree entered into a sale-operating leaseback of nonintegral equipment on which the gain is amortized into income over the lease term.
  - An acquiree is required to defer revenue under SOP 97-2, *Software Revenue Recognition,* on a software sale with extended payment terms.

The EITF noted that a liability for a performance obligation related to an acquiree's revenue arrangement should be recognized based on the fair value of the performance obligation at the date of acquisition as required in FAS 141, *Business Combinations.*

An acquirer may recognize an asset and a liability as a result of an arrangement acquired in a business combination. For example, an entity acquires a building and a lease obligation related to that building in a business combination. The fair value of the building should be presented as an asset and the estimated fair value of the assumed lease obligation should be presented separately as a liability in the balance sheet.

The income statement presentation model in Issue 01-9, *Accounting for Consideration Given by a Vendor to a Customer (Including a Reseller of the Vendor's Products),* applies to amortization of an exclusivity arrangement acquired in a business combination only if the acquiree had not negotiated the arrangement independently of the acquirer. Amortization of an arrangement negotiated independently by an acquirer should be reported as an expense.

EXAMPLE

Company A, which sells cleaning supplies to Company X, discusses paying a fee to Company X for the right to become its exclusive vendor for cleaning supplies. At the same time, Company A agrees to acquire Company B, which is in the same business as Company A. Shortly before the business combination is consummated, Company B enters into an exclusivity arrangement with Company X that is identical to the agreement discussed with Company A. Under this scenario, Company A's amortization of the fair value of the exclusivity arrangement negotiated by Company B and acquired in Company A's business combination with Company B should be accounted for as a reduction of Company A's consolidated revenue.

STUDY QUESTION

18. Under FAS 141, assumed liabilities of the acquiree are accounted for:

  a. At their historical value

  b. At discounted future value

  c. As part of the purchase price

  d. As deferred revenue

FASB/SEC STAFF ANNOUNCEMENTS

Topic D-54, *Accounting by the Purchaser for a Seller's Guarantee of the Adequacy of Liabilities for Losses and Loss Adjustment Expenses of an Insurance Enterprise Acquired in a Purchase Business Combination*

When an insurance enterprise is acquired in a purchase business combination, the seller may provide the buyer with guarantees to indemnify the purchaser for unanticipated increases in identified and unidentified liabilities that exist at the acquisition date. Such guarantees often are provided to cover losses and loss adjustment expenses for coverage with long payout periods, because of the difficulty of estimating the ultimate liability and timing of the payout.

Although similar guarantees may be provided in business combinations of other types of business enterprises, the FASB's announcement is limited to liabilities of short-duration insurance contracts of insurance enterprises in purchase business combinations. The FASB staff cautioned that the announcement does not apply to business combinations accounted for as poolings or to transactions outside the scope of APB 16, such as spinoffs or initial public offerings.

The FASB staff provided the following guidance on the purchaser's accounting:

- Paragraphs 22–24 of FAS 113 do not apply in accounting for reserve guarantees. The FASB staff believes that such guarantees should be accounted for the same as other guarantees of the existence of assets or the adequacy of liabilities that may be provided in business combinations between non-insurance enterprises.
- In accordance with FAS 60, *Accounting and Reporting by Insurance Enterprises,* the practitioner should recognize in income in the period in which they occur (a) changes in the liabilities for losses and loss adjustment expenses and (b) differences between estimates and payments for claims, including acquired liabilities subject to the reserve guarantee.
- Recognize a receivable for the amount due from the seller under the reserve guarantee, subject to an assessment of collectibility, with a corresponding credit to income.
- Include subsequent changes in the balance of the receivable in income in the period in which the estimates change (or payments are received, if differences arise between estimates and payments); such changes should not affect the acquirer's accounting for the business combination.

This announcement applies to arrangements in which a seller obtains reinsurance from a third-party reinsurer who will directly indemnify the acquirer for increases in liabilities for losses and expenses to adjust losses that existed at the date a purchase business combination was consummated and others with similar but not identical circumstances as those discussed in the announcement, based on the specific facts and circumstances. To apply the provisions of this announcement:

- An **acquiree** has to agree to participate in unexpected increases in liabilities for losses and in the expense of adjusting losses that exist at the consummation of a purchase business combination, or to indemnify the acquirer without retaining a direct obligation in such increases, for example, by obtaining a reinsurance arrangement.

- An arrangement that guarantees unexpected increases in liabilities that existed at the date a purchase business combination is consummated should occur **simultaneously** with, and be contingent on, the purchase business combination. Such a guarantee arrangement must commit to all the significant terms at the time a purchase business combination is consummated. The provisions of FAS 113 would apply, however, if the terms can be amended at a later date. If the acquirer retains any risk for increases in the acquiree's liabilities after a purchase business combination has been consummated, the arrangement was not simultaneous with the transaction.

OBSERVATION

The FASB has observed that selling enterprises should follow the provisions of FAS 113, *Accounting and Reporting for Reinsurance of Short-Duration and Long-Duration Contracts,* if applicable, in accounting for reinsurance arrangements entered into before or after a purchase business combination, even if the purchaser is identified as the direct beneficiary of the reinsurance arrangement. Using the pooling-of-interests method to account for a business combination is prohibited under the provisions of FAS 141, *Business Combinations,* which supersedes the guidance in APB 16, *Business Combinations.*

SEC Observer Comment. The SEC staff prefers a presentation of the gross effects of a reserve guarantee. The receivable from the seller should be presented separately from the related liability in the balance sheet or in the notes to the financial statements or in SEC Industry Guide 6 disclosures. Although the staff prefers that (a) expenses associated with increased reserves be reported as a component of other claim losses and loss adjustment expenses and (b) the effect of the reserve guarantee not be used to reduce the balance of other claim losses and loss adjustment expenses, the staff would not object to a net presentation in the income statement of the components in (b) if the effects of the reserve guarantee are separately disclosed in the notes to the financial statements, in the SEC Industry Guide 6 disclosures including the reconciliation of claims reserves, and in the loss ratio information. Management's Discussion and analysis also should clearly disclose the effect of such an arrangement on operations and cash flows.

Topic D-87, *Determination of the Measurement Date for Consideration Given by the Acquirer in a Business Combination When That Consideration Is Securities Other Than Those Issued by the Acquirer*

In response to questions on this topic, the FASB staff announced that the date a purchase business combination is consummated should be the measurement date for securities, other than those issued by the acquirer, that are transferred to shareholders in a business combination. The staff believes that this accounting conforms to the guidance in paragraph 94 of APB 16. Further, the staff believes it is also consistent with the guidance in FAS 125, because the acquirer controls the securities until the transaction is consummated. The assets are not isolated from the transferor and its creditors and the transferee does not have the right to exchange or pledge the securities until the transaction is consummated.

The staff notes that using the consummation date as the measurement date avoids issues related to fixing the value of the securities if FAS 115 or APB 18 requires that the carrying value of the investment be adjusted for changes in fair value or for the investee's operating results. This announcement applies to purchase business combinations consummated after March 16, 2000.

Topic D-100, *Clarification of Paragraph 61(b) of FASB Statement No. 141 and Paragraph 49(b) of FASB Statement No. 142*

The FASB staff provided the following guidance to clarify the application of paragraph 61(b) of FAS 141 and paragraph 49(b) of FAS 142, *Goodwill and Other Intangible Assets*. The FASB formally cleared this staff announcement at its October 10, 2001, meeting.

Paragraph 61(b) of FAS 141 requires entities that had consummated purchase business combinations before July 31, 2001, to reclassify and account separately from goodwill for the carrying amounts of (1) recognized intangible assets that qualify for recognition under the criteria in paragraph 39 of the Statement and (2) unidentifiable intangible assets that were recognized in accordance with FAS 72, *Accounting for Certain Acquisitions of Banking or Thrift Institutions*.

The transition guidance in paragraph 61(b) should be applied as follows to all intangible assets acquired in a purchase business combination consummated before July 31, 2001, including those with indefinite useful lives:

■ Acquirer should account for the intangible asset separately from goodwill. This accounting should be applied by entities that separately identified intangible assets acquired in a purchase business combination, estimated their fair values at acquisition, determined their useful lives, and recognized deferred taxes related to those assets. Even though the carrying amounts of those intangible assets may have been combined with goodwill for external reporting purposes, the entity maintained separate subsidiary ledgers for goodwill and for the individual intangible assets to which they posted periodic amortization and charges for impairment.

- Acquirer should not change the amount of the purchase price allocated to goodwill. This accounting applies to entities that recognized intangible assets acquired in a purchase business combination as a single asset with goodwill. Even though the acquired intangible assets had been separately identified and their fair values were estimated at acquisition, separate accounting records were not maintained for those assets and the combined asset (goodwill) was amortized over its estimated composite useful life.

The FASB staff also noted the following:

- Core deposit intangible (CDI) assets of an acquired financial institution should not be recognized with goodwill, because the staff believes that they meet the criteria for separate recognition in paragraph 39 of FAS 141.
- Failure to reclassify acquired intangible assets might affect the amount of future losses recognized as a result of an impairment of goodwill, because those losses would be measured as the difference between the carrying amount of goodwill, which includes the **carrying amount** of intangible assets, and the implied fair value of goodwill, which would not include the **fair value** of the intangible assets.
- FAS 141 does not affect the requirement in paragraph 5 of FAS 72 that financial institutions recognize and amortize the unidentifiable intangible asset that results when the fair value of liabilities assumed in the acquisition of another financial institution exceed the fair value of the tangible and intangible assets acquired.

OBSERVATION

As a result of the issuance of FAS 147, *Acquisitions of Certain Financial Institutions,* which amends the scope of FAS 72, acquisitions of all financial institutions, except for transactions between mutual enterprises, must be accounted for in accordance with the guidance in FAS 141 and FAS 142. Guidance for transactions between mutual enterprises is being addressed in a separate project.

STUDY QUESTIONS

19. According to Topic D-54, when an insurance enterprise is acquired in a purchase business combination, all of the following are applicable for guarantees to buyers indemnifying them from unanticipated increases in liabilities *except:*

  a. Spinoffs

  b. Business combinations accounted for as poolings

  c. Initial public offerings

  d. All of the above are inapplicable for purposes of guarantees under Topic D-54

20. Failure to reclassify acquired intangible assets might affect the amount of future losses recognized as a result of impaired goodwill because those losses would be measured as the difference between the carrying amount of goodwill and the implied fair value of goodwill. *True or False?*

CONCLUSION

This chapter has drawn from many source documents in Levels B and C of the GAAP hierarchy. The only Level B pronouncement is a brief document addressing two questions about business combinations. The literature in Level C covers a wide variety of specialized topics, with concentrations of issues in new basis accounting and combinations of entities under common control. This literature provides important clarifications to Level A GAAP and additional guidance in applying it to the many complex transactions that take place when businesses combine.

MODULE 2 — CHAPTER 3
Pension Plans—Employers

LEARNING OBJECTIVES

This chapter examines accrual accounting intricacies for various types of pension plans used today. After exploring how plan assets are managed under FAS 87, the chapter breaks net periodic pension costs into their components. The text details how and when plan assets are measured. The timely topic of disclosures required in financial statements—including interim statements—for pension plans is examined in depth. Finally, the chapter explains accounting processes for specific types of plans, such as multiemployer plans, multiple-employer plans, non-U.S. pension plans, and plans in business combinations.

Upon completion of this chapter, the professional will be able to:

■ Apply concepts of FAS 87 in recording entries for pension events;

■ Perform calculations to determine the net periodic pension cost;

■ Value pension plan assets;

■ Prepare disclosures regarding pension plans for financial statements;

■ Understand treatment of specific types of pension plans across multiple employers, foreign companies, and mergers among plan sponsors.

OVERVIEW

GAAP for employers' accounting for pension plans center on the determination of annual pension expense (identified as net periodic pension cost) and the presentation of an appropriate amount of pension liability in the statement of financial position. Net periodic pension cost has often been viewed as a single homogeneous amount, but it is actually made up of several components that reflect different aspects of the employer's financial arrangements, as well as the cost of benefits earned by employees.

In applying principles of accrual accounting for pension plans, the Financial Accounting Standards Board (FASB) emphasizes three fundamental features:

■ *Delayed recognition*—Changes in the pension obligation and changes in the value of pension assets are recognized not as they occur, but systematically and gradually over subsequent periods.

■ *Net cost*—The recognized consequences of events and transactions affecting a pension plan are reported as a single net amount in the employer's financial statements. This approach results in the aggregation of items that would be presented separately for any other part of the employer's operations: the compensation cost of benefits, the interest cost resulting from deferred payment of those benefits, and the results of investing pension assets.

■ *Offsetting*—Pension assets and liabilities are shown net in the employer's statement of financial position, even though the liability has not been settled. The assets may still be controlled and substantial risks and rewards associated with both are clearly borne by the employer.

GAAP for accounting for pensions by employers may be found in the following pronouncements:

FAS 87   *Employers' Accounting for Pensions;* and
FAS 132(R)   *Employers' Disclosures about Pensions and Other Postretirement Benefits.*

BACKGROUND

Employment is based on an explicit or implicit exchange agreement. The employee agrees to provide services for the employer in exchange for a current wage, a pension benefit, and frequently other benefits such as death, dental, or disability. Although pension benefits and some other benefits are not paid currently, they represent deferred compensation that must be accounted for as part of the employee's total compensation package.

Pension benefits usually are paid to retired employees or their survivors on a periodic basis, but they may be paid in a single lump sum. Other benefits, such as death and disability, may also be provided through a pension plan. Most pension plans also provide benefits upon early retirement or termination of service.

A pension plan may be **contributory** or **noncontributory;** that is, the employees may be required to contribute to the plan (contributory), or the entire cost of the plan may be borne by the employer (noncontributory). A pension plan may be **funded or unfunded;** that is, the employees and/or the employer may make cash contributions to a pension plan trustee (funded), or the employer may make only credit entries on its books reflecting the pension liability under the plan (unfunded). Pension plans are accounted for on the accrual basis, and any difference between net periodic pension cost charged against income and the amount actually funded is recorded as an accrued or prepaid pension cost.

OBSERVATION

A qualified pension plan under the Employee Retirement Income Security Act (ERISA) has to be funded. Every year the plan actuary must determine the minimum funding for the defined benefit pension plan. If the plan fails to meet the minimum funding requirement, a penalty tax is imposed on the employer on the funding deficiency.

Although interest cost on the pension liability and the return (or loss) on a pension plan's assets will increase or decrease net periodic pension cost, they are considered financial costs rather than employee compensation costs. Financial costs can be controlled by the manner in which the employer provides financing for the pension plan. An employer can eliminate interest cost by funding the plan completely or by purchasing annuity contracts to settle all pension obligations. The return on plan assets can be increased by the contribution of more assets to the pension fund.

STUDY QUESTION

> **1.** Pension plans use the _____ method of accounting.
>   **a.** Cash
>   **b.** Hybrid
>   **c.** Accrual
>   **d.** None of the above is used for pension plans

Pension Plan Accounting

The assets of a pension plan usually are kept in a trust account, segregated from the assets of the employer. Contributions to the pension trust account are made periodically by the employer and, if the plan is contributory, by the employees. The plan assets are invested in stocks, bonds, real estate, and other types of investments. Plan assets are increased by contributions and earnings and gains on investments and are decreased by losses on investments, payment of pension benefits, and administrative expenses. The employer usually cannot withdraw plan assets placed in a trust account. An exception arises, however, when the plan assets exceed the pension obligation and the plan is terminated. In this event, the pension plan agreement may permit the employer to withdraw the excess amount of plan assets, providing that all other existing pension plan obligations have been satisfied by the employer. Under GAAP, pension plan assets that are not effectively restricted for the payment of pension benefits or segregated in a trust are not considered pension plan assets.

Accounting and reporting for a pension plan (defined benefit plan) as a separate reporting entity are covered by FAS 35, *Accounting and Reporting by Defined Benefit Pension Plans.*

Deferred Compensation Plan

A **deferred compensation plan** is a contractual agreement that specifies that a portion of the employee's compensation will be set aside and paid in future periods as retirement benefits. FAS 87, *Employers' Accounting for Pensions,* covers deferred compensation plans that are in substance pension plans.

Postemployment and postretirement benefits generally are considered a form of deferred compensation to an employee because an employer provides these types of benefits in exchange for an employee's services. Thus, these benefits must be measured properly and recognized in the financial statements and, if the amount is material, financial statement disclosure may be required.

STUDY QUESTION

2. Reporting rules for defined benefit pension plans as separate entities are given in:
   a. FAS 35
   b. FAS 87
   c. FAS 132
   d. FAS 132 (revised 2003)

OVERVIEW OF FAS 87

Scope and Applicability

Most of the provisions of FAS 87 address **defined benefit pension plans** of single employers. A defined benefit pension plan is one that contains a pension benefit formula, which generally describes the amount of pension benefit that each employee will receive for services performed during a specified period of employment (FAS 87, par. 11). The amount of the employer's periodic contribution to a defined benefit pension plan is based on the total pension benefits (projected to employees' normal retirement dates) that could be earned by all eligible participants.

In contrast, a **defined contribution pension plan** does not contain a pension benefit formula, but generally specifies the periodic amount that the employer must contribute to the pension plan and how that amount will be allocated to the eligible employees who perform services during that same period. Each periodic employer contribution is allocated among separate accounts maintained for each employee, and pension benefits are based solely on the amount available in each employee's account at the time of his or her retirement.

For the purposes of FAS 87, any plan that is not a defined contribution pension plan is considered a defined benefit pension plan (see the definition of *defined benefit pension plan* in Appendix D of FAS 87).

FAS 87 requires that its provisions be applied to any arrangement, expressed or implied, that is similar in substance to a pension plan, regardless of its form or method of financing. Thus, a pension plan arrangement does not have to be in writing if the existence of a pension plan is implied by company policy. A qualified plan, however, has to be in writing under ERISA, as well as for federal and state tax purposes. Frequently, defined contribution pension plans provide for some method of determining defined benefits for employees, as may be the case with some **target benefit plans**. A target benefit plan is a defined contribution plan. The benefit defined in the document is only for the purpose of determining the contribution to be allocated to each participant's account. It is not intended to promise any benefit in the future. If, in substance, a plan does provide defined benefits for employees, it is accounted for as a defined benefit pension plan.

Actuarial Assumptions

Actuarial assumptions are factors used to calculate the estimated cost of pension plan benefits. Employee mortality, employee turnover, retirement age, administrative expenses of the pension plan, interest earned on plan assets, and the date on which a benefit becomes fully vested are some of the more important actuarial assumptions (FAS 87, par. 39).

Under FAS 87, each significant actuarial assumption must reflect the best estimate for that particular assumption. In the absence of evidence to the contrary, all actuarial assumptions are made on the basis that the pension plan will continue in existence (going-concern concept) (FAS 87, par. 43).

Discount rates used in actuarial valuations reflect the rates at which the pension benefits could be settled effectively. In selecting appropriate interest rates, employers should refer to current information on rates used in annuity contracts that could be purchased to settle pension obligations, including annuity rates published by the Pension Benefit Guaranty Corporation (PBGC) or the rates of return on high-quality fixed-income investments that are expected to be available through the maturity dates of the pension benefits (FAS 87, par. 44).

An **actuarial gain or loss** is the difference between an actuarial assumption and actual experience. Under FAS 87, actuarial gains and losses are not included in net periodic pension cost in the year in which they arise, but may be recognized in subsequent periods if certain criteria are met (FAS 87, par. 29).

OBSERVATION

In accounting for pension plans—particularly defined benefit plans—the CPA relies heavily on the expertise of actuaries. Actuaries are educated in mathematics, modeling, and other areas that permit them to deal with the many uncertainties required to make estimates related to an enterprise's pension plan that are necessary for both funding and financial reporting. Actuarial assumptions are one area in which the CPA is particularly vulnerable, because of the significant impact that different actuarial assumptions may have on the elements of the financial statements. Auditors who are relying on the work of actuaries should consult SAS 73, *Using the Work of Specialist* (AU 336).

STUDY QUESTION

3. All of the following are actuarial assumptions *except:*
   a. Date of full vesting of benefits
   b. Interest earned on plan assets
   c. Retirement age
   d. All of the above are actuarial assumptions

Pension Plan Assets

The resources of a pension plan may be converted into:

- Plan assets that are invested to provide pension benefits for the participants of the plan, such as stocks, bonds, and other investments (FAS 87, par. 19); or
- Plan assets that are used in the operation of the plan, such as real estate, furniture, and fixtures (FAS 87, par. 51).

Plan assets must be segregated in a trust or otherwise effectively restricted so that the employer cannot use them for other purposes. Under FAS 87, plan assets do not include amounts accrued by an employer as net periodic pension cost, but not yet paid to the pension plan. Plan assets may include securities of the employer if they are freely transferable (FAS 87, par. 19).

Pension plan assets that are held as investments to provide pension benefits are measured at fair value (FAS 87, par. 23). Pension plan assets that are used in the operation of the plan are measured at cost, less accumulated depreciation or amortization (FAS 87, par. 51). All plan assets are measured as of the date of the financial statements or, if used consistently from year to year, as of a date not more than three months prior to that date (FAS 87, par. 52).

For the purposes of FAS 87, plan liabilities that are incurred, other than for pension benefits, may be considered reductions of plan assets (Appendix D of FAS 87, under definition of *plan assets*).

Recording Pension Events

Under FAS 87, an enterprise makes two primary types of entries in its records each accounting period:

- To record pension expense (called **net periodic pension cost** in FAS 87 and discussed later in this chapter); and
- To record funding of the pension plan.

Depending on the circumstances, a third entry to record an additional pension liability may be required.

Basic Entries to Record Pension Events

Maddux Co. determines its net periodic pension cost to be $10,000 for 20X5, its first year of operation. An equal amount is funded by transferring cash to the insurance company that administers the plan. No additional entry for an additional pension liability is required. The entries to record these events areas follow:

Pension expense	$10,000
Accrued/prepaid pension cost	$10,000
Accrued/prepaid pension cost	10,000
Cash	10,000

In this case, the pension expense is fully funded and no accrued/prepaid pension cost balance exists. If less than $10,000 had been funded, the balance in accrued/prepaid pension cost would have been a liability. If more than $10,000 had been funded, the balance in accrued/prepaid pension cost would have been an asset.

As the figure shows, the accrued/prepaid pension cost carries the accumulated balance resulting from under- or overfunding of pension expense. The transfer of cash to the plan administrator is treated as a retirement of the pension liability. The pension asset and pension liability are effectively offset, and neither is presented in the employer's statement of financial position.

If the additional pension liability entry had been required, an intangible pension asset generally would have been debited and accrued/prepaid pension cost credited. The amount of the intangible pension asset is limited, however, to the amount of unrecognized prior service cost that may cause a negative element of stockholders' equity to emerge (i.e., excess of additional pension liability over unrecognized prior service cost). That procedure is explained later in this chapter.

Most of the provisions of FAS 87 pertain to the computation of the amount to be recorded in the first journal entry type in the above illustration as net periodic pension cost. This computation requires numerous worksheet calculations, which are illustrated throughout FAS 87.

Pension Plan Terminology

Key terms that are important for an understanding of accounting for pensions in accordance with FAS 87 are discussed below.

Projected Benefit Obligation. The **projected benefit obligation** is the actuarial present value, as of a specified date, of the total cost of all employees' vested and nonvested pension benefits that have been attributed by the pension benefit formula to services performed by employees to that date.

The projected benefit obligation includes the actuarial present value of all pension benefits (vested and nonvested) attributed by the pension benefit formula, **including consideration of future employee compensation levels** (FAS 87, Appendix D). Vested benefits are pension benefits that an employee has an irrevocable right to receive at a date specified in the pension agreement, even if the employee does not continue to work for the employer (FAS 87, Appendix D). In the event a pension plan is discontinued, a vested benefit obligation remains a liability of the employer.

Payments of pension benefits decrease both the projected benefit obligation and the fair value of plan assets, whereas contributions to a plan decrease accrued pension cost (or increase the prepaid pension cost), and increase the fair value of plan assets.

The projected benefit obligation does not appear on the books of the employer. However, the employer maintains a worksheet record of the projected benefit obligation.

Accumulated Benefit Obligation. An **accumulated benefit obligation** is an alternative measure of the pension obligation; it is calculated like the projected benefit obligation, except that current or past compensation levels instead of future compensation levels are used to determine pension benefits (FAS 87, Appendix D). Under FAS 87, an employer must recognize an additional minimum liability in its statement of financial position, if its accumulated benefit obligation exceeds the fair value of pension plan assets as of a specified date. The amount of the additional minimum liability must at least equal the employer's **unfunded accumulated benefit obligation,** which is the amount by which the accumulated benefit obligation exceeds the fair value of plan assets (FAS 87, par. 36). In the event a pension plan is discontinued, the balance of any unfunded accumulated benefit obligation remains a liability of the employer.

> **OBSERVATION**
>
> Basically, there are two types of pension benefit formulas: pay-related benefit and nonpay-related benefit. For a nonpay-related benefit formula, the accumulated benefit obligation and the projected benefit obligation are the same.

Fair Value of Plan Assets. The **fair value of plan assets** is the amount that a pension plan could reasonably be expected to receive from a current sale of plan assets, which are held to provide pension benefits, between a willing buyer under no compulsion to buy and a willing seller under no compulsion to sell (FAS 87, Appendix D). Plan assets that are used in the operation of the pension plan (building, equipment, furniture, fixtures, etc.) are valued at cost less accumulated depreciation or amortization (FAS 87, par. 51).

Pension plan assets are recorded on the books of the pension plan. However, an employer maintains worksheet records of the cost and fair value of all pension plan assets.

Funded Status of Plan. For the employer's accounting purposes, the **funded status of plan** is the difference between the projected benefit obligation and the fair value of plan assets as of a given date (FAS 87, Appendix B). If the projected benefit obligation exceeds the fair value of the plan assets, a pension plan liability exists. If the fair value of plan assets exceeds the projected benefit obligation, a pension plan asset exists.

Unrecognized Prior Service Cost. The **Unrecognized prior service cost** is the portion of prior service cost that has not been recognized by the employer in net periodic pension cost of any period. Upon the initial adoption of a pension plan or through a plan amendment, certain employees may be granted pension benefits for services performed in prior periods. These retroactive pension benefits are referred to as **prior service costs,** which usually are granted by the employer with the expectation that they will produce future economic benefits, such as reducing employee turnover, improving employee productivity, and minimizing the need to increase future employee compensation. Under FAS 87, an employer is required to amortize any prior service cost in equal amounts over the future periods of active employees who are expected to receive the benefits (FAS 87, par. 24).

An employer does not record unrecognized prior service cost on its books but maintains worksheet records of such amounts.

Unrecognized Net Gain or Loss. An **unrecognized net gain or loss** is the amount of actuarial gain or loss for a period that has not been recognized by the employer in net periodic pension cost of any period.

Actuarial gains or losses arise from the difference between (1) the actual and expected amount of projected benefit obligation at the end of a period, and/or (2) the actual and expected amount of the fair value of pension plan assets at the end of the period. Under FAS 87, actuarial gains or losses are not recognized by the employer in the period in which they arise, but they may become subject to recognition in subsequent periods if certain criteria are met (FAS 87, par. 29).

An unrecognized net gain or loss that, as of the beginning of the year, exceeds 10 percent of the greater of (1) the projected benefit obligation or (2) the market-related value of plan assets is subject to recognition. Recognition for the year is equal to the amount of unrecognized net gain or loss in excess of 10 percent of the greater of the projected benefit obligation or the value of plan assets, divided by the average remaining service period of active employees expected to receive benefits under the plan. This frequently is referred to as the **corridor test** in applying FAS 87 (FAS 87, par. 32).

Actuarial gains and losses are recognized on the books of a pension plan as they occur. However, an employer does not record actuarial gains or losses on its books but maintains worksheet records of such amounts.

Unrecognized Net Obligation (or Net Asset) at Date of Initial Application of FAS 87. The **unrecognized net obligation or net asset at date of initial application of FAS 87** is the difference between the projected benefit obligation and the fair value of plan assets, plus previously recognized unfunded accrued pension cost or minus previously recognized prepaid pension cost at the time FAS 87 was adopted. This unrecognized net obligation or net asset represents the difference between the funded status of a plan (projected benefit obligation less the fair value of plan assets) and the total amount of accrued or prepaid pension cost existing on the books of the employer as of the date of the initial application of FAS 87 (FAS 87, par. 77).

The unrecognized net obligation or net asset as of the date of initial application of FAS 87 is amortized on a straight-line basis over the average remaining service period of employees expected to receive benefits under the plan, except that (1) if the amortization period is less than 15 years, the employer may elect to use 15 years, and (2) if the plan is composed of all or substantially all inactive participants, the employer shall use those participants' average remaining life expectancy as the amortization period (FAS 87, par. 77).

The amount of the employer's unrecognized obligation or net asset is included in the projected benefit obligation as of the date of the employer's initial application of FAS 87. However, an employer does not record its unrecognized net obligation or net asset on its books as of the date of the initial application of FAS 87, but maintains a worksheet record of such amount.

Accrued or Prepaid Pension Cost. The **accrued pension cost** is the total amount of net periodic pension cost that has been recognized but not funded. A **prepaid pension cost** is the total amount that has been funded in excess of the total amount of the net periodic pension cost that has been recognized.

An accrued or prepaid pension cost is recorded on the books of the employer.

STUDY QUESTION

4. The difference between calculating the projected benefit obligation and accumulated benefit obligation measures is that the latter calculates pension benefits by:

a. Future compensation levels

b. Current or past compensation levels

c. Actuarial present value of all vested or unvested pension contributions

d. None of the above

NET PERIODIC PENSION COST

The employer's **net periodic pension cost** represents the net amount of pension cost for a specified period that is charged against income. Under FAS 87, the components of net periodic pension cost are the following:

- Service cost;
- Interest cost on the projected benefit obligation;
- Actual return on plan assets;
- Amortization of unrecognized prior service cost (if any);
- Recognition of net gain or loss (if required by FAS 87); and
- Amortization of the unrecognized net obligation or net asset existing at the date of initial application of FAS 87 (FAS 87, par. 20).

All of the components of net periodic pension cost are not necessarily recognized on the books of the employer when they arise.

EXAMPLE

The total prior service cost that results from a plan amendment is determined in the period in which it arises. Under the provisions of FAS 87, however, the employer recognizes cost in equal amounts over the future service periods of each active employee who is expected to receive the benefits of the plan amendment that gave rise to the prior service cost (FAS 87, par. 24).

Net periodic pension cost is estimated in advance at the beginning of a period based on actuarial assumptions relating to:

- The discount rate on the projected benefit obligation;
- The expected long-term rate of return on pension plan assets; and
- The average remaining service periods of active employees covered by the pension plan.

At the end of the period, adjustments are made to account for the differences (actuarial gains or losses), if any, between the estimated and actual amounts (FAS 87, par. 29).

The actuarial assumptions used to calculate the previous year's net periodic pension cost are used to calculate that cost in subsequent interim financial statements, unless more current valuations of plan assets and obligations are available or a significant event has occurred, such as a plan amendment, which usually would require new valuations (FAS 87, par. 52).

The components of net periodic pension cost that are either partially recognized or not recognized at all on the employer's books in the period in which they arise are:

- Unrecognized prior service cost;
- Unrecognized net asset gain or loss; and
- Unrecognized net obligation or net asset existing at the date FAS 87 is initially applied.

The following figure shows how the different components of net periodic pension cost are estimated.

Computing Net Periodic Pension Cost	
Service cost component	$2,000
Interest cost component	3,000
Estimated return on plan assets	(2,500)
Amortization of unrecognized prior service cost	1,000
Amortization of unrecognized net (gain) or loss	1,000
Amortization of initial unrecognized net obligation (asset)	1,500
Total net periodic pension cost	$6,000

For simplicity, an assumption is made that there are no differences (actuarial gains or losses) between the estimated and actual amounts at the end of the period, and that the employer made no contributions to the pension fund during the period.

		Beginning of Period	End of Period
(a)	Projected benefit obligation	$(115,000)	$(120,000)
(b)	Fair value of plan assets	65,000	67,500
(c)	Funded status of plan	$(50,000)	$(52,500)
(d)	Unrecognized prior service cost	10,000	9,000
(e)	Unrecognized net (gain) or loss	5,000	4,000
(f)	Unrecognized net obligation or (net asset) at date of initial application of FAS 87	35,000	33,500
(g)	(Accrued) or prepaid pension cost	$0	$(6,000)

The following journal entry is recorded by the employer for net periodic pension cost:

Net periodic pension cost	$6,000
Accrued pension cost	$6,000

The following explains the changes in the accounts that were affected by the net periodic pension cost accrual.

(a) *Projected benefit obligation* An increase in the projected benefit obligation of $5,000, representing the service cost component of $2,000 and interest cost component of $3,000 for the period. The projected benefit obligation is not recorded in the employer's books but is important information in accounting for pension cost.

(b) *Fair value of plan assets The* $2,500 increase in the fair value of plan assets between the beginning and end of the period represents the increase in the fair value of plan assets for the period. The fair value of plan assets is not recorded in the employer's books, but is important information in accounting for pension cost.

(c) *Funded status of plan The* $2,500 decrease in the funded status of the plan, between the beginning and end of the period, is the difference between the $5,000 increase in the projected benefit obligation for the period and the $2,500 increase in the fair value of plan assets for the period.

(d) Unrecognized prior service cost The $1,000 decrease in the unrecognized prior service cost between the beginning and end of the period is the amount of amortization of prior service cost that has been recognized by the employer as a component of net periodic pension cost.

The unrecognized prior service cost is not recorded on the books of the employer, but worksheet records are maintained for such amounts. Thus, the employer reduces the worksheet balance of the unrecognized prior service cost by $1,000.

(e) Unrecognized net gain or loss The $1,000 decrease in the unrecognized net gain or loss (actuarial gain or loss) between the beginning and end of the period is the amount of amortization that has been recognized by the employer as a component of net periodic pension cost.

The unrecognized net gain or loss (actuarial gain or loss) is not recorded on the books of the employer, but worksheet records are maintained for such amounts. Thus, the employer reduces the worksheet balance of the unrecognized net gain or loss by $1,000.

(f) Unrecognized net obligation or net asset at date of initial application of FAS 87 The $1,500 decrease in the unrecognized net obligation between the beginning and the end of the period is the amount of amortization that has been recognized by the employer as a component of net periodic pension cost for the period. The unrecognized net obligation or net asset is not recorded on the books of the employer, but worksheet records are maintained for such amounts. Thus, the employer reduces the worksheet balance of the unrecognized net obligation or net asset by $1,500.

> (g) *Accrued or prepaid pension cost* The $6,000 increase in the accrued or prepaid pension cost between the beginning and the end of the period is the amount of the net periodic pension cost for the period that has not been funded by employer contributions.
>
> Accrued pension cost is the total amount of net periodic pension cost that has been recognized to date but not funded by contributions to the pension plan. Prepaid pension cost is the total amount that has been funded by contributions to date, in excess of the total amount of net periodic pension cost that has been recognized.

STUDY QUESTION

> **5.** All of the following are used in the actuarial assumptions to estimate net periodic pension cost before the beginning of a period *except:*
>
> **a.** Unrecognized net asset gain or loss
> **b.** Discount rate on the projected benefit obligation
> **c.** Average remaining service periods of covered active employees
> **d.** Expected long-term rate of return on plan assets

Service Cost Component

In a defined benefit pension plan, FAS 87 requires that a pension benefit formula be used to determine the amount of pension benefit earned by each employee for services performed during a specified period. Under FAS 87, **attribution** is the process of assigning pension benefits or cost to periods of employee service, in accordance with the pension benefit formula (FAS 87, par. 21).

The **service cost component of net periodic pension cost** is defined as the actuarial present value of pension benefits attributed by the pension benefit formula to employee service during a specified period (FAS 87, par. 21).

> **EXAMPLE**
>
> A pension benefit formula may state that an employee shall receive, at the retirement age stated in the plan, a pension benefit of $20 per month for each year of service for life.

Future Values of Benefits. To compute the total future value of the pension benefit for the year, the monthly benefit is multiplied by the number of months in the employee's life expectancy at retirement age. This number of months is determined by reference to mortality tables. The actuarial present value of all employees' future pension benefits that are earned during a period is computed and included as the service cost component of the net periodic pension cost for the same period (FAS 87, par. 40).

If the terms of the pension benefit formula provide for benefits based on estimated future compensation levels of employees, estimates of those future compensation levels are used to determine the service cost component of net periodic pension cost. For example, if the pension benefit formula states that an employee's benefit for a period is equal to 1 percent of his or her final pay, an estimate of the employee's final pay is used to calculate the benefit for the period. Assumed compensation levels should reflect the best estimate of the future compensation levels of the employee involved and be consistent with assumed discount rates to the extent that they both incorporate expectation of the same future economic conditions (FAS 87, par. 202). Thus, future compensation levels in final-pay plans or career-average-pay plans are reflected in the service cost component of net periodic pension cost. Assumed compensation levels also shall reflect changes because of general price levels, productivity, seniority, promotion, and other factors (FAS 87, par. 46).

Plan Amendments. Changes resulting from a plan amendment that has become effective and automatic benefit changes specified by the terms of the pension plan, such as cost-of-living increases, are included in the determination of service cost for a period (FAS 87, par. 48).

An employer's substantive commitment to make future plan amendments in recognition of employees' prior services may indicate pension benefits in excess of those reflected in the existing pension benefit formula. Such a commitment may be evidenced by a history of regular increases in nonpay-related benefits, benefits under a career-average-pay plan, or other evidence. In this event, FAS 87 requires that the pension plan be accounted for based on the employer's substantive commitment, and that appropriate disclosure be made in the employer's financial statements (FAS 87, par. 41).

A plan's pension benefit formula might provide no benefits for the first 19 years of an employee's service and a vested benefit of $1,000 per month for life in the 20th year of an employee's service. This benefit pattern is no different than providing a benefit of $50 per month for 20 years and requiring 20 years before the benefits vest. If a pension plan benefit formula attributes all or a disproportionate portion of total pension benefits to later years, the employee's **total projected benefit** is calculated and used as the basis of assigning the total pension benefits under the plan. In this event, the employee's total projected benefit is assumed to accumulate in proportion to the ratio of the total completed years of service to date to the total completed years of service as of the date the benefit becomes fully vested (FAS 87, par. 42). An employee's total projected benefit from a pension plan is the actuarial present value of the total cost of pension benefits that the employee is likely to receive under the plan. If the pension benefit formula is based on future compensation, future compensation is used in calculating the employee's total projected benefit.

> **OBSERVATION**
>
> Under current pension law, the maximum time a single employer can make an employee wait before receiving vested benefits is 5 years. For a multi-employer plan, the longest period is 10 years.

STUDY QUESTION

6. Assumed compensation levels used to determine estimated future employee compensation in a pension benefit formula use all of the following expectations for compensation *except:*

   a. General price levels

   b. Seniority

   c. Productivity

   d. All of the above are used in developing assumed compensation levels

Unstated Manner of Accumulation. In the event a pension benefit formula does not indicate the manner in which a specific benefit relates to specific services performed by an employee, the benefit shall be assumed to accumulate as follows (FAS 87, par. 42):

- **If the benefit is includible in vested benefits**—the benefit is accumulated in proportion to the ratio of total completed years of service to date to the total completed years of service as of the date the benefit becomes fully vested.

- A vested benefit is a benefit that an employee has an irrevocable right to receive. For example, an employee is entitled to receive a vested benefit whether or not he or she continues to work for the employer; and

- **If the benefit is not includible in vested benefits**—the benefit is accumulated in proportion to the ratio of completed years of service to date to the total projected years of service. (An example of a benefit that is not includible in vested benefits is a death or disability benefit that is payable only if death or disability occurs during the employee's active service.)

Interest Cost Component

The two factors used to determine the actuarial present value of a future pension benefit are:

- The probability that the benefit will be paid to the employee (through the use of actuarial assumptions); and

- The time value of money (through the use of discounts for interest cost).

The probability that a pension benefit will be paid is based on actuarial assumptions such as employee mortality, employee turnover, and the date the benefits become vested.

EXAMPLE

An employer's liability for a retirement fund of $56,520 that is due in 10 years is not equal to a present liability of $56,520. At an 8 percent discount rate the $56,520 has a present value of only $26,179. The $26,179 increases each year by the employer's interest cost of 8 percent, and in 10 years grows to $56,520, if the 8 percent interest rate does not change.

FAS 87 requires an employer to recognize, as a component of net periodic pension cost, the interest cost on the projected benefit obligation. The interest cost is equal to the increase in the amount of the projected benefit obligation because of the passage of time (FAS 87, par. 22).

OBSERVATION

FAS 87 specifies that the interest cost component of net periodic pension cost shall *not* be considered to be interest for the purposes of applying the provisions of FAS 34, *Capitalization of Interest Cost*.

Actual Return on Plan Assets Component

The **actual return on plan assets** is equal to the difference between the fair value of plan assets at the beginning and end of a period, adjusted for employer and employee contributions (if a contributory plan) and pension benefit payments made during the period (FAS 87, par. 23). **Fair value** is the amount that a pension plan could reasonably be expected to receive from a current sale of an investment between a willing buyer under no compulsion to buy and a willing seller under no compulsion to sell. Plan assets that are used in the operation of the pension plan (building, equipment, furniture, fixtures, etc.) are valued at cost, less accumulated depreciation or amortization (FAS 87, par. 51).

A return on plan assets decreases the employer's cost of providing pension benefits to its employees, whereas a loss increases pension cost. Net periodic pension income can result from a significantly high return on pension plan assets during a period.

FAS 87 requires an employer to recognize, as a component of net periodic pension cost, the actual return (or loss) on pension plan assets (FAS 87, par. 16).

STUDY QUESTION

---

7. The actual return on plan assets is calculated using the difference between the fair value of plan assets at the beginning and end of a period adjusted for:

a. Changes in mortality rates listed in mortality tables during the period

b. Changes in interest rates on the assets during the period

c. Employer and employee contributions and pension benefits paid during the period

d. None of the above is used; the difference is the actual return on plan assets

---

AMORTIZATION OF UNRECOGNIZED PRIOR SERVICE COST COMPONENT

Upon the initial adoption of a pension plan or as the result of a plan amendment, employees may be granted pension benefits for services performed in prior periods. These **retroactive pension benefits** are assumed to have been granted by the employer in the expectation that they will produce future economic benefits, such as reducing employee turnover, improving employee productivity, and minimizing the need for increasing future employee compensation. The cost of pension benefits that are granted retroactively to employees for services performed in prior periods is referred to as **prior service cost** (FAS 87, par. 24).

Portion Included in Net Periodic Pension Cost. Under FAS 87, only a portion of the total amount of prior service cost arising in a period—including retroactive benefits that are granted to retirees—is included in net periodic pension cost. FAS 87 requires that the total prior service cost arising in a period from an adoption or amendment of a plan be amortized in equal amounts over the future service periods of **active** employees who are expected to receive the retroactive benefits (FAS 87, par. 25).

> **OBSERVATION**
>
> Because retirees are not expected to render future services, the cost of their retroactive benefits cannot be recognized over their remaining service periods. FAS 87 requires that the total prior service cost arising from a plan adoption or amendment, including the cost attributed to the benefits of retirees, shall be amortized in equal amounts over the future service periods of **only** the active employees who are expected to receive benefits.

If substantially all of the participants of a pension plan are inactive, the prior service cost attributed to the benefits of the inactive participants shall be amortized over the remaining life expectancy of those participants (FAS 87, par. 25).

> **OBSERVATION**
>
> The last sentence of paragraph 25 of FAS 87 addresses the method of amortizing that portion of the cost of retroactive plan amendments that affects benefits of inactive participants of a plan composed of substantially all inactive participants. However, the paragraph does not address the method of amortizing the portion of the cost of the same retroactive plan amendments that affect benefits of the active participants of the same plan. Two alternatives appear to be available. The first is that the cost of the active participants' benefits is charged to income of the period of the plan amendment. The second is that the cost of the **active** participants' benefits is amortized in the same manner as if the plan were not composed of substantially all inactive participants. In this event, the cost attributed to the retroactive benefits of the **active** participants of a plan composed of substantially all **inactive** participants is amortized in equal amounts throughout the future service periods of each active employee who is expected to receive the retroactive benefits.

STUDY QUESTION

8. To include the expense of benefits granted to retirees in the calculation of net periodic pension cost, the total prior service cost arising during a period is:

   a. Amortized in equal amounts over future service periods of only the active employees expected to receive benefits
   b. Amortized in equal amounts over the retirees' past service periods
   c. Amortized in equal amounts over future service periods for the total number of retirees receiving benefits
   d. None of the above is the method used

Alternative Amortization. FAS 87 permits the consistent use of an alternative amortization approach that more rapidly reduces the amount of unrecognized prior service cost. For example, straight-line amortization of unrecognized prior service cost over the average future service period of active employees who are expected to receive benefits under the plan is acceptable. If an alternative method is used to amortize unrecognized prior service cost, it must be disclosed in the financial statements (FAS 87, par. 26).

Effect of Regular Amendments. Some companies have a history of increasing pension benefits through regular plan amendments. In these cases, the period in which an employer expects to realize the economic benefits from retroactive pension benefits that were previously granted is shorter than the entire remaining future service period of all active employees. Under this circumstance, FAS 87 requires that a more rapid rate of amortization be applied to the remaining balance of the unrecognized prior service cost to reflect the earlier realization of the employer's economic benefits and to allocate properly the cost to the periods benefited (FAS 87, par. 27).

An amendment to a pension plan usually increases the cost of employees' pension benefits and increases the amount of the projected benefit obligation. However, a pension plan amendment may decrease the cost of employees' pension benefits, which results in a decrease in the amount of the projected benefit obligation. Any decrease resulting from a pension plan amendment shall be applied to reduce the balance of any existing unrecognized prior service cost and any excess shall be amortized on the same basis as increases in unrecognized prior service cost (FAS 87, par. 28).

Gains and Losses Component

Gains and losses are changes in the amount of either the projected benefit obligation or pension plan assets, resulting from the differences between estimates or assumptions used and actual experience. Thus, a gain or loss can result from the difference between (1) the expected and actual amounts of the projected benefit obligation at the end of a period, and/or (2) the expected and actual amounts of the fair value of pension plan assets at the end of a period. Technically, both of these types of gains and losses are considered **actuarial gains and losses.** Under FAS 87, however, a gain or loss resulting from a change in the projected benefit obligation is referred to as an **actuarial gain or loss,** whereas a gain or loss resulting from a change in the fair value of pension plan assets is referred to as a **net asset gain or loss.** For the purposes of FAS 87, the sources of these gains and losses are not distinguished separately, and they include amounts that have been realized as well as amounts that are unrealized (FAS 87, par. 29).

Under FAS 87, the gains and losses component of net periodic pension cost consists of (1) the difference between the expected and actual returns on pension plan assets (net asset gain or loss), and (2) if required, amortization of any unrecognized gain or loss from previous periods (FAS 87, par. 34).

As discussed previously, the actual return on pension plan assets is equal to the difference between the fair value of pension plan assets at the beginning and end of a period, adjusted for any contributions and pension benefit payments made during that period. Fair value is the amount that a pension plan could reasonably be expected to receive from a current sale of an investment between a willing buyer under no compulsion to buy and a willing seller under no compulsion to sell.

Computing Expected Return. The expected return on pension plan assets during the period is computed by multiplying the **market-related value** of plan assets by the **expected long-term rate of return.** The expected long-term rate of return is an actuarial assumption of the expected long-term rate of return that will be earned on plan assets during the period. Under FAS

87, the current rate of return earned on plan assets and the likely reinvestment rate of return should be considered in estimating the long-term rate of return on plan assets. The expected long-term rate of return on plan assets should reflect the average rate of earnings expected on plan investments (FAS 87, par. 45).

To reduce the volatility of changes in the fair value of pension plan assets and the resulting effect on net periodic pension cost, FAS 87 requires the use of a market-related value for plan assets to compute the expected return on such assets during a period. Market-related value is used only to compute the expected return on pension plan assets for the period (Expected return = Market-related value × Expected long-term rate of return) (FAS 87, par. 30).

Under FAS 87, the market-related value of a plan asset can be either: (1) the actual fair value of the pension plan asset; or (2) a calculated value that recognizes, in a systematic and rational manner, the changes in the actual fair value of the pension plan asset during a period of not more than five years (FAS 87, par. 30). Thus, in computing the market-related value of a pension plan asset, an enterprise may use actual fair value or a calculated value based on a five-year moving average of the changes in the actual fair value of the pension plan asset. In this event, the calculated market-related value would include only 20 percent of the total changes in the actual fair value of the pension plan asset that have occurred during the past five years.

> **EXAMPLE**
>
> If the actual fair value of a plan asset at the end of each of the last six years was $8,000, $10,000, $12,000, $14,000, $16,000, and $13,000, the net gain for the most recent five years is $5,000 ($2,000 + $2,000 + $2,000 + $2,000 − $3,000 = $5,000). In this event, only 20 percent of the $5,000 gain ($1,000) is included in computing the calculated market-related value of the pension plan asset for the current year.

The difference between the actual fair value of a pension plan asset and its calculated market-related value is the amount of net gain or loss from previous years that has not yet been recognized in the calculated market-related value.

Market-related value may be computed differently for each class of plan assets, but the method of computing it must be applied consistently from year to year for each class of plan assets. For example, fair value may be used for bonds and other fixed income investments, and a calculated market-related value for stocks and other equities (FAS 87, par. 30).

Illustration of Computing Market-Related Value

For computing the market-related value of a particular class of plan assets as of the end of each period, an employer uses a calculated value that includes 20 percent of the gains and losses on the plan assets that have occurred over the last five years. The total market-related value of this particular class of plan assets at the beginning of calendar year 20X5 was $100,000. The total fair value of the plan assets was $120,000 at the beginning of 20X5 and $130,000 at the end of 20X5. Actual gains and losses for the past five years as of the beginning of 20X5 were: 20X0 $10,000; 20X1 $(8,000); 20X2 $12,000; 20X3 $10,000; 20X4 $(4,000); the result is a net gain of $20,000 for these five years. Employer's contributions to the plan for 20X5 are estimated at $2,000 and benefit payments expected to be paid from the plan in 20X5 are also $2,000. The expected long-term rate of return on plan assets for 20X5 is 10 percent. The computation of the estimated market-related value as of December 31, 20X5, for this particular class of plan assets is determined as follows:

Market-related value at the beginning of period	$100,000
Add:	
Expected return on assets for 20X5 (market-related value, multiplied by expected long-term rate of return	10,000
20% of the net gain or loss for the last five years 20% × $20,000)	4,000
Employer's contribution	2,000
Benefit payments made from plan	(2,000)
Estimated market-related value, Dec. 31, 20X5	$114,000

NOTE

A The difference between the fair value ($130,000) and market-related value ($114,000) of plan assets at the end of 20X5 is $16,000. This difference represents the amount of net gain from the five years to the beginning of 20X5 that has not yet been recognized in the market-related value of plan assets.

The expected return on plan assets is based on market-related values, which do not include all of the net asset gains and losses from previous years (unless market-related values are equal to fair values). Thus, net asset gains and losses may include both (1) gains and losses of previous years that have been included in market-related value, and (2) gains and losses of previous years that have not yet been included in market-related value (FAS 87, par. 31).

As mentioned above, FAS 87 does not require the recognition of any gains and losses as components of net periodic pension cost of the period in which they arise, except to the extent that the net asset gain or loss for the period offsets or supplements the actual return of pension plan assets for the period. In subsequent years, however, all gains and losses, except those that have not yet been recognized in the market-related values of pension plan assets, are subject to certain minimum amortization provisions of FAS 87.

STUDY QUESTION

9. The expected return on pension plan assets during a period is calculated by multiplying the market-related value of plan assets by:

    a. Long-term interest rates divided by the anticipated future benefit distributions

    b. Expected long-term rate of return

    c. Historic rate of return of plan assets

    d. None of the above

Recognition of Net Gains or Losses. FAS 87 requires recognition of unrecognized net gains or losses based on beginning-of-the-year balances. An unrecognized net gain or loss that, as of the beginning of the year, exceeds 10 percent of (1) the projected benefit obligation, or (2) the market-related value of plan assets, whichever is greater, is subject to recognition. The minimum recognition for the year is calculated by dividing the average remaining service period of active employees who are expected to receive benefits under the plan into the amount of unrecognized net gain or loss that, as of the beginning of the year, exceeds 10 percent of (1) the projected benefit obligation, or (2) the market-related value of plan assets, whichever is greater. If substantially all of a plan's participants are inactive, however, the average remaining life expectancy of the inactive participants is divided into the excess unrecognized net gain or loss subject to amortization. The computation of the minimum amortization required by FAS 87 is made each year based on beginning-of-the-year balances of unrecognized net gains or losses (FAS 87, par. 32).

In lieu of the minimum amortization of unrecognized gains and losses specified by FAS 87, an employer may use an alternative amortization method provided that the method (1) is systematic and applied consistently, (2) is applied to both gains and losses similarly, (3) reduces the unamortized balance by an amount greater than the amount that would result from the minimum amortization method provided by FAS 87, and (4) is disclosed in the financial statements (FAS 87, par. 33).

Illustration of Computing Market-Related Value

ABC Corporation had an unrecognized net obligation of $400 upon the initial adoption of FAS 87. ABC Corp. amortized $40 of this transition obligation in 20X5. The net asset (gain) or loss for 20X5, resulting from changes in actuarial assumptions, was a loss of $400, which was deferred as an unrecognized net loss for the year. The market-related value of pension plan assets at 20X6 is $1,600, and the average remaining service life of active employees is 10 years.

The expected net periodic pension cost for 20X6 is $340, determined as follows: the sum of service cost $200, interest cost $240 (10%), amortization of unrecognized net asset loss $20, and amortization of unrecognized net obligation $40, less a 10% expected return on plan assets of $160 (Expected return = Market-related value of plan assets of $1,600 × Expected long-term rate of return of 10%). No contributions were made to the pension plan in 20X6.

	Actual 12/31/X5	Expected 12/31/X6	Actual 12/31/X6
(1) Projected benefit obligation	$(2,400)	$(2,840)	$(2,900)
(2) Fair value of plan assets	1,640	1,800	1,750
Funded status of plan	$ (760)	$(1,040)	$(1,150)
Unrecognized prior service cost	0	0	0
Unrecognized net (gain) or loss	400	380	490
Unrecognized net obligation existing at 1/1/X1	360	320	320
(Accured)/prepaid pension cost	$0	$(340)	$(340)

(1) The difference between the actual projected benefit obligation for 20X5 and the expected projected benefit obligation for 20X6 is $440, which consists of the expected service cost of $200, and the expected interest cost of $240. However, the actual projected benefit for 20X6 increased $500 over the actual projected benefit for 20X5. The difference between the expected increase in the projected benefit obligation of $440 and the actual increase of $500 represents a $60 actuarial loss. The $60 loss occurred because the actuarial assumptions used were different from actual experience.

The $40 amortization of the unrecognized net obligation does not affect the projected benefit obligation because the full amount of the net obligation was recognized in the projected benefit obligation as of the date of the initial application of FAS 87.

(2) The difference between the actual fair value of plan assets for 20X5 and the expected fair value of plan assets for 20X6 is $160, which represents the 10 percent expected return on plan assets (market-related value of plan assets of $1,600 × 10 percent). However, the actual fair value of plan assets for 20X6 of $1,750 increased only $110 over the actual fair value of plan assets of $1,640 for 20X5. The difference between the expected increase in the fair value of plan assets of $160 and the actual increase of $110 represents a $50 net asset loss for the period. The loss occurred because the actual rate of return on pension plan assets was less than the expected rate of return.

Cost Components of Net Periodic Pension Cost for 20X6

FAS 87, as amended by FAS 132, *Employers' Disclosures about Pensions and Other Postretirement Benefits* (revised 2003), requires financial statement disclosure of the amount of net periodic pension cost for the period. The disclosure shall indicate separately the service cost component, the interest cost component, the expected return on plan assets for the period, the amortization of the unrecognized transition obligation or asset, gains and losses recognized, prior service cost recognized, and gain or loss recognized due to a settlement or curtailment (FAS 132, par. 5d).

Service cost	$200
Interest cost	240
Expected return on plan assets	(160)
Amortization of unrecognized net obligation	40
Amortization of prior service cost	0
Recognized net actuarial loss	20
Net periodic pension cost	340

NOTE

A net asset gain or loss is not recognized in the period in which it arises (FAS 87, par. 29). In this case, the net asset loss is $50—the difference between the expected return on plan assets, $160, and the actual return on plan assets, $110. The expected return on plan assets is included as a component of net periodic pension cost. Recognition of the net asset loss is deferred to future periods.

Computation of the Amortization of the Unrecognized Gain or Loss for 20x6

Unrecognized net (gain) or loss 1/1/X6	$400
Add asset gain or subtract asset loss not yet recognized in market-related values at 1/1 [difference between fair value of plan assets ($1,640) and market-related value ($1,600)	40
Unrecognized net (gain) or loss subject to the minimum amortization provisions of FAS 87	440
10% of the greater of the projected benefit obligation or market-related value at 1/1	(240)
Unrecognized net (gain) or loss subject to amortization	$200
Amortization for 20X6 (over the 10-year average remaining service life of active employees)	$ 20

> **NOTE**
>
> The unrecognized net (gain) or loss at 1/1 must be adjusted to exclude asset gains and losses not yet reflected in market-related values, because gains and losses are not required to be amortized (FAS 87, par. 31).

> **NOTE**
>
> The $60 loss that occurred in 20X6 as a result of the difference between the expected and actual projected benefit obligation for 20X6, and the $50 loss that occurred in 20X6 as a result of the difference between the expected and actual fair value of plan assets for 20X6, will become subject to the minimum amortization provisions of FAS 87 as of 1/1/X7. The computation of the amount of unrecognized net (gain) or loss as of 1/1/X7, is as follows:
>
> | | | |
> |---|---:|---:|
> | Unrecognized net asset (gain) or loss 1/1/X6 | | $400 |
> | Less: Amortization for 20X6 | | 20 |
> | Unrecognized net asset (gain) or loss 12/31/X6 | | 350 |
> | Add: Actuarial net (gain) or loss for 20X6 | | $60 |
> | Net asset (gain) or loss for 20X6 | 50 | 110 |
> | Unrecognized net (gain) or loss as of 1/1/X7 | | $490 |

Amortization of the Unrecognized Net Obligation or Net Asset (As of the Date of Initial Application of FAS 87)

The **funded status** of a pension plan for employer accounting purposes is equal to the difference between the projected benefit obligation and the fair value of pension plan assets. The funded status indicates whether the employer has underfunded or overfunded the pension plan.

The unrecognized net obligation or net asset of a pension plan is determined by the employer as of the date of its financial statements of the beginning of the year in which FAS 87 is first applied or, if used consistently from year to year, as of a date not more than three months prior to that date. The unrecognized net obligation or net asset is equal to the difference between the projected benefit obligation and fair value of pension plan assets, plus previously recognized unfunded accrued pension cost or less previously recognized prepaid pension cost. In the event there is no accrued or prepaid pension cost on the employer's statement of financial position as of the date of transition to FAS 87, the funded status of the pension plan and the unrecognized net obligation or net asset are exactly equal (FAS 87, par. 77).

An unrecognized net obligation or net asset is amortized by the employer on a straight-line basis over the average remaining service period of employees expected to receive benefits under the plan, as of the date of initial application of FAS 87, except under the following circumstances (FAS 87, par. 77):

- If the amortization period is less than 15 years, an employer may elect to use 15 years.
- If the plan is composed of all or substantially all inactive participants, the employer shall use those participants' average remaining life expectancy as the amortization period.

The above amortization method is also used to recognize, as of the date of the initial application of FAS 87, any unrecognized net obligation or net asset of a defined contribution pension plan.

STUDY QUESTION

---

10. An unrecognized net obligation or net asset as of the date on which FAS 87 is first applied is amortized:

- **a.** On a straight-line basis over the average remaining service period of all employees, including retirees
- **b.** On an accelerated basis of 10 years when obligations for inactive employees (retirees) are included
- **c.** On a straight-line basis over the average remaining service period of employees expected to receive benefits
- **d.** None of the above is the amortization approach

RECOGNITION OF LIABILITIES AND ASSETS

If an employer's total contribution to its pension plan for the period is not equal to the amount of net periodic pension cost as determined by the provisions of FAS 87, the difference is recognized by the employer either as a liability or as an asset (i.e., accrued/prepaid pension cost). A **liability** (unfunded accrued pension cost) is recognized if the amount of contribution is **less** than the amount of net periodic pension cost. If the amount of contribution is **more** than the amount of net periodic pension cost, an **asset** (prepaid pension cost) is recognized (FAS 87, par. 35).

An employer's **unfunded accumulated benefit obligation** is the amount by which the accumulated benefit obligation exceeds the amount of the fair value of plan assets as of a specific date. Under FAS 87, an **additional minimum li-**

ability must be recognized in the employer's statement of financial position if an unfunded accumulated benefit obligation exists and:

- An asset has been recognized as prepaid pension cost;
- A liability has been recognized as unfunded accrued pension cost in an amount that is less than the amount of the existing unfunded accumulated benefit obligation; or
- No accrued or prepaid pension cost has been recognized.

If an asset has been recognized as prepaid pension cost, the additional minimum liability is the amount of the existing unfunded accumulated benefit obligation plus the amount of the prepaid pension cost. If a liability has been recognized as unfunded accrued pension cost in an amount that is less than the amount of the existing unfunded accumulated benefit obligation, the additional minimum liability is the amount of the existing unfunded accumulated benefit obligation reduced by the amount of the unfunded accrued pension cost. If no accrued or prepaid pension cost has been recognized, the additional minimum liability is the amount of the existing unfunded accumulated benefit obligation (FAS 87, par. 36).

If an additional minimum liability is required to be recognized, generally an intangible asset in the same amount as the additional minimum liability is recognized. However, the amount of the intangible asset cannot exceed the total amount of any existing unrecognized prior service cost and any unrecognized net obligation. In the event that the intangible asset exceeds the total existing unrecognized prior service cost and unrecognized net obligation, the excess is reported in other comprehensive income, net of related tax benefits (FAS 87, par. 37).

> **OBSERVATION**
>
> Limiting the intangible asset to the amount of unrecognized prior service cost is based on the circumstances that give rise to the need to record an additional pension liability. When a pension plan is amended and benefits to employees are increased, the company's pension obligation immediately increases. The amount of pension assets probably will increase slowly over time, however, because pension plan funding usually is tied to the amount of pension expense recognized, and the recognition of prior service cost will be made gradually as that cost is amortized as a component of net periodic pension cost. In this circumstance, it is logical to limit the amount of the intangible pension asset to the amount of unrecognized prior service cost, which is a surrogate measure of the unamortized cost of the "employee goodwill" acquired upon amendment of the pension plan.

When a new determination of the amount of additional liability is made to prepare a statement of financial position, the related intangible asset and separate component of equity are adjusted or eliminated, as necessary (FAS 87, par. 38).

STUDY QUESTION

---

11. FAS 87 dictates that an additional minimum liability must be recognized in the employer's statement of financial position if an unfunded accumulated benefit obligation exists and all of the following conditions apply *except:*

a. No accrued or prepaid pension cost has been recognized.

b. A liability has been recognized as unfunded accrued pension cost that is less than the existing unfunded accumulated benefit obligation.

c. An asset has been recognized as a prepaid pension cost.

d. All of the conditions apply.

MISCELLANEOUS CONSIDERATIONS

Measurement of Plan Assets

All pension plan assets that are held as investments to provide pension benefits are measured at their fair values as of the date of the financial statements or, if used consistently from year to year, as of a date not more than three months prior to that date (FAS 87, par. 52). **Fair value** is the amount that a pension plan could reasonably be expected to receive for a current sale of an investment between a willing buyer under no compulsion to buy and a willing seller under no compulsion to sell. If an active market exists for a plan investment, fair value is determined by the market price. If an active market does not exist for a particular plan investment, selling prices for similar investments, if available, should be considered appropriately. If no market price is available, an estimate of the fair value of the plan investment may be based on its projected cash flow, taking into account current discount rates and investment risk. (FAS 87, par. 49).

Pension plan assets that are used in the actual operation of a plan are valued at amortized cost. Thus, buildings, leasehold improvements, furniture, equipment, and fixtures that are used in the everyday operation of a pension plan are valued at historical cost, less accumulated depreciation or amortization (FAS 87, par. 51).

Unless more current amounts are available for both the obligation and plan assets, the amount of additional minimum liability reported in interim financial statements shall be the same amount as reported by the employer in its previous year-end statement of financial position, adjusted for subsequent accruals and contributions (FAS 87, par. 52).

The same assumptions used to calculate the previous year-end net periodic pension cost are used to calculate the net periodic pension cost in subsequent interim and annual financial statements, unless more current valuations of plan assets and obligations are available or a significant event has occurred, such as a plan amendment that usually would require new valuations (FAS 87, par. 53).

STUDY QUESTION

> **12.** Pension plan assets held as investments should be valued at their fair values, but if an active market does not exist for an investment, the value used is:
>
> **a.** An estimate based on comparable investments
> **b.** Amortized cost
> **c.** Historical cost
> **d.** None of the above is used

Financial Statement Disclosure

The disclosure requirements that were originally included in FAS 87 (as well as in other pronouncements concerning pension and other postretirement benefits) were replaced by the disclosure requirements of FAS 132, *Employers' Disclosures about Pensions and Other Postretirement Benefits,* and again subsequently by FAS 132(R) (revised 2003). In addition to simplifying and streamlining disclosures about pensions, FAS 132(R) (revised 2003) consolidates the disclosures about pensions, settlement, and curtailment of pension plans, and retirement benefits other than pensions into a single set of requirements.

> **PRIVATE COMPANIES PRACTICE**
>
> An auditor is only concerned with misappropriation of asset (theft or defalcation) that results in a material financial statement misstatement. Immaterial theft, for example, is not important to the auditor, per se. However, if an immaterial theft has occurred, the auditor should be concerned about the bigger picture and whether the occurrence of the theft suggests a deficiency in internal control.

FAS 132(R) retains virtually all of the disclosure requirements of FAS 132 and requires additional disclosures in response to concerns expressed by users of financial statements. The incremental disclosures required by FAS 132(R) relate to types of plan assets, investment strategy, measurement dates, plan obligations, cash flows, and components of net periodic benefit cost recognized in interim periods.

Disclosures about Pension Plans and Other Postretirement Plans. Paragraph 5 of FAS 132(R) requires the following information to be provided for each period for which an income statement is presented:

- Reconciliation of beginning and ending balances of the benefit obligation showing separately the effects of
    - Service cost,
    - Interest cost,
    - Contributions by plan participants,
    - Actuarial gains and losses,
    - Changes in foreign currency exchange rates,
    - Benefits paid,
    - Plan amendments,
    - Business combinations,
    - Divestitures,
    - Curtailments,
    - Settlements,
    - Special termination benefits;
- Reconciliation of beginning and ending balances of the fair value of plan assets, showing separately the effects of:
    - Actual return on plan assets,
    - changes in foreign currency exchange rates,
    - Contributions by the employer,
    - contributions by plan participants,
    - Benefits paid,
    - business combinations,
    - divestitures,
    - Settlements;

- Funded status of the plan, amounts not recognized in the statement of financial position, and amounts recognized in the statement of financial position, including:
  - Amount of any unamortized prior service cost,
  - Amount of any unrecognized net gain or loss,
  - Amount of any remaining unamortized, unrecognized net obligation or net asset existing at the initial application of FAS 87 or FAS 106, Employers' Accounting for Postretirement Benefits Other Than Pensions,
  - Net pension or other postretirement benefit prepaid assets or accrued liabilities,
  - Any intangible asset and the amount of accumulated other comprehensive income;
- Information about plan assets:
  - For each major category of plan assets (such as equity or debt securities, real estate and other assets) the percentage of the fair value of total plan assets held as of the measurement date
  - Narrative description of investment policies and strategies
  - Narrative description of the basis used to determine the overall expected long-term rate-of-return-on-asset assumption
  - Additional asset categories and additional information about specific assets within a category are encouraged, if useful in understanding the risks associated with each asset category and its expected long-term rate of return;
- For defined benefit pension plans:
  - The accumulated benefit obligation,
  - The benefits expected to be paid in each of the next five fiscal years and in the aggregate for the five fiscal years thereafter,
  - The employer's best estimate of contributions expected to be paid to the plan during the next fiscal year;
- The amount of net periodic benefit cost recognized, showing separately:
  - The service cost component,
  - The interest cost component,
  - The expected return on plan assets,
  - amortization of the unrecognized transition obligation or transition asset,
  - amount of recognized gains or losses, the amount of prior service cost recognized,
  - Amount of gains or losses recognized due to a plan settlement or curtailment;
- Amount included within other comprehensive income for the period from a change in the additional pension liability recognized pursuant to FAS 87;

- On a weighted-average basis, the following assumptions:
  - Assumed discount rates,
  - Rates of compensation increase,
  - Expected long-term rates of return on plan assets;
- The measurement dates used to determine pension and other postretirement benefit measurements for the pension plans and other postretirement plans that make up at least the majority of plan assets and benefit obligations;
- Assumed healthcare cost trend rates for the next year used to determine expected cost of benefits covered by the plan, and a general description of the direction and pattern of change in the assumed trend rates thereafter;
- The effect of a 1-percent increase and a 1-percent decrease in the assumed healthcare cost trend rates on the aggregate of the service and interest cost components of net periodic postretirement healthcare benefit costs and the accumulated postretirement benefit obligation for healthcare benefits;
- Amounts and types of securities of the employer and related parties included in the plan assets,
- the approximate future annual benefits of plan participants covered by insurance contracts issued by the employer or related parties,
- any significant transactions between the employer or related parties and the plan during the period;
- Any alternative method used to amortize prior service amounts or unrecognized net gains and losses;
- Any substantive commitments used as the basis for accounting for the benefit obligation;
- The cost of providing special or contractual termination benefits recognized during the period and a description of the nature of the event; and
- Explanation of any significant change in the benefit obligation or plan assets not otherwise apparent from the other disclosures

STUDY QUESTION

---

13. FAS 132(R) requires disclosure on the income statement of the benefits expected to be paid in each of the next _____ fiscal year(s) and the contributions expected to be received into the plan for the next _____ year(s).

   a. Three; two
   b. Five; five
   c. Two; two
   d. Five; one

Disclosures by Employers with Two or More Plans. Employers that sponsor two or more plans shall aggregate information for all defined benefit pension plans and for all other defined benefit postretirement plans unless disaggregating in groups is considered to provide more useful information. Disclosures about pension plans having assets in excess of the accumulated benefit obligation generally may be aggregated with disclosures about pension plans with accumulated obligations in excess of assets. The same is true for other postretirement benefit plans. If aggregate disclosures are presented, the following information is required:

- The aggregate benefit obligation and aggregate fair value of plan assets for plans with benefit obligations in excess of plan assets; and
- The aggregate pension accumulated benefit obligation and aggregate fair values of plan assets for pension plans with accumulated benefit obligations in excess of plan assets.

Reduced Disclosures for Nonpublic Companies. Under FAS 132(R), a nonpublic entity is not required to present the complete set of information required for public entities. The disclosures required for a nonpublic entity are as follows:

- The benefit obligation, fair value of plan assets, and funded status of the plan;
- Employer contributions, participant contributions, and benefits paid;
- Information about plan assets:
  - For each major category of plan assets (e.g., equity securities, debt securities, real estate), the percentage of the fair value of total plan asset held as of the measurement date used for each statement of financial position presented,
  - A narrative description of investment policies and strategies,
  - A narrative description of the basis used to determine the overall expected long-term rate-of-return-on-assets assumption,
  - Disclosure of additional asset categories and additional information about specific assets within a category is encouraged if that information is useful in understanding the risks associated with each asset category and the overall expected long-term rate of return on assets;
- For defined benefit pension plans, the accumulated benefit obligation
- The benefits expected to be paid in each of the next five fiscal years and in the aggregate for the five fiscal years thereafter;
- The employer's best estimate of contributions expected to be paid to the plan during the next fiscal year;

- The amount recognized in the statements of financial position, including net pensions and other postretirement benefit prepaid assets or accrued liabilities and any intangible asset and the amount of accumulated other comprehensive income;
- The amount of net periodic benefit cost recognized and the amount included within other comprehensive income arising from a change in the minimum pension liability;
- On a weighted-average basis, the following assumptions used in the accounting for the plan:
  - Discount rates,
  - Rates of compensation increase,
  - Expected long-term rates of return on plan assets;
- The measurement dates used to determine pension and other postretirement benefit measurements for the pension plans and other postretirement benefit plans that make up the majority of plan assets and benefit obligations;
- The assumed healthcare trend rates for the year used to measure the expected cost of benefits covered by the plan, and a general description of the direction and pattern of change in the assumed trend rates thereafter, and the ultimate trend rates and when those rates are expected to be achieved;
- The amounts and types of securities of the employer and related parties included in plan assets;
- The approximate amount of future annual benefits of plan participants covered by insurance contracts issued by the employer or related parties;
- Significant transactions between the employers and related parties and the plan during the period;
- The nature and effect of significant nonroutine events, such as amendments, combinations, divestitures, curtailments, and settlements.

A nonpublic entity that has more than one defined benefit pension plan or more than one other defined benefit postretirement plan shall provide the required information separately for pension plans and other postretirement benefit plans.

STUDY QUESTION

14. Although the disclosure requirements are the same for public and non-public companies regarding how assumed healthcare cost trend rates are used to determine expected cost of plan benefits, the difference in reporting between the two types is that:

a. Public companies must also project trend rates for the next two years.

b. Public companies must describe ultimate trend rates and when they are expected to be achieved.

c. Private companies must give specific descriptions of the direction and pattern of changes in the assumed trend rates after five years.

d. Public companies must also describe the effect of a 1-percent increase and a 1-percent decrease in the assumed healthcare cost trend rates on the aggregate of the service.

Disclosures in Interim Financial Reports. A publicly traded entity shall disclose the following information in its financial statements that include an income statement:

■ The amount of net periodic benefit cost recognized for each period for which an income statement is presented with separate disclosure of the components of net periodic benefit cost; and

■ The total amount of the employee's contributions paid, or expected to be paid, during the current year if significantly different from amounts previously disclosed

A nonpublic entity shall disclose in interim periods for which a complete financial statement is presented:

■ The total amount of the employer's contributions paid and expected to be paid if significantly different; and

■ The employer's best estimate of contributions expected to be paid during the next fiscal year (paragraph 10 of FAS 132(R)).

Employers with Two or More Pension Plans

If an employer sponsors more than one defined benefit pension plan, the provisions of FAS 87 are applied separately to each plan. An employer shall not apply the assets of one plan to reduce or eliminate the unfunded accrued pension cost and/or minimum additional liability of another plan, unless the employer clearly has the right to do so. An excess of plan assets over the accumulated benefit obligation or prepaid pension cost of one plan cannot be applied to reduce or eliminate a liability of another plan that is required to be recognized by FAS 87 (FAS 87, par. 55).

Annuity Contracts

All or part of an employer's obligation to provide pension plan benefits to individuals may be transferred effectively to an insurance company by the purchase of annuity contracts. An **annuity contract** is an irrevocable agreement in which an insurance company unconditionally agrees to provide specific periodic payments, or a lump-sum payment to another party, in return for a specified premium. Thus, by use of an annuity contract, an employer can effectively transfer to an insurance company its legal obligation to provide specific employee pension plan benefits. Under FAS 87, a contract is not considered an annuity contract if the insurance company is one that does business primarily with the employer and its related parties (a captive insurer) or there is reasonable doubt that the insurance company will meet its obligation. (FAS 87, par. 57).

Types of Contracts. An annuity contract may be participating or nonparticipating. In a participating annuity contract, the insurance company's investing activities with the funds received for the annuity contract generally are shared, in the form of dividends, with the purchaser (the employer or the pension fund). A contract is not considered an annuity contract, under FAS 87, unless all the risks and rewards associated with the assets and obligations assumed by the insurance company are actually transferred to the insurance company by the employer (FAS 87, par. 57).

The cost incurred for currently earned benefits under an annuity contract is the cost of those benefits, except for the cost of participating rights of participating annuity contracts, which must be accounted for separately (see below). Thus, the service cost component of net periodic pension cost for the current period is the cost incurred for nonparticipating annuity contracts that cover all currently earned benefits (FAS 87, par. 58). FAS 87 contains provisions that address accounting for the cost of pension benefits not covered by annuity contracts (FAS 87, par. 59).

The projected benefit obligation and the accumulated benefit obligation do not include the cost of benefits covered by annuity contracts. Except for the cost of participation rights, pension plan assets do not include the cost of any annuity contracts (FAS 87, par. 60).

The difference in cost between a participating and a nonparticipating annuity contract usually is attributable to the cost of the participation right. The cost of a participation right, at the date of its purchase, is recognized as a pension plan asset. In subsequent periods, a participation right is included in plan assets at its fair value, if fair value is reasonably determinable. If fair value is not reasonably determinable, a participation right is included in plan assets at its amortized cost and systematically amortized over the expected dividend period stated in the contract. In this event, amortized cost may not exceed the net realizable value of the participation right (FAS 87, par. 61).

STUDY QUESTION

15. The cost of a participation right at the date of its purchase is recognized as a _____, but in subsequent periods it is included in plan assets _____.

a. Liability; at fair value
b. Fair value; at its amortized cost
c. Pension plan asset; at fair value
d. None of the above describes the cost recognition

Other Contracts with Insurance Companies. The purchase of insurance contracts that are, in substance, annuity contracts, is accounted for in accordance with FAS 87. The purchase of other types of insurance contracts are accounted for as pension plan assets and reported at fair value. The best evidence of fair value for some insurance contracts may be their contract values. Under FAS 87, the cash surrender value or conversion value of an insurance contract is presumed to be its fair value (FAS 87, par. 62).

Multiemployer Plans

A **multiemployer plan** is a pension plan to which two or more unrelated employers make contributions, usually pursuant to one or more collective-bargaining agreements. In a multiemployer pension plan, assets contributed by one employer are not segregated in separate accounts or restricted to provide benefits only to employees of that employer. Thus, assets contributed by one employer in a multiemployer plan may be used to provide benefits to employees of other participating employers (FAS 87, par. 67).

The net periodic pension cost of an employer participating in a multiemployer plan is the amount of the required contribution for the period. An employer participating in a multiemployer plan shall also recognize as a liability any of its contributions that are due and unpaid (FAS 87, par. 68).

> **OBSERVATION**
>
> A withdrawal from a multiemployer pension plan may result in a loss contingency if the withdrawing employer has a potential liability to the plan for a portion of its unfunded benefit obligation. Under FAS 87, if it is probable or reasonably possible that the loss contingency will develop into an actual loss, the withdrawing employer shall account for the loss contingency in accordance with the provisions of FAS 5, *Accounting for Contingencies* (FAS 87, par. 70).

An employer participating in a multiemployer plan shall disclose the following information (FAS132(R), par. 12):

- The amount of contributions to multiemployer plans during the period—amounts contributed to pension and postretirement benefit plans do not have to be disaggregated; and
- A description of any changes in pension or postretirement benefit plans that would affect comparability, including a discussion of the nature and effects of the change—examples include a change in the rate of employer contributions, business combinations, and divestitures

Multiple-Employer Plans

Some pension plans to which two or more unrelated employers contribute are not multiemployer plans, but are groups of single-employer plans combined to allow participating employers to pool assets for investment purposes and to reduce the cost of plan administration. Under FAS 87, multiple-employer plans are considered single-employer plans and each employer's accounting shall be based on its respective interest in the plan (FAS 87, par. 71).

Non-U.S. Pension Plans

FAS 87 does not make any special provision for non-U.S. pension plans. In some foreign countries, it is customary or required for an employer to provide benefits for employees in the event of a voluntary or involuntary severance of employment. In this event, if the substance of the arrangement is a pension plan, it is subject to the provisions of FAS 87 (for example, benefits are paid for substantially all terminations) (FAS 87, par. 73).

Business Combinations

The total cost of a business combination accounted for by the purchase method must be allocated to the individual assets acquired and liabilities assumed (FAS 141, *Business Combinations*). Each identifiable asset is assigned a cost equal to its fair value. Liabilities are accounted for at the present value of the amount that will eventually be paid and, if certain criteria are met, appropriate consideration should be given to contingent assets and liabilities (FAS 141, *Business Combinations*, pars. 40 and 41).

When a single-employer defined benefit pension plan is acquired as part of a business combination accounted for by the purchase method, an excess of the projected benefit obligation over the plan assets is recognized as a liability and an excess of plan assets over the projected benefit obligation is recognized as an asset. The recognition of a new liability or new asset by the purchaser, at the date of a business combination accounted for by the purchase method, results in the elimination of any (1) previously existing unrecognized net gain or loss, (2) unrecognized prior service cost, and (3) unrecognized net obligation or net asset that existed at the date of initial application of FAS 87 (FAS 87, par. 74).

In subsequent periods, the differences between the purchaser's net pension cost and contributions will reduce the new liability or new asset recognized at the date of combination to the extent that the previously unrecognized net gain or loss, unrecognized prior service cost, or unrecognized net obligation are considered in determining the amounts of contributions to the plan. In addition, the effects of an expected plan termination or curtailment shall be considered by the purchaser in calculating the amount of the projected benefit obligation at the date of a business combination accounted for by the purchase method (FAS 87, par. 74).

DEFINED CONTRIBUTION PENSION PLANS

A defined contribution pension plan has the following characteristics (FAS 87, par. 63):

- It provides for employers' contributions that are defined in the plan,
- It does not contain any provision for defined pension benefits for employees
- It does not contain a defined benefit pension formula.
- It provides pension benefits based on the amount of the employer's defined contributions provides for individual accounts for each plan participant
- It contains the terms that specify how contributions are determined for each participant's individual account.
- Periodic employer contributions are allocated to each participant's individual account in accordance with the terms of the plan
- Pension benefits are based solely on the amount available in each participant's account at the time of his or her retirement.
- The amount available in each participant's account at the time of his or her retirement is the total of:
  - The amounts contributed by the employer
  - Plus the returns earned on investments of those contributions,
  - Plus forfeitures of other participants' benefits that have been allocated to the participant's account,
  - Less any allocated administrative expenses.

Under FAS 87, the net periodic pension cost of a defined contribution pension plan is the amount of contributions made or due in a period on behalf of participants who performed services during that same period. Contributions for periods after an individual retires or terminates shall be estimated and accrued during periods in which the individual performs services (FAS 87, par. 64).

The amount of the unrecognized net obligation of a defined contribution pension plan, at the date of initial application of FAS 87, is amortized on a straight-line basis over the average remaining service period of employees expected to receive benefits under the plan, except:

- If the amortization period consists of fewer than 15 years, the employer may elect to use 15 years; and
- If the plan is composed of all or substantially all inactive participants, the employer shall use those participants' average remaining life expectancy as the amortization period (FAS 87, par. 77).

An employer who sponsors one or more defined contribution pension plans shall disclose the amount of cost recognized for defined contribution pension and other postretirement benefit plans during the period. This disclosure shall include the nature and effect of any significant changes during the period affecting comparability—examples include a change in the rate of employer contributions, business combinations, or divestitures (FAS 132(R), par.11).

Illustration of Calculation of the Additional Pension Liability

	As of End of Period		
	Year 1	Year 2	Year 3
Accumulated benefit obligation	$(3,762)	$(4,884)	$(4,884)
Fair value of plan assets	3,945	4,515	4,866
(Unfunded) or over funded accumulated benefit obligation	$ (267)	$ (369)	$ 18
Projected benefit obligation	$(5,637)	$(7,326)	$(7,272)
Fair value of plan assets	3,495	4,515	4,866
Funded status of plan	(2,142)	(2,811)	(2,406
Unrecognized prior service cost	2,145	3,942	3,516
Unrecognized net (gain) or loss	(753)	(1,671)	(1,380)
Unrecognized net obligation at date of initial application of FAS 87	840	780	720
(Accrued) or prepaid pension cost	$ 90	$ 240	$ 450
(Accrued) or prepaid pension cost at beginning of period	$ 0	$ 90	$ 240
Less: Net periodic pension cost	912	1,005	1,191
Add: Contributions paid	1,002	1,155	1,401
(Accrued) or prepaid pension cost at end of period	$ 90	$ 240	$ 450
(Unfunded) or overfunded accumulated benefit obligation (computed above)	$(267)	$ 369)	$ 18
Required adjustment for additional minimum liability (see accompanying note)	(357)	(252)	609
Intangible asset	357	252	(609)
Cumulative balance of the additional minimum liability	(357)	(609)	0

NOTE

The adjustment necessary to record the additional minimum liability is equal to the unfunded accumulated benefit obligation, plus the amount of any prepaid pension cost or less the amount of any accrued pension cost (at the end of the period), less the previous balance of the additional minimum liability from the preceding year. Thus the adjustment in year 1 is $357, which is equal to the unfunded accumulated benefit obligation of $267, plus the prepaid pension cost of $90 at the end of the period (there was no previous balance of the additional minimum liability from the preceding year).

The adjustment for year 2 is $252, which is equal to the unfunded accumulated benefit obligation of $369, plus the amount of prepaid pension cost of $240 at the end of the period, less the preceding year's balance of the additional minimum liability of $357.

In year 3, the balance of the unfunded accumulated benefit obligation was an $18 debit, which results in no unfunded accumulated benefit obligation. Thus, the adjustment consisted of eliminating the preceding year's balance of $609.

The additional minimum liability that was required in all three years did not exceed the unrecognized prior service cost plus the unrecognized net obligation. Thus, no portion of the required additional minimum liability had to be reported as a separate component of stockholders' equity.

CONCLUSION

This chapter described how pension plan accounting functions in today's post-Enron realm of financial statements. In particular, the chapter explained the Financial Accounting Standards Board rules expressed in FAS 87 and FAS 132 for proper inclusion of pension plan assets and liabilities and recounted the types of disclosures necessary in statements based on the pension plan type. Central to the discussion and proper calculation of costs related to retirement plans are the components of the net periodic pension costs, as illustrated in this chapter.

Employers and their financial advisors should develop a working knowledge of FASB rules to ensure their plans are represented in financial statements in compliance with GAAP.

MODULE 2 — CHAPTER 4

FAS 109: Accounting for Income Taxes

Accounting for income tax is complicated in part by its many applications in specialized or rarely seen areas. The professional literature on the subject is diffuse and fragmented, with six authoritative pronouncements in the "level A" GAAP hierarchy alone, and another twenty-three in the lower levels. This chapter addresses, in a si ngle source, the most important principles in accounting for income taxes and illustrates their application in commonly observed situations, while bypassing many of the exotic and seldom-seen scenarios that congest the literature. A comprehensive illustration, with example worksheets, demonstrates in clear fashion the calculation, recording and financial statement presentation of current and deferred income taxes.

LEARNING OBJECTIVES

Upon completion of this chapter, the professional will be able to:
- Apply the liability method of accounting for income taxes;
- Differentiate taxable temporary differences from deductible ones;
- Recognize and measure deferred tax assets and liabilities;
- Analyze how to present temporary differences in financial statements.

OVERVIEW

The tax consequences of many transactions recognized in financial statements are included in determining income taxes currently payable in the same accounting period. Sometimes, however, tax laws differ from the recognition and measurement requirements of financial reporting standards. Differences arise between the tax bases of assets or liabilities and their reported amounts in the financial statements. These differences are called **temporary differences** and they give rise to deferred tax assets and liabilities.

Temporary differences ordinarily reverse when the related asset is recovered or the related liability is settled. A **deferred tax liability** or **deferred tax asset** represents the increase or decrease, respectively, in taxes payable or refundable in future years as a result of temporary differences and carryforwards at the end of the current year.

The objectives of accounting for income taxes are to recognize:
- The amount of taxes payable or refundable for the current year.
- The deferred tax liabilities and assets that result from future tax consequences of events that have been recognized in the enterprise's financial statements or tax returns.

GAAP for accounting for income taxes are in the following pronouncements:

APB 2	*Accounting for the "Investment Credit"*
APB 4	*Accounting for the "Investment Credit"*
APB 10	Paragraph 6, "Tax Allocation Accounts—Discounting"
	Paragraph 7, "Offsetting Securities against Taxes Payable"
APB 23	*Accounting for Income Taxes—Special Areas*
FAS 109	*Accounting for Income Taxes*
FIN 18	*Accounting for Income Taxes in Interim Periods*

BACKGROUND

FAS 109, *Accounting for Income Taxes,* superseded FAS 96 and addresses financial accounting and reporting for income taxes. FAS 109 changed accounting for income taxes from the deferred method, required by APB 11, *Accounting for Income Taxes,* to the asset/liability method, commonly referred to as simply the **liability method.**

The **deferred method** placed primary emphasis on the matching of revenues and expenses. Income tax expense was determined by applying the current income tax rate to pretax accounting income. Any difference between the resulting expense and the amount of income taxes payable was an adjustment to deferred income taxes. The deferred method focused first on the income statement, and adjustments to balance sheet elements were determined by the measurement of income tax expense.

The **liability method** places primary emphasis on the valuation of current and deferred tax assets and liabilities. The amount of income tax expense recognized for a period is the amount of income taxes currently payable or refundable, plus or minus the change in aggregate deferred tax assets and liabilities. The method focuses first on the balance sheet, and the amount of income tax expense is determined by changes in the elements of the balance sheet.

STUDY QUESTION

1. The primary emphasis of the deferral method was:

a. Making adjustments to the balance sheet elements, then focusing on the income statement

b. Matching revenues and expenses, resulting in adjustments to deferred income taxes

c. Valuing current and deferred tax assets and liabilities

d. None of the above was the primary emphasis of the deferral method

THE LIABILITY METHOD

FAS 109 requires income taxes to be accounted for by the liability method. Its main effects on financial statements include the following:

■ Emphasis is on the recognition and measurement of deferred tax assets and liabilities. Deferred income tax expense is determined residually (i.e., as the difference between the beginning and required ending balances in deferred tax assets and liabilities for the period).

■ Deferred tax asset and liability amounts are remeasured when tax rates change to approximate more closely the amounts at which those assets and liabilities will be realized or settled.

■ Deferred tax assets are recognized for operating loss carryforwards and other carryforwards. Deferred tax assets are subject to reduction by a valuation allowance if evidence indicates that it is **more likely than not** that some or all of the deferred tax assets will not be realized. Determining this valuation allowance is similar to accounting for reductions in receivables to net realizable value.

■ Disclosure requirements result in the presentation of a significant amount of information in the notes to the financial statements.

STUDY QUESTION

---

2. FAS 109 requires deferred tax asset and liability amounts to be remeasured when:

  a. Annual tax returns are submitted
  b. The disposition of the asset or liability occurs
  c. Tax rates change
  d. None of the above occasions the remeasurement

GENERAL PROVISIONS OF FAS 109

Scope

FAS 109 requires what traditionally has been referred to as **comprehensive income tax allocation,** as opposed to partial allocation or nonallocation. This means that the income tax effects of all revenues, expenses, gains, losses, and other events that create differences between the tax bases of assets and liabilities and their amounts for financial reporting are required to be recognized (FAS 109, par. 3).

FAS 109 is applicable to (FAS 109, par. 4):

■ Domestic federal income taxes and foreign, state, and local taxes based on income.

■ An enterprise's domestic and foreign operations that are consolidated, combined, or accounted for by the equity method.

- Foreign enterprises in preparing financial statements in accordance with U.S. GAAP.

Three important financial statement issues are specifically set aside and not covered by FAS 109 (FAS 109, par. 5):
- Accounting for the investment tax credit (ITC).
- Accounting for income taxes in interim periods.
- Discounting deferred income taxes.

Accounting for the ITC and accounting for income taxes in interim periods are covered by existing authoritative pronouncements, which FAS 109 does not affect. Accounting for the ITC is covered in APB 2, *Accounting for the "Investment Credit,"* and APB 4, *Accounting for the "Investment Credit,"* and accounting for income taxes in interim periods is discussed in APB 28, *Interim Financial Reporting,* and FIN 18, *Accounting for Income Taxes in Interim Periods.* The issue of discounting deferred income taxes is beyond the scope of FAS 109.

STUDY QUESTION

---

3. Which of the following is covered by FAS 109?

   a. Accounting for income taxes in interim periods

   b. Discounting deferred income taxes

   c. Preparing financial statements for foreign enterprises in accordance with GAAP

   d. None of the above is an issue that is not covered by FAS 109

Basic Principles of the Liability Method

The objectives of accounting for income taxes are identified in terms of elements of the balance sheet (FAS 109, par. 6):
- To recognize the amount of taxes currently payable or refundable.
- To recognize the deferred tax assets and liabilities for the future tax consequences of events that have been recognized in the financial statements or in tax returns.

This emphasis on the balance sheet is consistent with the liability method of accounting for income taxes incorporated in FAS 109.

Four basic principles are particularly important for understanding the liability method and the procedures described in FAS 109 for accounting for income taxes. Each basic principle focuses on the elements of the balance sheet relating to income taxes (FAS 109, par. 8):
- Recognize a **tax liability or asset** for the amount of taxes currently payable or refundable.

- Recognize a **deferred tax liability or asset** for the estimated future tax effects of temporary differences or carryforwards.
- Measure **current** and **deferred tax assets** and **liabilities** based on provisions of enacted tax laws.
- Reduce the amount of any deferred **tax assets** by a valuation allowance, if necessary, based on available evidence.

  The following are exceptions to these basic principles (FAS 109, par. 9):

- Certain exceptions to the requirements for recognition of deferred tax assets and liabilities for the areas addressed by APB 23, *Accounting for Income Taxes—Special Areas,* as amended by FAS 109, paragraphs 31–34, notably the investments in foreign subsidiaries and joint ventures.
- Special transitional procedures for temporary differences related to deposits in statutory reserve funds by U.S. steamship enterprises.
- Accounting for leveraged leases as required by FAS 13, *Accounting for Leases,* and FIN 21, *Accounting for Leases in a Business Combination.*
- Prohibition of the recognition of a deferred tax liability or asset related to goodwill for which amortization is not deductible for tax purposes.
- Accounting for income taxes under ARB 51, *Consolidated Financial Statements.*
- Prohibition of the recognition of a deferred tax liability or asset for differences related to assets and liabilities accounted for under FAS 52, *Foreign Currency Translation.*

Temporary Differences

Deferred tax assets and liabilities that result from temporary differences are based on the assumption that assets and liabilities in an entity's balance sheet eventually will be realized or settled at their recorded amounts (FAS 109, par. 11).

Categories. The following major categories of temporary differences refer to events that result in differences between the tax bases of assets and liabilities and their reported amounts in the financial statements (FAS 109, par. 11):

- Revenues or gains that are taxable after they are recognized in accounting income (e.g., receivables from installment sales).
- Expenses or losses that are deductible for tax purposes after they are recognized in accounting income (e.g., a product warranty liability).
- Revenues or gains that are taxable before they are recognized in accounting income (e.g., subscriptions received in advance).
- Expenses or losses that are deductible for tax purposes before they are recognized in accounting income (e.g., cost recovery deductions under MACRS or other tax provisions that differ from depreciation expense under GAAP.).

Other less common examples of temporary differences are:
- Investment tax credits accounted for by the deferred method.
- Business combinations accounted for by the purchase method.

STUDY QUESTION

> **4.** Most categories of temporary differences refer to events that result in differences between:
>
> **a.** The tax bases of assets and liabilities and their amounts as reported in financial statements
> **b.** Taxable and deductible transactions
> **c.** Recognized and unrecognized assets or liabilities
> **d.** None of the above

Taxable and Deductible Temporary Differences. An important distinction in applying the procedures required to account for income taxes by the asset/liability method under FAS 109 is the difference between taxable and deductible temporary differences. A **taxable temporary difference** is one that will result in the payment of income taxes in the future when the temporary difference reverses. A **deductible temporary difference** is one that will result in reduced income taxes in future years when the temporary difference reverses (FAS 109, par. 13). Taxable temporary differences give rise to deferred tax liabilities; deductible temporary differences give rise to deferred tax assets.

EXAMPLE

The following are taxable temporary differences:

	Explanation	Deferred Tax
Depreciable assets	Use of MACRS for tax purposes and straight-line for accounting purposes makes the tax basis of asset less than the accounting basis	Liability to be paid as MACRS deduction becomes less than straight-line depreciation
Installment sale receivable	Sales recognized for accounting purposes at transaction date and deferred for tax purposes until collection, resulting in a difference between the tax and accounting bases of the installment receivable	Liability to be paid when the sale is recognized for tax purposes

The following are deductible temporary differences:

	Explanation	Deferred Tax
Warranty liability	Expense recognized on accrual basis for accounting purposes and on cash basis for tax purposes, resulting in a liability that is recognized for financial reporting purposes but has a zero basis for tax purposes	Asset to be recovered when deduction is recognized for tax purposes
Accounts receivable/ allowance for doubtful accounts	Expense recognized on an accrual basis for accounting purposes and deferred for tax purposes	Asset to be recovered when uncollectible account is written off for tax purposes

The expanded definition of **temporary differences** in FAS 109 includes some items that do not appear in the company's balance sheet. For example, a company may expense organization costs when they are incurred but recognize them as a tax deduction in a later year. Between the two events, no balance sheet item exists for this type of temporary difference (FAS 109, par. 15).

The identification of temporary differences may require significant professional judgment. Similar items may be temporary differences in one instance and not in another. For example, the excess of the cash surrender value of life insurance over premiums paid is a temporary difference and results in deferred taxes if the cash surrender value is expected to be recovered by surrendering the policy, but it is not a temporary difference and does not result in deferred taxes if the asset is expected to be recovered upon the death of the insured (FAS 109, par. 14). Management intent and professional judgment are important factors in making the appropriate determination of the nature of assets and liabilities of this type.

OBSERVATION

Developing a system for identifying and tracking the amounts of all temporary differences and carryforwards is an important implementation issue for FAS 109. Theoretically, differences should be identified by comparing items and amounts in the entity's balance sheets for accounting purposes and for tax purposes. Many companies do not maintain tax-basis balance sheets, although this may be the most logical way to identify and track temporary differences in the relatively complex situations in which FAS 109 is applied.

Permanent Differences

FAS 109 carries forward the APB 11 concept of **permanent differences**, although that term is not used. FAS 109 points out that certain differences between the tax basis and the accounting basis of assets and liabilities will not result in taxable or deductible amounts in future years, and no deferred tax asset or liability should be recognized (FAS 109, par. 14).

> **OBSERVATION**
>
> Examples of permanent differences include interest income from tax exempt municipal bonds and the 50 percent meal disallowance. These items are income and expense, respectively, for financial statement purposes that will never be taxable or deductible for federal income tax purposes.

STUDY QUESTION

5. A deductible temporary difference is one that will give rise to _____, whereas a taxable temporary difference gives rise to _____.

   a. Deferred tax liabilities; deferred tax assets
   b. Future tax liabilities; deferred tax assets
   c. Deferred tax liabilities; future tax assets
   d. Deferred tax assets; deferred tax liabilities

Recognizing and Measuring Deferred Tax Assets and Liabilities

The emphasis placed on the balance sheet by the liability method of accounting for income taxes is evident from the focus on the recognition of deferred tax liabilities and assets. The change in these liabilities and assets is combined with the income taxes currently payable or refundable to determine income tax expense (FAS 109, par. 16).

Five steps are required to complete the annual computation of deferred tax liabilities and assets (FAS 109, par. 17):

1. Identify the types and amounts of existing temporary differences and the nature and amount of each type of operating loss and tax credit carryforward and the remaining length of the carryforward period.
2. Measure the total deferred tax liability for taxable temporary differences using the applicable tax rate.
3. Measure the total deferred tax asset for deductible temporary differences and operating loss carryforwards using the applicable tax rate.
4. Measure deferred tax assets for each type of tax credit carryforward.
5. Reduce deferred tax assets by a valuation allowance if it is more likely than not that some or all of the deferred tax assets will not be realized.

Valuation Allowance and Tax-Planning Strategies

Determining the need for and calculating the amount of the valuation allowance requires the following steps at the end of each accounting period

(FAS 109, par. 21):

1. Determine the amount of the deferred tax asset recognized on each deductible temporary difference, operating loss, and tax credit carryforward. (These are not offset by the deferred tax liability on taxable temporary differences.)
2. Assess the sources of future taxable income that may be available to recognize the deductible differences and carryforwards by considering the following:
   a. Taxable income in prior carryback year(s) if a carryback is permitted under tax law
   b. Future reversals of existing taxable temporary differences
   c. Tax planning strategies that would make income available at appropriate times in the future that would otherwise not be available
   d. Future taxable income exclusive of reversing differences and carryforwards.

OBSERVATION

The four sources of income are organized differently here than in FAS 109 in order to emphasize the implementation of the standard. In identifying income to support the recognition of deferred tax assets (and thereby supporting a case that an allowance is not required), a logical approach is to consider sources of income in order from the most objective to the least objective. Income in prior carryback years is most objective, followed by the income from the reversal of taxable temporary differences, income resulting from tax planning strategies, and finally, future income from other sources.

---

3. Based on all available evidence, make a judgment concerning the realizability of the deferred tax asset.
4. Record the amount of the valuation allowance or the change in the valuation allowance.

EXAMPLE

Assuming that the allowance is being recorded for the first time or is being increased for $100,000, the valuation allowance is shown as this:

Income tax expense	$100,000	
Allowance to reduce deferred tax asset to lower recoverable value		$100,000

OBSERVATION

FAS 109 relaxes the criteria for recognizing deferred tax assets by requiring the recognition of deferred tax assets for all deductible temporary differences and all operating loss and tax credit carryforwards. An important adjunct to this provision, however, is the requirement to determine the need for, and amount of, a valuation allowance to reduce the deferred tax asset to its realizable value. The valuation allowance aspects of FAS 109 require significant judgment on the part of accountants and auditors of financial statements. A valuation allowance is required if it is more likely than not that some or all of the deferred tax assets will not be realized. *More likely than not* is defined as a likelihood of more than 50 percent.

Applicable Tax Rate. Reference to the applicable tax rate is made in the four steps identified above. The **applicable tax rate** is that rate expected to apply to taxable income in the periods in which the deferred tax liability or asset is expected to be settled or realized based on enacted tax law. If the entity's taxable income is low enough to make the graduated tax rates a significant factor, the entity uses the average graduated tax rate applicable to the amount of estimated annual taxable income in the periods in which the deferred tax liability or asset is expected to be settled or realized (FAS 109, par. 18). For example, if a company has taxable temporary differences of $20,000 that are expected to reverse in a year when no other income is expected, the applicable tax rate under current tax law is 15 percent and the deferred tax liability is:

$$\$20,000 \times 15\% = \$3,000$$

If the taxable temporary differences total $60,000, graduated tax rates become a factor (the tax rate changes at $50,000); deferred taxes are $10,000:

$$\$50,000 \times 15\% = \$\ 7,500$$
$$\underline{\$10,000 \times 25\% = \ \ \ \ 2,500}$$
$$\$10,000$$

The average applicable tax rate is 16.67%.

$$\$10,000 \div \$60,000 = 16.67\%$$

OBSERVATION

Determining the applicable tax rate may be a very simple task, or it may require careful analysis and professional judgment. When an entity has been consistently profitable at sufficiently high levels that graduated tax rates are not a significant factor, use the single flat tax rate at which all income is used to compute the amount of deferred taxes on cumulative temporary differences. If a company experiences intermittent tax loss and tax income years, or if the company is consistently profitable at a level low enough that the graduated tax rates are a significant factor, greater judgment is required to determine the applicable tax rate under FAS 109.

Deferred tax assets and liabilities are remeasured at the end of each accounting period and adjusted for changes in the amounts of cumulative temporary differences and for changes in the applicable income tax rate, as well as for other changes in the tax law (FAS 109, par. 27). As a result of this procedure, the deferred tax provision is a combination of two elements:

- The change in deferred taxes because of the change in the amounts of temporary differences.
- The change in deferred taxes because of a change in the tax rate caused by new enacted rates or a change in the applicability of graduated tax rates (or other changes in the tax law).

Treating the change in income tax rates in this manner is consistent with accounting for a change in estimate under APB 20, *Accounting Changes.*

STUDY QUESTION

6. The minimum requirement to be considered more likely than not for valuation allowances is:

   a. 40 percent
   b. 50 percent
   c. 60 percent
   d. 75 percent

Tax-Planning Strategies. Tax planning strategies must be considered in determining the need for, and the amount of, the valuation allowance for deferred tax assets. Tax planning strategies are actions that management takes to prevent operating loss carryforwards or credit carryforwards from expiring before they are used. They usually include either:

- Shifting estimated future taxable income between future years, such as to load taxable income into a year in the near future when an operating loss carryover is scheduled to expire, so as to get the benefit of the carryover before it expires.

■ Shifting the anticipated reversals of temporary differences, so as to move them into a nearer future year, thus creating more taxable income in a subsequent future year when a carryforward is scheduled to expire.

> **OBSERVATION**
>
> It is important to draw a distinction between routine business practices and tax planning strategies. A **tax-planning strategy** is an action that a company might not ordinarily take, but would take to reap the tax benefit of a carryforward that would otherwise expire unused. Tax planning strategies do not include actions taken in the ordinary course of business, such as a routine practice of structuring sales as installment sales in order to defer taxable income.

FAS 109 describes tax-planning strategies as actions that (FAS 109, par. 22):
■ Are prudent and feasible.
■ The entity might not ordinarily take, but **would** take to prevent an operating loss or tax credit carryforward from expiring before it is used.
■ Would result in the realization of deferred tax assets.

Examples include actions the entity could take to accelerate taxable income to use expiring carryforwards, to change the character of taxable or deductible amounts from ordinary income or loss to capital gain or loss, and to switch from tax-exempt to taxable investments.

In determining the need for a valuation allowance, the accountant must consider both negative and positive evidence about the company's ability to recognize the tax benefit of a carryforward in a future period.

Negative Evidence. Negative evidence supports a conclusion that the tax benefit will not be recognized, and thus that a valuation allowance is necessary. If negative evidence is present, such as cumulative losses in recent years, it is difficult to conclude that a valuation allowance is unnecessary. Other examples of negative evidence are (FAS 109, par. 23):
■ A history of operating loss or tax credit carryforwards expiring before they are used.
■ Losses expected in the near future.
■ Unsettled circumstances that, if unfavorably resolved, would adversely affect future operations and profit levels on a continuing basis in future years.
■ A carryback or carryforward period that is so brief that it significantly limits the probability of realizing deferred tax assets.

Positive Evidence. Positive evidence supports a conclusion that a valuation allowance is not required. Examples of positive evidence are (FAS 109, par. 24):

■ Existing contracts or firm sales backlog that will produce more than enough taxable income to realize the deferred tax asset based on existing sales prices and cost structures.

■ An excess of appreciated asset value over the tax basis of the entity's net assets in an amount sufficient to realize the deferred tax asset.

■ A strong earnings history exclusive of the loss that created the future deductible amount, coupled with evidence indicating that the loss is an aberration rather than a continuing condition.

OBSERVATION

Projecting the reversal of temporary differences for each future year individually is commonly referred to as **scheduling.** Does FAS 109 require scheduling? On the one hand, the requirement to recognize deferred tax assets and liabilities for all taxable and deductible temporary differences, as well as for all carryforwards, seems to diminish or eliminate the need to schedule. Also, using a flat tax rate in determining the amount of deferred tax assets and liabilities, as described earlier, diminishes the need to schedule individual future years. On the other hand, scheduling may help determine the need for, and amount of, a valuation allowance, including the consideration of tax-planning strategies. To determine the availability of taxable income in the appropriate years—to take advantage of deferred tax assets and to make the judgments concerning the valuation allowance—projecting taxable income from known or estimated sources by year may still be important.

Professional judgment is required in considering the relative impact of negative and positive evidence to determine the need for, and amount of, the valuation allowance for deferred tax assets. The weight given the effect of negative and positive evidence should be commensurate with the extent to which it can be objectively verified. The more negative evidence exists, the more positive evidence is needed to conclude that a valuation allowance is not required (FAS 109, par. 25).

The effect of a change in the valuation allowance that results from a change in circumstances--which in turn causes a change in judgment about the realizability of the related deferred tax asset--is included in income from continuing operations with limited exceptions (FAS 109, par. 26).

STUDY QUESTIONS

7. Which of the following is **not** an example of negative evidence?
   a. A brief carryback or carryforward period that limits realization of deferred tax assets
   b. A history of expired operating losses or tax credit carryforwards not used
   c. An excess of appreciated asset value over the tax basis of the entity's net assets of an amount sufficient to realize the deferred tax asset
   d. All of the above are examples of negative evidence.

8. All of the following are examples of positive evidence **except:**
   a. Losses expected in the near future
   b. Evidence that the loss is an aberration rather than a continuing condition plus a strong earnings history exclusive of the loss that generated the future deductible amount
   c. Existing contracts or a firm sales backlog that will generate enough taxable income to realize the deferred tax asset
   d. All of the above are examples of positive evidence

SPECIALIZED APPLICATIONS OF FAS 109

Several specialized applications of FAS 109 are summarized briefly here.

Change in Tax Status

An enterprise's tax status may change from nontaxable to taxable or taxable to nontaxable. A deferred tax liability or asset shall be recognized for temporary differences at the date that a nontaxable enterprise becomes a taxable enterprise. A deferred tax liability or asset shall be eliminated at the date an enterprise becomes a nontaxable enterprise (FAS 109, par. 28).

Regulated Enterprises

Regulated enterprises are **not** exempt from the requirements of FAS 109. Specifically, FAS 109 (FAS 109, par. 29):

- Prohibits net-of-tax accounting and reporting.
- Requires recognition of a deferred tax liability for tax benefits that flow through to customers when temporary differences originate and for the equity component of the allowance for funds used during construction.
- Requires adjustment of a deferred tax liability or asset for an enacted change in tax laws or rates.

If as a result of an action by a regulator, it is probable that the future increase or decrease in taxes payable for the last two items above will be restored from or returned to customers through future rates, an asset or a liability is recognized for that probable future revenue or reduction in future revenue in accordance with FAS 71, *Accounting for the Effects of Certain Types of Regulation.* That asset or liability is a temporary difference for which a deferred tax liability or asset is required.

Business Combinations

A deferred tax asset or liability is recognized for differences between the assigned values (i.e., allocated portion of historical cost) and the tax bases of assets and liabilities resulting from a business combination (in contrast to the recording of these items on a net-of-tax basis, as required by APB 11). If a valuation allowance is recognized for the deferred tax asset for an acquired entity's deductible temporary differences, operating loss, or tax credit carryforward at the acquisition date, the tax benefits for those items that are first recognized in financial statements after the acquisition date are applied in the following order (FAS 109, par. 30):

1. Reduce to zero any goodwill related to the acquisition.
2. Reduce to zero other noncurrent intangible assets related to the acquisition.
3. Reduce income tax expense.

STUDY QUESTION

---

9. The *last* reduction applied to items recognized in financial statements after the acquisition date is:
   a. Income tax expense
   b. Noncurrent intangible assets
   c. Goodwill
   d. None of the above is the last reduction

Intraperiod Tax Allocation

An income tax expense or benefit for the year shall be allocated among continuing operations, discontinued operations, extraordinary items, and items charged or credited directly to shareholders' equity. The amount allocated to continuing operations is the tax effect of the pretax income or loss from continuing operations that occurred during the year, plus or minus income tax effects of:

- Changes in circumstances that cause a change in judgment about the realization of deferred tax assets.
- Changes in tax laws or rates.
- Changes in tax status.
- Tax deductible dividends paid to shareholders, except for dividends paid on unallocated shares held by an employee stock ownership plan (ESOP).

The remainder is allocated to items other than continuing operations (FAS 109, par. 35).

The tax effects of the following items are charged or credited directly to the related components of stockholders' equity (FAS 109, par. 36):

- Adjustments of the opening balance of retained earnings for certain changes in accounting principles or to correct an error.
- Gains and losses included in comprehensive income but excluded from net income.
- An increase or decrease in contributed capital.
- Expenses for employee stock options recognized differently for accounting and tax purposes.
- Dividends that are paid on unallocated shares held by an ESOP and that are charged to retained earnings.
- Deductible temporary differences and carryforwards that existed at the date of a quasi-reorganization.

Generally, the tax benefit of an operating loss carryforward or carryback is reported in the same manner as the source of the income or loss in the current year, and not in the same manner as (1) the source of the operating loss carryforward or taxes paid in a prior year, or (2) the source of expected future income that will result in realization of deferred tax assets for an operating loss carryforward from the current year. Exceptions to this general rule are:

- Tax effects of deductible temporary differences and carryforwards that existed at the date of a purchase business combination and for which a tax benefit is recognized initially in subsequent years in accordance with FAS 109, par. 30
- Tax effects of deductible temporary differences and carryforwards that are allocated to shareholders' equity in accordance with FAS 109, par. 36.

If there is only one item other than continuing operations, the portion of income tax expense or benefit that remains after the allocation to continuing operations is allocated to that item. If there are two or more items, the amount that remains after the allocation to continuing operations is allocated among those other items in proportion to their individual effects on income tax expense or benefit for the year (FAS 109, par. 38).

STUDY QUESTIONS

10. All of the following are specialized applications of FAS 109 *except:*

   a. Business combinations

   b. Regulated enterprises

   c. Entity's change in tax status between taxable and nontaxable

   d. All of the above are specialized applications of FAS 109

> **11.** For business combinations in which a valuation allowance is recognized for an acquired entity's deductible temporary differences, which of the following is the *last* in the order for tax benefits to be recognized in financial statements?
>
> **a.** Any goodwill related to the acquisition
> **b.** Other noncurrent intangible assets related to the acquisition
> **c.** Income tax expense
> **d.** None of the above is the last in the recognition order for tax benefits
>
> **12.** According to par. 34 of FAS 109, a deferred tax asset is recognized for an excess of the tax basis over the amount for accounting purposes of an investment in a subsidiary or corporate joint venture that is essentially permanent in duration only if it is apparent that the temporary difference will not reverse in the foreseeable future—that is, if it will become a permanent difference. *True or False?*

Quasi-Reorganizations

The tax benefits of deductible temporary differences and carryforwards as of the date of a quasi-reorganization ordinarily are reported as a direct addition to contributed capital if the tax benefits are recognized in subsequent years. The only exception is for enterprises that previously adopted FAS 96, *Accounting for Income Taxes,* and effected a quasi-reorganization involving only the elimination of a deficit in retained earnings by a noncurrent reduction in contributed capital prior to adopting FAS 109. For those enterprises, subsequent recognition of the tax benefit of prior deductible temporary differences and carryforwards is included in income, reported as required by FAS 109, and then reclassified from retained earnings to contributed capital (FAS 109, par. 39).

Separate Financial Statements of a Subsidiary

The allocation of income taxes among the members of a group of entities that file a consolidated tax return must be based on a method that is systematic, rational, and consistent with the broad principles established in FAS 109, although FAS 109 does not require a single allocation method. A method that allocates current and deferred taxes to members of the group by applying FAS 109 to each member as if it were a separate taxpayer meets those criteria. Examples of methods that are **not** consistent with the broad principles of FAS 109 include (FAS 109, par. 40):

- A method that allocates only current taxes payable to a member of the group that has taxable temporary differences.
- A method that allocates deferred taxes to a member of the group using a method fundamentally different from the asset and liability method.

- A method that allocates no current or deferred tax expense to a member of the group that has taxable income because the consolidated group has no current or deferred tax expense.

Miscellaneous Topics

The following pronouncements are essentially unchanged by FAS 109:

- APB 10, paragraph 6
- APB 10, paragraph 7
- APB 23
- FIN 18

APB 10, *Omnibus Opinion—1966,* indicates that deferred taxes should not be discounted (paragraph 6), and that offsetting of assets and liabilities (including tax assets and liabilities) is prohibited unless a legal right of setoff exists (paragraph 7).

APB 23, covered earlier in this chapter, indicates several situations in which deferred taxes are not recognized for certain temporary differences unless it becomes apparent that those differences will reverse in the foreseeable future.

FIN 18 provides guidance in accounting for income taxes in interim periods in accordance with the provisions of APB 28. APB 28 generally requires an estimated annual effective tax rate to be used to determine the interim period income tax provision.

OBSERVATION

The special applications of FAS 109 discussed in this section illustrate the pervasive nature of accounting for income taxes. Income tax considerations affect many parts of the financial statements and many kinds of business transactions. This dimension of accounting for income taxes makes FAS 109 an important pronouncement and accounts, at least partially, for the long and difficult process of making the transition from the deferred method under APB 11 to the asset/liability method under FAS 109.

FINANCIAL STATEMENT PRESENTATION AND DISCLOSURE ISSUES

FAS 109 requires deferred tax assets and liabilities to be presented in a classified balance sheet in current and noncurrent categories. The following policies are included for applying this requirement (FAS 109, pars. 41 and 42):

- If the temporary difference giving rise to the deferred tax asset or liability is reflected in a balance sheet asset or liability, the classification of the deferred tax is governed by that related asset or liability. For example, the temporary difference for depreciable assets is classified as noncurrent because the related asset (i.e., property, plant and equipment) is noncurrent.

■ If the deferred tax does not relate to an underlying asset or liability on the balance sheet, classification is based on the expected timing of reversal. For example, if organization costs are expensed when incurred for accounting purposes but deferred and deducted later for tax purposes, there is no related balance sheet asset or liability.

■ For a particular taxpaying component of an enterprise and within a particular tax jurisdiction (e.g., federal and state), all current deferred tax liabilities and assets are offset and presented as a single amount; the same procedure is followed for all noncurrent deferred tax liabilities and assets. Deferred tax liabilities and assets that are attributable to different taxpaying components of the enterprise or to different tax jurisdictions are **not** offset.

OBSERVATION

The classification of deferred tax assets and liabilities as current or noncurrent based on the underlying asset is conceptually inferior to classifying them based on the expected timing of the receipt or payment of taxes. The latter approach is conceptually stronger in terms of the intent of the current/noncurrent classification—namely, to isolate as current those assets and liabilities expected to have cash flow consequences in the near future. Classifying a deferred tax asset or liability based on the underlying asset or liability appears to have been part of an effort by the FASB to reduce complexity and eliminate, to the extent possible, procedures that would require scheduling of taxable income for individual future years in determining the amounts of deferred tax assets and liabilities and their classifications.

STUDY QUESTION

13. Deferred tax liabilities and assets that are attributable to different taxpaying components of the enterprise or to different tax jurisdictions may be offset in the balance sheet. *True or False?*

Disclosures

The following components of the net deferred tax liability or asset recognized in an enterprise's balance sheet must be disclosed (FAS 109, par. 43):

■ The total of all deferred tax liabilities for taxable temporary differences.
■ The total of all deferred tax assets for deductible temporary differences and loss and tax credit carryforwards.
■ The total valuation allowance recognized for deferred tax assets.
■ The net change during the year in the total valuation allowance.

> **OBSERVATION**
>
> Publicly traded companies must disclose the approximate tax effect of each significant type of temporary difference and carryforward. Nonpublic entities must disclose the types of significant temporary differences and carryforwards, but need not show the tax effects of each.

Earlier, several exceptions were identified under APB 23 for which deferred taxes are not recognized. Whenever a deferred tax liability is not recognized because of those exceptions, the following information is required to be disclosed (FAS 109, par. 44):

- A description of the types of temporary differences for which a deferred tax liability has not been recognized and the types of events that would cause those temporary differences to become taxable.
- The cumulative amount of each type of temporary difference.
- The amount of the unrecognized deferred tax liability for temporary differences related to investments in foreign subsidiaries and foreign corporate joint ventures that are essentially permanent in duration if determination of that liability is practicable, or a statement that determination is not practicable.
- The amount of the deferred tax liability for temporary differences other than those in the previous item above that is not recognized based on exceptions granted by APB 23

Disclosure of significant components of income tax expense attributable to continuing operations for each year presented is required in the financial statements or related notes. FAS 109 (par. 45) lists the following as examples of significant components:

- Current tax expense or benefit.
- Deferred tax expense or benefit.
- Investment tax credit.
- Government grants (to the extent recognized as reductions in income tax expense).
- Tax benefits of operating loss carryforwards.
- Tax expense that results from allocating tax benefits (1) directly to contributed capital or (2) to reduce goodwill or other noncurrent intangible assets of an acquired entity.
- Adjustments to a deferred tax liability or asset for enacted changes in tax laws or rates or for a change in the tax status of the enterprise.
- Adjustments of the beginning balance of the valuation allowance because of a change in circumstances that causes a change in judgment about the realizability of the related deferred tax asset in the future.

> **OBSERVATION**
>
> The effect of two unique features of the liability method can be seen in the disclosure requirements listed above. The adjustment for the changes in tax laws or rates or change in tax status requires disclosure of the amount of the adjustment to deferred tax assets and liabilities for enacted changes in tax laws or rates. The final item listed requires disclosure of the amount of the adjustment of the beginning balance of the valuation allowance on deferred tax assets made as a result of a change in judgment about the realizability of that item.

The amount of income tax expense or benefit allocated to continuing operations and amounts separately allocated to other items shall be disclosed for each year for which those items are presented.

Several distinctions are made in the disclosures required of public versus nonpublic enterprises. The two most significant ones are summarized as follows (FAS 109, pars. 43 and 47):

Disclosures Required of Public Versus Nonpublic Companies

	Public	Nonpublic
Temporary difference and carryforwards	Approximation of tax effect of each type	Description of types
Statutory reconciliation	Reconciliation in percentages or dollars	Description of major reconciling items

Companies with operating loss and tax credit carryforwards must disclose the amount and expiration dates.

Disclosure is also required for any portion of the valuation allowance for deferred tax assets for which subsequently recognized tax benefits will be allocated (1) to reduce goodwill or other noncurrent intangible assets of an acquired entity or (2) directly to contributed equity (FAS 109, par. 48).

An entity that is a member of a group that files a consolidated tax return shall disclose the following in its separately issued financial statements (FAS 109, par. 49):

- The aggregate amount of current and deferred tax expense for each statement of earnings presented and the amount of any tax-related balances due to or from affiliates as of the date of each statement of financial position presented.
- The principal provisions of the method by which the consolidated amount of current and deferred tax expense is allocated to members of the group and the nature and effect of any changes in that method during the year.

STUDY QUESTIONS

14. FAS 109 lists all of the following as examples of significant components of income tax attributable to continuing operations, which must be disclosed *except:*

   a. Government grants, to the extent that they reduce tax expense
   b. Amounts and expiration dates of carryforwards
   c. Deferred tax expense or benefit
   d. Adjustments to a deferred tax liability for enacted changes in tax rates..

15. The major difference in disclosures required for public companies as opposed to private ones for temporary differences and carryforwards under FAS 109 is that:

   a. Public companies must list and describe the types of differences and carryforwards, whereas nonpublic companies have no requirement.
   b. Nonpublic companies must approximate the tax effect of temporary differences and carryforwards, whereas public companies must describe the types of such items.
   c. Public companies must include approximations of the tax effect of temporary differences and carryforwards, but private companies need only describe the types of these items.
   d. None of the above is the major difference.

Illustration of Major Provisions of FAS 109

This illustration considers Power Company for three consecutive years, with the objective of preparing the year-end income tax accrual and income tax information for the company's financial statements. Power Company's first year of operations is 20X6. During that year, the company reported $160,000 of pretax accounting income. Permanent and temporary differences are combined with pretax financial income to derive taxable income, as follows:

Pretax financial income	$160,000
Permanent difference:	
Interest on municipal securities	(5,000)
Pretax financial income subject to tax	$155,000
Temporary differences:	
Depreciation	(28,000)
Warranties	10,000
Revenue received in advance	7,000
Taxable income	$144,000

The $5,000 interest on municipal securities represents nontaxable income, and the $28,000 depreciation temporary difference represents the excess of accelerated write-off for tax purposes over straight-line depreciation for financial reporting purposes. Warranties are expensed at the time of sale on an estimated basis but are deductible for income tax purposes only when paid. In 20X6, $10,000 more was accrued than paid. Revenue received in advance is taxable at the time received but is deferred for financial reporting purposes until earned. In 20X6, $7,000 was received that was not earned by year-end. Depreciation is a **taxable temporary difference** that reduces current tax payable and gives rise to a deferred tax liability. The warranties and revenue received in advance are **deductible temporary differences** that increase current tax payable and give rise to deferred tax assets.

Exhibit A presents analyses that facilitate the preparation of the year-end tax accrual, as well as information for the financial statements. Similar analyses are used for each of the three years in this Illustration. The analysis in the upper portion of Exhibit A "rolls forward" the amount of the temporary differences from the beginning to the end of the year. Because 20X6 is the first year for Power Company, the beginning balances are all zero. The change column includes the amounts used in the earlier calculation to determine taxable income from pretax accounting income. The numbers without parentheses are deductible temporary differences; those in parentheses are taxable temporary differences. The company is in a net taxable temporary difference position at the end of the year because the net amount of temporary differences is $(11,000), due to the large amount of the depreciation difference.

The lower portion of Exhibit A converts these temporary differences to amounts of deferred income taxes based on those differences. Again, the beginning balances are all zero and the ending balances are computed at 34 percent, the assumed income tax rate for 20X6 in this Illustration. The amounts in parentheses are deferred tax liabilities, based on taxable temporary differences. The numbers without parentheses are deferred tax assets, based on deductible temporary differences.

EXHIBIT A:

**Analysis of Cumulative Temporary Differences
and Deferred Taxes, 20X6**

Cumulative Temporary Differences (TD)

	Beginning Balance 20X6	Change	Ending Balance 20X6
Deductible TD:			
Warranties	0	$ 10,000	$ 10,000
Revenue received in advance	0	7,000	7,000
(Taxable) TD:			
Depreciation	0	(28,000)	(28,000)
	0	$(11,000)	$(11,000)

Deferred Income Taxes

	Beginning Balance @—%	Ending Balance @34%	Change	Classification Current	Classification Noncurrent
Assets:					
Warranties	0	$ 3,400	$ 3,400		$ 3,400
Revenue received in advance	0	2,380	2,380	$2,380	
(Liabilities):					
Depreciation	0	(9,520)	(9,520)		(9,520)
	0	$(3,740)	$(3,740)	$2,380	$(6,120)

The classification columns on the lower right side of Exhibit A separate the ending balances into current and noncurrent for balance sheet classification purposes. This distinction is based on the asset or liability (if one exists) underlying the temporary difference. If no such asset or liability exists, classification is based on the timing of the expected cash flow. In this case, the warranty period is assumed to be five years, so the related temporary difference is noncurrent, as is depreciation, because of the noncurrent classification of the underlying plant assets. The revenue received in advance is expected to be earned in the coming period, and thus is a current asset.

The December 31, 20X6, entry to record the income tax accrual for Power Company is as follows:

Dec. 31, 20X6

Income tax expense ($48,960 + $3,740)	$52,700	
Deferred income tax—Current	2,380	
Income tax payable ($144,000 × 34%)		$48,960
Deferred income tax—Noncurrent		6,120

Notice that the amounts of deferred income taxes—current and noncurrent—are taken from the lower analysis in Exhibit A. The income tax payable is determined by multiplying the $144,000 taxable income by the 34 percent tax rate. An important point to understand is that income tax expense is determined last: It is the net of the other three numbers and can be computed only after the remaining elements of the entry have been determined.

An important step to complete before moving to 20X7 is a proof of the numbers obtained, commonly referred to as a **statutory rate reconciliation.** For 20X6, this calculation is as follows:

Pretax financial income @ statutory rate ($160,000 × 34%)	$54,400
Less: Permanent differences ($5,000 × 34%)	(1,700)
Income tax expense	$52,700

Effects of these calculations on the balance sheet and income statement will be considered after all three years of analysis are completed.

Power Company's second year of operations is 20X7, in which pretax financial income is $150,000. Municipal interest is $12,000 and temporary differences for depreciation and warranties are $(35,000) and $12,000, respectively. Of the revenue received in advance in 20X6, $5,000 is earned and an additional $9,000 is received in 20X7 that is expected to be earned in 20X8. A new temporary difference is the litigation loss that results from the $10,000 accrual on an estimated basis for accounting purposes. This loss will be deductible for tax purposes when the suit is settled, which is expected to occur in 20X8.

Taxable income for 20X7 is determined as follows:

Pretax financial income	$150,000
Permanent difference:	
Interest on municipal securities	(12,000)
Pretax financial income subject to tax	$138,000
Temporary differences:	
Depreciation	(35,000)
Warranties	12,000
Revenue received in advance ($9,000 – $5,000)	4,000
Litigation loss	10,000
Taxable income	$129,000

Exhibit B includes a 20X7 analysis similar to the 20X6 analysis in Exhibit A. During 20X7, new tax legislation increases the income tax rate for 20X7 and all future years to 40 percent. The amounts in 20X7 simply are moved forward from the end of 20X6. In the lower portion of Exhibit B, the change column is calculated by determining the change required to move the beginning balance to the desired ending balance. The litigation loss is classified as current because of its expected settlement in 20X8, when it will be deductible for income tax purposes.

EXHIBIT B:

Analysis of Cumulative Temporary Differences and Deferred Taxes, 20X7

Cumulative Temporary Differences (TD)

	Beginning Balance 20X7	Change	Ending Balance 20X7
Deductible TD:			
Warranties	$ 10,000	$12,000	$ 22,000
Revenue received in advance	7,000	4,000	11,000
Litigation	0	10,000	10,000
(Taxable) TD:			
Depreciation	(28,000)	(35,000)	(63,000)
	$(11,000)	$ (9,000)	$(20,000)

Deferred Income Taxes

	Beginning Balance @34%	Ending Balance @40%	Change	Classification Current	Classification Noncurrent
Assets:					
Warranties	$ 3,400	$ 8,800	$ 5,400		$ 8,800
Revenue received in advance	2,380	4,400	2,020	$4,400	
Litigation loss	0	4,000	4,000	4,000	
(Liabilities):					
Depreciation	(9,520)	(25,200)	(15,680)		(25,200)
	$(3,740)	$ (8,000)	$ (4,260)	$8,400	$(16,400)

The entry to record income taxes at the end of 20X7 is as follows:

Dec. 31, 20X7

Income tax expense ($51,600 + $4,260)	$55,860	
Deferred income tax—Current ($8,400 – $2,380)	6,020	
Income tax payable ($129,000 × 40%)		$51,600
Deferred income tax—Noncurrent ($16,400 – $6,120)		10,280

Notice that the debits and credits to deferred income tax—current and noncurrent, respectively—are calculated as the changes in those accounts. It is not necessary to deal with that consideration in 20X6 because it was the company's first year. The desired ending balances of current and noncurrent deferred income taxes from Exhibit B are compared with the balances from Exhibit A and the differences are debited or credited into the deferred tax accounts, as appropriate, to produce the desired ending balances. For example, deferred income tax—noncurrent must have a credit (liability) balance of $16,400 at the end of 20X7. The account began with a credit balance of $6,120, requiring a credit of $10,280 in the year-end tax accrual. Similarly, the required debit (asset) balance for deferred income taxes—current is $8,400; with a debit balance of $2,380 at the end of 20X6, the adjustment is $6,020 ($8,400 − $2,380). This illustrates the basic approach of the liability method of accounting for income taxes: The desired balance sheet figures are determined first and the expense is recognized in the amount required to meet the balance sheet objective.

The statutory rate reconciliation has an additional component in 20X7, because of the tax rate change from 34 percent to 40 percent. This change has the effect of increasing deferred taxes and, therefore, tax expense, as indicated in the following reconciliation:

Pretax financial income at statutory rate ($150,000 × 40%)	$ 60,000
Less: Permanent differences ($12,000 × 40%)	(4,800)
Plus: Tax increase on beginning cumulative temporary differences [$11,000 × (40% − 34%)]	660
Income tax expense	$ 55,860

Notice that the adjustment for the tax increase is calculated only for the beginning balance of cumulative temporary differences. The temporary differences originating in 20X7 have already been taxed at 40 percent. As indicated earlier, the balance sheet and income statement presentation of deferred tax information will be considered after the analysis for 20X8.

During the third year of this Illustration, Power Company's activities took a significant downturn. Because of negative economic trends and a loss of several important contracts, the company reported a pretax financial *loss* of $275,000.

An analysis of the pretax financial loss, permanent and temporary differences, and the amount of loss for tax purposes are analyzed as follows:

Pretax financial (loss)	$(275,000)
Permanent difference:	
Interest on municipal securities	(15,000)
Pretax financial (loss) subject to tax	$(290,000)
Temporary differences:	
Depreciation	(40,000)
Warranties	18,000
Revenue received in advance ($15,000 – $10,000)	5,000
Litigation loss	(10,000)
Taxable (loss)	$(317,000)

This analysis is similar to those for 20X6 and 20X7, except for the negative amount entered as pretax financial loss. Revenue of $10,000 received in advance that was previously taxed was recognized in accounting income and an additional $15,000 was received that was deferred for accounting purposes, but taxed currently. The litigation of 20X7 was completed and the $10,000 loss was deducted for tax purposes.

Notice that the loss for tax purposes is $317,000. Assume that Power Company decides to carry back the loss to the extent possible and receive a refund for income taxes paid in the carryback period. While the loss can be carried back three years, in this case the company has existed for only two years, so the loss can be carried back only to 20X6 and 20X7. For Power Company for 20X8, the amount of the refund to be received is $100,560:

20X6:	$144,000	×	34%	=	$	48,960
20X7:	$129,000	×	40%	=		51,600
						$100,560

The determination of deferred tax balances in Exhibit C is similar to those in the two previous exhibits with modifications necessary to include the loss carryforward of $44,000, which is determined by subtracting the amount of loss that is carried back from the total loss for tax purposes for 20X8:

$$\$317,000 - (\$144,000 + \$129,000) = \$44,000$$

Notice that a category for the loss carryforward has been added to the analysis at the top of Exhibit C and the $44,000 loss carryforward in 20X8 has been included. The loss carryforward gives rise to a deferred tax asset, as indicated in the analysis at the bottom of Exhibit C. This item is classified as noncurrent on the assumption that, given the large loss encountered by Power Company in 20X8, it will be several years before the company returns to profitable operations and is able to recognize the benefit of the loss carryforward. That item is treated in the same manner as a deductible temporary difference for purposes of determining deferred tax assets and liabilities.

OBSERVATION

Accumulating the information required to implement FAS 109 is facilitated by preparing a workpaper like those in Exhibits A, B, and C. Such a work-paper includes the following major components:

1. A record of the cumulative temporary differences and carryforwards, including:
   a. Separation of temporary differences into taxable and deductible categories
   b. Beginning balances, the increase or decrease in the cumulative temporary differences, and the ending balances
2. A record of cumulative amounts of carryforwards identified by year
3. A record of deferred income taxes, including:
   a. Separate classifications of deferred tax liabilities and assets
   b. Beginning balances, ending balances, and the resulting changes in deferred taxes for the year
   c. The classification of the ending balances of deferred tax assets and liabilities into current and noncurrent balance sheet categories

The journal entry to record income taxes at the end of 20X8 is as follows:

Dec. 31, 20X8

Receivable for past income taxes
    [($144,000 × 34%) + ($129,000 × 40%)] $100,560
Deferred income tax—Noncurrent
    ($16,400 – $7,600)   8,800
  Deferred income tax—Current
    ($8,400 – $6,400) $ 2,000
  Income tax benefit ($100,560 + $6,800)   107,360

As shown in the two right-hand columns of Exhibits B and C, the balances of both deferred income taxes—current (debit) and deferred income taxes—non-current (credit) declined from 20X7 to 20X8. The two most significant differences are the reversal of the temporary difference from the litigation loss and the inclusion of the loss carryforward, both of which are relatively large amounts.

In the journal entry above, income tax expense has been replaced by the account income tax benefit, which indicates the positive impact (loss reduction) of using the 20X8 loss to receive the refund of 20X6 and 20X7 income taxes and to offset income taxes that would otherwise have to be paid after 20X8.

The 20X8 statutory rate reconciliation can now be prepared as follows:

Pretax financial (loss) at statutory rate [($275,000) × 40%]	$(110,000)
Less: Permanent differences ($15,000 × 40%)	(6,000)
Plus: Loss carryback at 34% [$144,000 × (40% – 34%)]	8,640
Income tax (benefit)	$(107,360)

The last item in the reconciliation, identified as "loss carryback at 34 percent," is required because the 20X6 part of the carryback was determined at 34 percent, the 20X6 income tax rate, rather than the current (20X8) rate of 40 percent.

Now that the three-year analysis of the cumulative temporary differences and the loss carryforward, the related deferred tax assets and liabilities, and the year-end journal entries to record income taxes is completed, attention should be focused on the amounts that will be presented in the balance sheet and income statement. That information is presented in Exhibit D. For each year, a portion of deferred taxes appears in the current asset section of the balance sheet. This amount represents the net amount of deferred taxes on temporary differences on assets and liabilities that are classified as current in the balance sheet. In addition, in 20X8, a current asset is presented for the $100,560 receivable of 20X6 and 20X7 taxes resulting from the 20X8 carryback. For 20X6 and 20X7, a current liability is presented for income taxes payable—$48,960 and $51,600 in 20X6 and 20X7, respectively.

Among noncurrent liabilities, each year includes a deferred tax amount that represents deferred taxes resulting from temporary differences classified as noncurrent, and from the loss carryforward. The amount of noncurrent deferred taxes declines between 20X7 and 20X8 because of the loss carryforward, which partially offsets the large deferred tax liability related to the depreciation temporary difference for the first time in 20X8.

The income statement presentation for each year displays pretax financial income (loss), followed by income tax expense (benefit), separated into current and deferred components. In 20X6 and 20X7, income tax expense reduces the amount of net income reported, as would be expected given the profitability reported by the company in those years. In 20X8, however, the benefit of the carryback and carryforward results in a reduction in the amount of loss that would otherwise have been reported because of the refund of past taxes and the anticipation of reduced taxes in the future, when the carryforward is realized.

To examine the accounting procedures required when a valuation allowance is established for deferred tax assets, return to Exhibit C. Assume that, after careful consideration, management determines it is more likely than not that 25 percent of the deferred tax assets will not be realized. This requires a valuation allowance of $10,000, determined as follows, based on the information from Exhibit C:

Current deferred tax assets:		
Revenue received in advance		$ 6,400
Noncurrent deferred tax assets:		
Warranties	$16,000	
Loss carryforward	17,600	33,600
		$40,000
Valuation allowance: 25% × $40,000		$10,000
Allocation to current/noncurrent:		
Current: ($6,400/$40,000) × $10,000		$ 1,600
Noncurrent: ($33,600/$40,000) × $10,000		8,400
		$10,000

This allocation results in a $1,600 reduction in the current deferred tax asset and a $8,400 addition to the net noncurrent deferred tax liability. In the following comparative analysis, the impact of the valuation allowance is determined as indicated in the right-hand column, and is compared with the figures presented earlier without a valuation allowance in the left-hand column.

	Without Valuation Allowance	With Valuation Allowance
Current deferred tax asset	$ 6,400	$ 6,400
Less: Allowance	0	(1,600)
	$ 6,400	$ 4,800
Noncurrent deferred tax liability:		
Asset component	$33,600	$ 33,600
Less: Allowance	0	(8,400)
	$33,600	$ 25,200
Liability component	(41,200)	(41,200)
	$ (7,600)	$(16,000)
Total deferred tax	$ (1,200)	$(11,200)

The difference between the totals in the two columns is $10,000, exactly the amount of the valuation allowance.

The journal entry to record income taxes at the end of 20X8 under these revised assumptions, and including the valuation allowance, is as follows:

Dec. 31, 20X8

Receivable for past income taxes		
[($144,000 × 34%) + ($129,000 × 40%)]	$100,560	
Deferred income tax—Noncurrent		
($16,400 – $7,600)	8,800	
Allowance to reduce deferred tax assets		
to lower recoverable value		$10,000
Deferred income tax—Current		
($8,400 – $6,400)		2,000
Income tax benefit		
($100,560 + $6,800 – $10,000)		97,360

The statutory rate reconciliation for 20X5, including the recognition of the valuation allowance, is as follows:

Pretax financial income (loss) at statutory rate	
[($275,000) × 40%]	$(110,000)
Less: Permanent differences ($15,000 × 40%)	(6,000)
Plus: Loss carryback at 34% [$144,000 × (40% – 34%)]	8,640
Increase in valuation allowance	10,000
Income tax (benefit)	$ (97,360)

The valuation allowance is evaluated at the end of each year, considering positive and negative evidence about whether the asset will be realized. At that time, the allowance will either be increased or reduced; reduction could result in the complete elimination of the allowance if positive evidence indicates that the value of the deferred tax assets is no longer impaired and the allowance is no longer required.

EXHIBIT C:

**Analysis of Cumulative Temporary Differences
and Deferred Taxes, 20X8**

Cumulative Temporary Differences (TD)

	Beginning Balance 20X8	Change	Ending Balance 20X8
Deductible TD:			
Warranties	$ 22,000	$ 18,000	$ 40,000
Revenue received in advance	11,000	5,000	16,000
Litigation	10,000	(10,000)	0
(Taxable) TD:			
Depreciation	(63,000)	(40,000)	(103,000)
Loss Carryforward:			
20X3 Loss*	0	44,000	44,000
	$(20,000)	$ 17,000	$ (3,000)

Deferred Income Taxes

	Beginning Balance @40%	Ending Balance @40%	Change	Classification Current	Classification Noncurrent
Assets:					
Warranties	$ 8,800	$16,000	$ 7,200		$16,000
Revenue received in advance	4,400	6,400	2,000	$6,400	
Litigation loss	4,000	0	(4,000)		
Loss carryforward	0	17,600	17,600		17,600
(Liabilities):					
Depreciation	(25,200)	(41,200)	(16,000)		(41,200)
	$(8,000)	$(1,200)	$6,800	$6,400	$(7,600)

* [$317,000 – ($144,000 + $129,000)]

EXHIBIT D:

**Financial Statement Presentation
of Income Taxes, 20X6–20X8**

Balance Sheet

	20X6	20X7	20X8
Current assets:			
Receivable for past income taxes			$ 100,560
Deferred income taxes	$ 2,380	$ 8,400	6,400
Current liabilities:			
Income taxes payable	48,960	51,600	
Noncurrent liabilities:			
Deferred income taxes	6,120	16,400	7,600

Income Statement

	20X6	20X7	20X8
Income (loss):			
Before income tax	$160,000	$150,000	$(275,000)
Income tax expense (benefit):			
Current	48,960	51,600	(100,560)
Deferred	3,740	4,260	(6,800)
	52,700	55,860	(107,360)
Net income (loss)	$107,300	$ 94,140	$(167,640)

CONCLUSION

This chapter has attempted to distill the complex provisions of FAS 109 and the other authoritative literature on accounting for income taxes into a succinct applications guide for the most commonly seen practice situations. It followed this sequential process from top to bottom, with text that explained the theory of how to differentiate the temporary differences that give rise to deferred income taxes, as well as how to calculate, record, and display them. The chapter concludes with a comprehensive illustration that demonstrates in a practical, worksheet-based format, how to put the theory into practice.

MODULE 2 — CHAPTER 5

Financial Instruments

LEARNING OBJECTIVES

The evolution of business models and financial markets has complicated the both the nature of financial instruments, and the measurement and reporting principles associated with them. This chapter distills the authoritative literature on this subject into a digestible source that is designed to assist accounting practitioners in putting these principles into practice.

Upon completion of this chapter, the professional will be able to:

■ Identify the various types of financial instruments, including derivative instruments.

■ Apply the recognition and measurement principles of FAS 133 to derivatives.

■ Understand the reporting requirements for derivative instruments and hedging activities.

■ Present proper disclosures for the fair value of financial instruments.

■ Understand the principles for estimating the fair value of financial instruments.

OVERVIEW

The term **financial instrument** is extremely broad and encompasses a wide variety of rights and obligations. A financial instrument is cash, an ownership interest in another entity, or a contract that imposes a contractual obligation on one entity and conveys a corresponding right to a second entity to require delivery (receipt) or exchange of a financial instrument (FAS 107, par. 3). Accounting principles for financial instruments are contained in numerous pronouncements. This chapter focuses on principles governing only the most active areas related to financial instruments—accounting for derivative instruments, offsetting of assets and liabilities arising from derivative transactions, and fair value disclosures for all financial instruments. GAAP established by the FASB for financial instruments are contained in the following:

FAS 107   *Disclosures About Fair Value of Financial Instruments*

FAS 126   *Exemption from Certain Required Disclosures About Financial Instruments for Certain Nonpublic Entities*

FAS 133   *Accounting for Derivative Instruments and Hedging Activities*

FAS 137   *Deferral of the Effective Date of FASB Statement No. 133*

FAS 138   *Accounting for Certain Derivative Instruments and Certain Hedging Activities*

FAS 149   *Amendment of FASB Statement No. 133 on Derivative Instruments and Hedging Activities*

FIN 39   *Offsetting of Amounts Related to Certain Contracts*

> **OBSERVATION**
>
> The accounting for financial instruments is becoming increasingly complex. Significant guidance for financial instruments also is contained in Emerging Issues Task Force (EITF) Issues, FASB Staff Implementation Guides, FASB Staff Positions (FSPs), and other literature.

BACKGROUND

Significant financial innovation and the rapid development of complex financial instruments prompted the FASB to undertake an involved and lengthy project to develop a set of accounting standards for financial instruments in 1986. Many financial instruments were described as **off-balance-sheet** instruments because they failed to meet one or more of the criteria for recognition. Before addressing the difficult recognition and measurement issues associated with financial instruments, the FASB developed standards to improve disclosures surrounding financial instruments. Initially, the FASB issued two broad pronouncements for financial instrument disclosures: FAS 105, *Disclosure of Information About Financial Instruments with Off-Balance-Sheet Risk and Financial Instruments with Concentrations of Credit Risk,* issued in 1990, and FAS 107, *Disclosures About Fair Value of Financial Instruments,* issued in 1991. Additionally, the FASB issued FAS 119, *Disclosure About Derivative Financial Instruments and Fair Value of Financial Instruments,* in 1994.

The FASB issued several pronouncements in the early and mid-1990s that addressed the recognition and measurement of financial instruments, including FAS 114, *Accounting by Creditors for Impairment of a Loan,* FAS 115, *Accounting for Certain Investments in Debt and Equity Securities,* FAS 118, *Accounting by Creditors for Impairment of a Loan—Income Recognition and Disclosures,* and FAS 125, which was later replaced by FAS 140, *Accounting for Transfers and Servicing of Financial Assets and Extinguishments of Liabilities.* A significant milestone in the FASB's financial instrument project was reached in 1998 with the issuance of FAS 133, *Accounting for Derivative Instruments and Hedging Activities.* FAS 133 was the result of extensive discussion and debate by the FASB on the subject of accounting for derivative instruments; it overhauled the fragmented preexisting accounting model for derivative instruments by establishing recognition and measurement standards for all derivatives, regardless of their use, based on fair value. FAS 133 replaced FAS 105, FAS 119, and amended FAS 107 as well as various other pronouncements.

ACCOUNTING FOR DERIVATIVE INSTRUMENTS AND HEDGING ACTIVITIES

FAS 133, *Accounting for Derivative Instruments and Hedging Activities,* was issued in June 1998 and was originally effective for fiscal periods (both years and quarters) beginning after June 15, 1999. This effective date was delayed one year to June 15, 2000, by FAS 137. FAS 133 subsequently was amended by FAS 138, *Accounting for Certain Derivative Instruments and Certain Hedging Activities,* primarily to ease implementation difficulties for a large number of the entities required to apply the standard. Both FAS 133 and FAS 138 are effective for fiscal periods beginning after June 15, 2000. FAS 149, *Amendment of Statement 133 on Derivative Instruments and Hedging Activities,* issued in 2003, further amended FAS 133 to clarify the definition of a derivative and to incorporate certain implementation guidance. FAS 149 generally is effective for contracts entered into or modified after June 30, 2003.

FAS 133, as amended, establishes accounting and reporting standards for derivative instruments, including derivative instruments that are embedded in other contracts, and hedging activities. (For simplicity, the remainder of this section refers only to FAS 133, although the discussion reflects all related amendments.) FAS 133 is based on the following fundamental principles (FAS 133, par. 3):

- Derivative instruments represent rights or obligations that meet the definitions of assets and liabilities and, therefore, should be reported in the financial statements.
- Fair value is the most relevant measure for financial instruments and the only relevant measure for derivative instruments.
- Only items that are assets or liabilities should be reported as such in the financial statements.
- Special accounting for items designated as being hedged should be provided only for qualifying items. One aspect of qualification is an assessment of the expectation of effective offsetting changes in fair value or cash flows during the term of the hedge for the risk being hedged.

Defining a Derivative and Its Scope

A **derivative instrument** is a financial instrument or other contract with all of the following characteristics:

- It has (1) one or more underlyings (An **underlying** is a specified interest rate, security price, commodity price, foreign exchange rate, index of prices or rates, or other variable including the occurrence or nonoccurrence of a specified event and (2) one or more notional amounts (a **notional amount** is a number of currency units, shares, bushels, pounds, or other unit specified in the contract) or payment provisions, or both. The interaction of the underlying and notional amount determine the amount of the settlement and, in some cases, whether a settlement is required.

- It requires no initial investment or an initial investment that is smaller than would be required for other types of contracts that would be expected to have a similar response to changes in market factors.
- Its terms require or permit net settlement; it can be readily settled net by a means outside the contract; or it provides for delivery of an asset that puts the recipient in a position not substantially different from net settlement (FAS 133, par. 6–9).

FAS 133 contains a number of exceptions to the definition of a derivative. Some of the scope exceptions were granted because the FASB recognized established accounting models already existed for certain instruments that would meet the definition of a derivative. Other scope exceptions were granted in order to simplify application of the standard. The following is a partial list of those scope exceptions (FAS 133, pars. 10–11):

- **Regular-way security trades** (i.e., security trades that require delivery of an existing security within a timeframe established by regulations in the marketplace or exchange in which the transaction is executed), if they cannot be net settled;
- Purchases and sales of **when-issued securities** or other securities that do not yet exist that meet certain specified conditions; and all security trades that are required to be recognized on a trade-date basis by other GAAP.
- Normal purchases and normal sales (i.e., contracts that provide for the purchase or sale of something other than a financial instrument or derivative instrument that will be delivered in quantities expected to be used or sold by the reporting entity over a reasonable period in the normal course of business).
- Certain insurance contracts.
- Certain financial guarantee contracts.
- Certain contracts that are not traded on an exchange.
- Derivatives that serve as impediments to sales accounting.
- Investments in life insurance (in specific circumstances).
- Certain investment contracts (in specific circumstances).
- Loan commitments for origination of any type of loan that are held by a potential borrower.
- Loan commitments issued to originate mortgage loans that will be classified as held for investment under FAS 65 (however, loan commitments issued to originate mortgage loans that will be classified as held for sale under FAS 65 are subject to FAS 133).
- Contracts issued or held by the reporting entity that are both indexed to the entity's own stock and classified in stockholders' equity.
- Contracts issued by the entity in connection with stock-based compensation arrangements.

- Contracts issued as contingent consideration in business combinations.
- Forward purchase contracts for the reporting entity's shares that require physical settlement that are covered by paragraphs 21 and 22 of FAS 150.

A contract that qualifies for a scope exception under FAS 133 should be accounted for in accordance with relevant GAAP.

OBSERVATION

The definition of a derivative and the scope exceptions in FAS 133 are complicated and highly interpretive. Practitioners encountering complex instruments that may be subject to FAS 133 should seek the advice of experts in the area of accounting for derivatives.

STUDY QUESTIONS

1. Which of the following is *not* a typical characteristic of derivative instruments?

   a. Notional amount specified in the contract

   b. Underlyings

   c. Payment provisions

   d. All of the above are characteristics of derivative instruments

2. All of the following are types of security transactions that qualify as scope exceptions to FAS 133 *except:*

   a. When-issued securities

   b. Mortgage-backed securities

   c. Regular-way securities

   d. All of the above qualify as scope exceptions

3. All of the following are types of contracts that qualify as scope exceptions to the definition of derivatives under FAS 133 *except:*

   a. Contracts issued as contingent consideration in business combinations

   b. Contracts issued in connection with stock-based compensation arrangements

   c. Forward purchase contracts requiring physical settlement that are covered by FAS 150

   d. All of the above qualify as scope exceptions

Embedded Derivatives

Contracts that do not in their entirety meet the definition of a derivative instrument (e.g., bonds, insurance policies, leases) may contain embedded derivative instruments as a result of implicit or explicit terms that affect some or all of the cash flows or the value of other exchanges required by the contract in a manner that makes them similar to a derivative instrument. An embedded derivative instrument should be separated from the host contract and accounted for as a derivative instrument in accordance with FAS 133, assuming the following conditions are met (FAS 133, par. 12):

- The economic characteristics and risks of the embedded derivative instrument are not clearly and closely related to the economic characteristics of the host contract.
- The hybrid instrument that embodies the embedded derivative instrument and the host contract is not remeasured at fair value under otherwise applicable generally accepted accounting principles.
- A separate instrument with the same terms as the embedded instrument would be a derivative subject to the requirements of FAS 133. However, this criterion is not met if the separate instrument with the same terms as the embedded derivative instrument would be classified in stockholders' equity absent the provisions in FAS 150 (FAS 133, par. 12).

> **OBSERVATION**
>
> Contracts that qualify for a scope exception under FAS 133 are not evaluated under FAS 133 for the existence of embedded derivatives. FAS 133 contains implementation guidance and illustrations related to the assessment of whether an embedded derivative is considered clearly and closely related to a host contract. The identification and bifurcation of embedded derivatives, especially for complex compound financial instruments, require a high level of expertise.

Recognition and Measurement of Derivatives

FAS 133 requires the recognition of all derivatives (both assets and liabilities) in the statement of financial position and the recognition of their measurement at fair value. In accordance with FAS 133, each derivative instrument is classified in one of the following four categories:

- No hedge designation.
- Fair value hedge.
- Cash flow hedge.
- Foreign currency hedge.

Changes in the fair value of derivative instruments in each category are accounted for as indicated in the following table (FAS 133, par. 18).

Derivative Designation	Accounting for Changes in Fair Value
No hedge designation	Included in current income
Fair value hedge	Included in current net income (with the offsetting gain or loss on the hedged item attributable to the risk being hedged)
Cash flow hedge	Included in other comprehensive income (outside net income)
Foreign currency hedge of a net investment in a foreign operation	Included in comprehensive income (outside of net income) as part of the cumulative translation adjustment

STUDY QUESTIONS

4. Under FAS 133, derivatives that are either assets or liabilities must be recognized in the:
   a. Statement of retained earnings
   b. Statement of financial position
   c. Income statement
   d. Statement of cash flows

5. Changes in fair value for foreign currency hedges are accounted for in which of the following?
   a. Current income
   b. Current net income
   c. Comprehensive income as part of the cumulative translation adjustment
   d. Other comprehensive income (outside net income)

6. Changes in fair value for cash flow hedges are accounted for in which of the following?
   a. Current income
   b. Current net income
   c. Comprehensive income as part of the cumulative translation adjustment
   d. Other comprehensive income (outside net income)

Derivatives Designated in Hedging Relationships

Fair Value Hedges. Certain instruments are designated as hedging the exposure to changes in the fair value of an asset or liability or an identified portion thereof that is attributed to a particular risk. A fair value hedge must meet all of the following criteria (FAS 133, par. 20, as amended by FAS 149):

■ At the inception of the hedge, the hedging relationship and the entity's risk management objective and strategy for undertaking the hedge are formally documented. Records must include identification of:

- The hedged instrument.
- The hedged item.
- The nature of the risk being hedged.
- How the hedging instrument's effectiveness in offsetting the exposure to changes in the fair value of the hedged item will be assessed.

■ Both at the inception of the hedge and on an ongoing basis, the hedging relationship is expected to be highly effective in achieving offsetting changes in fair value attributed to the hedged risk during the period that the hedge is designated. An assessment is required whenever financial statements or earnings are reported, and at least every three months.

■ If a written option is designated as hedging a recognized asset or liability or an unrecognized firm commitment, the combination of the hedged item and the written option provides at least as much potential for gains as the exposure to losses from changes in the combined fair values.

In a fair value hedge, the following criteria must be met for an asset or liability to qualify as a hedged item (FAS 133, par. 21):

■ Specific identification either as all or as a specified portion of a recognized asset or a recognized liability or an unrecognized firm commitment. The hedged item is a single asset or liability (or specified portion thereof) or is a portfolio of similar assets or a portfolio of similar liabilities (or a specified portion thereof).

■ Presentation of an exposure to changes in fair value attributable to the hedged risk that could affect reported earnings. (The reference to affecting reported earnings does not apply to an entity that does not report earnings as a separate caption in a statement of financial performance, such as a not-for-profit organization.)

The hedged item is not any of the following:

- An asset or liability that is remeasured with the changes in fair value attributable to the hedged risk reported currently in earnings
- An investment accounted for by the equity method
- A minority interest in one or more consolidated subsidiaries
- An equity investment in a consolidated subsidiary
- A firm commitment either to enter into a business combination or to acquire or dispose of a subsidiary, a minority interest, or an equity method investee
- An equity instrument issued by the entity and classified as stockholders' equity in the statement of financial position.

■ If the hedged item is all or a portion of a debt security that is classified as held-to-maturity by FAS 115, *Accounting for Certain Investments in Debt and Equity Securities,* the designated risk being hedged is the risk of changes in its fair value attributable to credit risk, foreign exchange risk, or both.

- If the hedged item is an option component of a held-to-maturity security that permits its prepayment, the designated risk being hedged is the risk of changes in the entire fair value of that option component.
- If the hedged item is a nonfinancial asset or liability other than a recognized loan servicing right or a nonfinancial firm commitment with financial components, the designated risk being hedged is the risk of changes in the fair value of the entire hedged asset or liability.
- If the hedged item is a financial asset or liability, a recognized loan servicing right, or a nonfinancial firm commitment with financial components, the designated risk being hedged is:
  - The risk of changes in the overall fair value of the entire hedged item
  - The risk of changes in its fair value attributable to changes in the designated benchmark interest rate (i.e., interest rate risk)
  - The risk of changes in its fair value attributable to changes in the related foreign currency exchange risk (i.e., foreign exchange risk)
  - The risk of changes in its fair value attributable to both changes in the obligor's creditworthiness and changes in spread over the benchmark interest rate with respect to the hedged item's credit section at inception (i.e., credit risk).

Changes in the fair value of derivative instruments that qualify as fair value hedges are recognized currently in earnings. The gain or loss on the hedged item attributable to the hedged risk adjusts the carrying amount of the hedged item and is recognized currently in earnings (FAS 133, par. 22).

OBSERVATION

Although FAS 133 generally requires accounting for derivative instruments at fair value, those qualifying as fair value hedges are the only types of hedges for which the change in value is included currently in determining net income. This accounting distinguishes fair value hedges from cash flow hedges and foreign currency hedges and can be expected to result in some volatility in reported income.

An entity shall discontinue prospectively accounting for a fair value hedge if **any** of the following occurs (FAS 133, par. 25):
- Any criterion of a fair value hedge, or hedged item, is no longer met.
- The derivative expires, or is sold, terminated, or exercised.
- The entity removes the designation of the fair value hedge.

An asset or liability that is designated as a fair value hedge is subject to the applicable GAAP requirement for assessment of impairment (asset) or recognition of an increased obligation (liability) (FAS 133, par. 27).

STUDY QUESTION

---

7. For a fair value hedge, if the hedged item is a debt security classified under FAS 115 as held-to-maturity, the risk being hedged is the risk of changes to fair value attributable to:

a. Credit risk and or foreign exchange risk
b. Interest rate risk
c. Risk of changes in the fair value of the entire hedged asset
d. Cash flow risk

Cash Flow Hedges. A derivative instrument may be designated as hedging the exposure to variability in expected future cash flows attributed to a particular risk. That exposure may be associated with an existing recognized asset or liability (e.g., variable rate debt) or a forecasted transaction (e.g., a forecasted purchase or sale). To qualify for cash flow hedge accounting, designated hedging instruments and hedged items or transactions must meet all of the following criteria (FAS 133, par. 28):

- At the inception of the hedge, there is formal documentation of the hedging relationship and the entity's risk management objective and strategy for undertaking the hedge. This must include identification of:
  - The hedging instrument
  - The hedged transaction
  - The nature of the risk being hedged
  - How the hedging instrument's effectiveness hedges the risk to the hedged transaction's variability in cash flows attributable to the hedged risk will be assessed.

- Both when the hedge is initiated and on an ongoing basis, the hedging relationship is expected to be highly effective in offsetting cash flows attributable to the hedged risk during the term of the hedge. When financial statements or earnings are reported, and at least every three months thereafter, an assessment is necessary.

- If a written option is designated as hedging the variability in cash flows for a recognized asset or liability, the combination of the hedged item and the written option provides at least as much potential for favorable cash flows as the exposure to unfavorable cash flows.

- If a hedging instrument is used to modify the interest receipts or payments associated with a recognized financial asset or liability from one variable rate to another variable rate, the hedging instrument must be a link between an existing designated asset with variable cash flows and an existing designated liability with variable cash flows and must be highly effective in achieving offsetting cash flows.

A forecasted transaction qualifies as a hedged transaction in a cash flow hedge if it meets all of the following additional criteria (FAS 133, par. 29):

- The forecasted transaction is specifically identified as a single transaction or a group of individual transactions. If a group, the individual transactions within the group must share the same risk exposure that is being hedged.
- The occurrence of the forecasted transaction is probable.
- The forecasted transaction is with a party external to the reporting entity.
- The forecasted transaction is not the acquisition of an asset or incurrence of a liability that will subsequently be remeasured with changes in fair value attributed to the hedged risk reported currently in earnings.
- If the variable cash flows of the forecasted transaction relate to a debt security that is classified as held-to-maturity under FAS 115, the risk being hedged is the risk of changes in its cash flows attributable to credit risk, foreign exchange risk, or both.
- The forecasted transaction does not involve a business combination subject to the provisions of FAS 141, *Business Combinations,* and is not a transaction involving:
  - A parent company's interest in consolidated subsidiaries
  - A minority interest in a consolidated subsidiary
  - An equity-method investment
  - An entity's own equity instruments.
- If the hedged transaction is the forecasted purchase or sale of a nonfinancial asset, the designated risk being hedged is one of these:
  - The risk of changes in the functional-currency-equivalent cash flows attributable to changes in the related foreign currency exchange rates
  - The risk of changes in the cash flows relating to all changes in the purchase price or sales price of the asset, regardless of whether that price and the related cash flows are stated in the entity's functional currency or a foreign currency.
- If the hedged transaction is the forecasted purchase or sale of a financial asset or liability, the interest payments on that financial asset or liability, or the variable cash inflow or outflow of an existing financial asset or liability, the designated risk being hedged is:
  - The overall risk of changes in the hedged cash flows related to the asset or liability
  - The risk of changes in its cash flows attributable to changes in the designated benchmark interest rates
  - The risk of changes in the functional-currency-equivalent cash flows attributable to changes in the related foreign currency exchange rates
  - The risk of changes in cash flows attributable to default, changes in the obligor's creditworthiness, and changes in the spread over the benchmark interest rate.

The effective portion of the gain or loss (i.e., change in fair value) on a derivative designated as a cash flow hedge is reported in other comprehensive income (outside net income). The ineffective portion is reported in earnings. Amounts in accumulated other comprehensive income are reclassified into earnings (net income) in the same period in which the hedged forecasted transaction affects earnings (FAS 133, par. 30).

> **OBSERVATION**
>
> Changes in the fair value of cash flow hedges are not included currently in determining net income as they are with fair value hedges. Rather, they are included in "other comprehensive income," outside the determination of net income.

An entity must discontinue prospectively accounting for cash flow hedges as specified above if **any** of the following occurs (FAS 133, par. 32):
- Any criterion for a cash flow hedge, or the hedged forecasted transaction, is no longer met.
- The derivative expires, or is sold, terminated, or exercised.
- The entity removes the designation of the cash flow hedge.

If a company discontinues cash flow hedge accounting, the accumulated amount in other comprehensive income remains and is reclassified into earnings when the hedged forecasted transaction affects earnings. Existing GAAP for impairment of an asset or recognition of an increased liability apply to the asset or liability that gives rise to the variable cash flows that were designated in the cash flow hedge (FAS 133, par. 34).

Foreign Currency Hedges. If the hedged item is denominated in a foreign currency, FAS 133 indicates that an entity may designate the following types of hedges as hedges of foreign currency exposure:
- A fair value hedge of an unrecognized firm commitment or a recognized asset or liability (including an available-for-sale security).
- A cash flow hedge of a forecasted transaction, an unrecognized firm commitment, the forecasted functional-currency equivalent cash flows associated with a recognized asset or liability, or a forecasted intercompany transaction.
- A hedge of a net investment in a foreign operation.

Foreign currency fair value hedges and cash flows hedges are generally subject to the fair value and cash flow hedge accounting requirements, respectively, covered earlier.

The change in fair value of a derivative instrument that qualifies as a hedge of net investment of a foreign operation is reported in other comprehensive income (outside net income) as part of the cumulative translation adjustment in accordance with FAS 52, *Foreign Currency Translation*, (FAS 133, par. 42).

OBSERVATION

Foreign currency hedges build on the standards for fair value and cash flow hedges presented earlier, and (for foreign currency hedges of net investments in foreign operations) on accounting for the cumulative translation adjustment requirements of FAS 52, *Foreign Currency Translation*. If a foreign currency hedge satisfies the FAS 133 criteria as a fair value or cash flow hedge, it is treated accordingly. If the foreign currency hedge is a hedge of net investment in a foreign operation, it is treated as a part of the cumulative translation adjustment. In this latter case, changes in fair value are included in other comprehensive income (much like a cash flow hedge) and are included in the cumulative translation adjustment rather than separately disclosed.

Required Disclosures

General. For instruments that qualify as hedging instruments, the following disclosures are required (FAS 133, par. 44):

■ Objectives for holding or issuing the instruments.
■ The context needed to understand these objectives.
■ The entity's strategies for achieving these objectives.
■ Distinction concerning the above between derivative instruments designated as fair value hedging instruments, cash flow hedging instruments, hedges of the foreign currency exposure of a net investment in a foreign operation, and all other derivatives.
■ The entity's risk management policy for each type of hedge, including a description of the items or transactions for which risks are hedged.
■ For instruments not designated as hedging instruments, the purpose of the derivative activity.

Fair Value Hedges. The following disclosures are required for derivative instruments—as well as nonderivative instruments that may give rise to foreign currency transaction gains or losses under FAS 52—that have been designated and qualify as fair value hedging instruments (FAS 133, par. 45a):

■ The net gain or loss recognized in earnings during the period representing:
  – The amount of the hedges' ineffectiveness
  – The component of the derivative instruments' gain or loss, if any, excluded from the assessment of hedge effectiveness
  – A description of where the net gain or loss is reported in the statement of income or other statement of financial performance.
■ The amount of net gain or loss recognized in earnings when a hedged firm commitment no longer qualifies as a fair value hedge.

Cash Flow Hedges. The following disclosures are required for derivatives that have been designated and qualify as cash flow hedging instruments and the related hedged transactions (FAS 133, par. 45b):

- The net gain or loss recognized in earnings during the reporting period representing:
  - The amount of the hedges' ineffectiveness
  - The component of the derivative instruments' gain or loss, if any, excluded from the assessment of hedge effectiveness
  - A description of where the net gain or loss is reported in the statement of income or other statement of financial performance.
- A description of the transactions or other events that will result in the reclassification into earnings of gains or losses that are reported in accumulated other comprehensive income and the estimated net amount of the existing gains or losses at the reporting date that is expected to be reclassified into earnings within the next 12 months.
- The maximum length of time over which the entity is hedging its exposure to the variability in future cash flows for forecasted transactions excluding those forecasted transactions related to the payment of variable interest on existing financial instruments.
- The amount of gains and losses reclassified into earnings as a result of the discontinuance of cash flow hedges, because it is probable that the original forecasted transactions will not occur by the end of the originally specified time period.

Hedges of a Net Investment in a Foreign Operation. The net amount of gains and losses included in the cumulative translation adjustment during the reporting period must be disclosed for derivative instruments, as well as nonderivative instruments that may give rise to foreign currency transaction gains or losses under FAS 52, that have been designated and qualify as hedging instruments for hedges of the foreign currency exposure of a net investment in a foreign operation. (FAS 133, par. 45c).

STUDY QUESTIONS

> 8. FAS 133 requires companies offering hedging instruments to make a general disclosure listing the objectives for holding or issuing such instruments, as well as the _____ the objectives.
>
>   a. Timeline and funding for attaining
>   b. Past experience with and past outcomes of
>   c. Context for understanding and strategies for achieving
>   d. Consideration of alternatives to hedging and process for developing

9. Disclosures required for cash flow hedges involving derivatives include all of the following *except:*

    a. The maximum length of time over which the entity is hedging exposure to the variability of future cash flows

    b. The amount of gains and losses reclassified into earnings as a result of discontinuing the cash flow hedges

    c. The amount of net gain (loss) recognized in earnings for the reporting period representing the hedges' ineffectiveness

    d. All of the above are required disclosures

REPORTING CASH FLOWS OF DERIVATIVE INSTRUMENTS THAT CONTAIN FINANCING ELEMENTS

An instrument accounted for as a derivative under FAS 133 that at its inception includes off-market terms, requires an up-front cash payment, or both, contains a financing element. If a significant financing element is present at inception, other than a financing element inherently included in an at-the-market derivative instrument with no prepayments, the borrower shall report all cash inflows and outflows associated with that derivative instrument as a financing activity as described in FAS 95, *Statement of Cash Flows* (FAS 133, par. 45A).

REPORTING CHANGES IN COMPONENTS OF COMPREHENSIVE INCOME

Changes in components of comprehensive income are the following:

- Within other comprehensive income, entities must display a separate classification of the net gain or loss on derivative instruments designated and qualifying as cash flow hedging instruments that are reported in comprehensive income (FAS 133, par. 46).
- As part of the disclosure of accumulated other comprehensive income in accordance with FAS 130, *Reporting Comprehensive Income*, entities must disclose the beginning and ending accumulated derivative gain or loss, the related net change associated with current period hedging transactions, and the net amount of any reclassification into earnings (FAS 133, par. 47).

OFFSETTING DERIVATIVE ASSETS AND LIABILITIES

FIN 39 specifies that offsetting of assets and liabilities in the balance sheet is improper except when the right of setoff exists. FIN 39 establishes four criteria that must be satisfied to establish a valid right of setoff. Generally, for an asset and liability to be offset and displayed as a net position, all four criteria of FIN 39 must be satisfied:

- Each party owes the other party determinable amounts.
- The reporting party has the right to set off the amount payable, by contract or other agreement, with the amount receivable.
- The reporting entity intends to net settle.
- The right of setoff is enforceable at law.

An exception to the general rule in FIN 39 exists for derivative contracts executed with the same counterparty under a master netting agreement. A **master netting agreement** is a contractual agreement entered into by two parties to multiple contracts that provides for the net settlement of all contracts covered by the agreement in the event of default under any one contract. For such derivative contracts, assets and liabilities may be offset and presented as a net amount even if the reporting entity does not meet the requirement in FIN 39 that the reporting entity has the intent to net settle. Offsetting derivative assets and liabilities under this exception is an election and the reporting entity must apply the election consistently.

STUDY QUESTION

> **10.** FIN 39 criteria for offsetting an asset and liability as a net position include all of the following *except:*
>
> **a.** Intention of the reporting entity to net settle
> **b.** The right of setoff being enforceable at law
> **c.** A master netting agreement is created to create the right of setoff
> **d.** Parties owe each other determinable amounts

DISCLOSURE OF INFORMATION ABOUT FAIR VALUE OF FINANCIAL INSTRUMENTS

Definitions and Scope

FAS 107, *Disclosures About Fair Value of Financial Instruments,* par. 3, defines **financial instrument** as cash, evidence of an ownership interest in an entity, or a contract that both:

- Imposes on one entity a contractual obligation (1) to deliver cash or another financial instrument to a second entity or (2) to exchange other financial instruments on potentially unfavorable terms with the second entity.
- Conveys to the second entity a contractual right (1) to receive cash or another financial instrument from the first entity or (2) to exchange other financial instruments on potentially favorable terms with the first entity.

Fair value is the amount at which the instrument could be exchanged in a current transaction between willing parties, not in a forced or liquidation sale. If a quoted market price is available for an instrument, that is considered its fair value and the amount to be disclosed is the product of the number of trading units multiplied by the quoted market price (FAS 107, par. 5).

FAS 107 requires disclosure of fair value information about financial instruments, whether or not those instruments are recognized in the financial statements, with certain exceptions. It applies to all entities. It does not change requirements for recognition, measurement, or classification of financial instruments in financial statements (FAS 107, par. 7).

General Disclosure Requirements

FAS 107 establishes specific disclosure requirements and certain procedures that must be followed in estimating the fair value of financial instruments, as follows:

- An entity shall disclose, either in the body of the financial statements or in the accompanying notes, the fair value of financial instruments for which it is practicable to estimate that value. An entity also shall disclose the method(s) and significant assumptions used to estimate the fair value of financial instruments (FAS 107, par. 10).

> **OBSERVATION**
>
> FAS 133 adds a note to FAS 107 that indicates that fair value information disclosed in the notes should be presented with the related carrying value in a form that makes it clear whether the fair value and the carrying value represent assets or liabilities and how the carrying amounts relate to information reported in the statement of financial position. If disclosure of fair value information is in more than one note, one of the notes must include a summary table that contains cross-referenced locations(s) of the remaining disclosures (FAS 107, par. 10, as amended by FAS 133).

- Quoted market prices, if available, are the best evidence of the fair value of financial instruments. If quoted market prices are not available, management's best estimate of fair value may be based on the quoted market price of a financial instrument with similar characteristics or on valuation techniques (for example, the present value of estimated future cash flows using a discount rate commensurate with the risks involved, option pricing models, or matrix pricing models) (FAS 107, par. 11).
- In estimating the fair value of deposit liabilities, a financial entity should not take into account the value of its long-term relationships with depositors, commonly known as **core deposit intangibles,** which are separate intangible assets, not financial instruments. For deposit liabilities with no defined maturities, the fair value to be disclosed is the amount pay-

able on demand at the reporting date. FAS 107 does not prohibit an entity from disclosing separately the estimated fair value of any of its nonfinancial intangible and tangible assets and nonfinancial liabilities (FAS 107, par. 12).

■ For trade receivables and payables, no disclosure is required under FAS 107 when the carrying amount approximates fair value (FAS 107, par. 13).

■ In disclosing the fair value of a financial instrument, amounts of instruments shall not be netted, even if the instruments are of the same class or otherwise related except as permitted by FIN 39, *Offsetting of Amounts Related to Certain Contracts,* and FIN 41, *Offsetting of Amounts Related to Certain Repurchase and Reverse Repurchase Agreements* (FAS 133, par. 531c).

■ If it is not practicable for an entity to estimate the fair value of a financial instrument, or a class of financial instruments, the entity shall disclose information pertinent to estimating the fair value, such as the carrying amount, effective interest rate, and maturity, and provide an explanation of why it is not practicable to estimate fair value (FAS 107, par. 14).

STUDY QUESTIONS

---

11. Which of the following does not affect the estimate of fair value of deposit liabilities?

   a. Core deposit intangibles

   b. Quoted market prices

   c. Management's best estimate of fair value

   d. All of the above affect the estimate of fair value

12. For disclosures of fair value of financial instruments under FAS 133, amounts of instruments should not be netted, even if instruments are related, except as permitted for certain types of instruments by:

   a. FAS 105

   b. FAS 52 and FAS 65

   c. FAS 107

   d. FIN 39 and FIN 41

Disclosures About Concentrations of Credit Risk

An entity shall disclose all significant credit risks from all financial instruments. Group **concentrations of credit risk** exist if a number of counterparties are engaged in similar activities and have similar economic characteristics that would cause their ability to meet contractual obligations to be affected in a similar way by changes in economic or other conditions. Following is information required to be disclosed about each significant concentration of credit risk (FAS 133, par. 531):

- Information about the shared activity, region, or economic characteristic that identifies the concentration.
- The maximum amount of loss due to credit risk (i.e., the loss that would result to parties to the financial instrument if the parties failed completely to perform and any security proved to be of no value).
- The entity's policy of requiring collateral to support financial instruments subject to credit risk, information about the entity's access to the collateral, and the nature and a brief description of collateral.
- The entity's policy of entering into master netting arrangements to mitigate credit risk of financial instruments, information about the arrangements for which the entity is a party, and a description of the terms of those agreements.

Encouraged Disclosures About Market Risk of All Financial Instruments

Entities are encouraged, but not required, to disclose quantitative information about the market risks of financial instruments that are consistent with the way it manages or adjusts those risks (FAS 107, par. 15(c), as amended by FAS 133).

Methods of disclosure are expected to vary among reporting entities. Possible ways of disclosing this information include (FAS 107, par. 15D, as amended by FAS 133):

- Details about current positions and activity during the period.
- The hypothetical effects on comprehensive income or net income of possible changes in market value.
- A gap analysis of interest rate repricing or maturity dates.
- The duration of the financial instruments.
- The entity's value at risk from derivatives and from other positions at the end of the reporting period and the average value of the risk during the period.

Situations Not Covered by FAS 107

Although FAS 107 is intended to require disclosure of fair value information about a wide spectrum of financial instruments, a number of instruments and other items are exempt. These exemptions fall into three categories (FAS 107, par. 8):

- Items subject to reporting and disclosure requirements of other authoritative pronouncements (e.g., pensions, extinguished debt, insurance contracts other than financial guarantees and investment contracts, leases, and equity method investments). FAS 107 does not change existing disclosure requirements for these items.
- Other items explained in terms of certain definitional problems that the FASB was unable to resolve at the time (e.g., insurance contracts other than those mentioned above, lease contracts, warranty obligations, and

unconditional purchase obligations that may have both financial and nonfinancial components) (FAS 107, par. 74). The FASB believes that definitional and valuation difficulties for these contracts and obligations require further consideration before decisions can be made about the appropriateness of fair value disclosure requirements.

■ The FAS 107 disclosures are intended to apply only to financial assets and liabilities, thereby excluding items such as minority interests in consolidated subsidiaries and an entity's own equity instruments included in stockholders' equity.

STUDY QUESTION

13. FAS 107 fair value disclosures do not apply to instruments such as warranty obligations and leases. *True or False?*

Optional Disclosures for Nonpublic Entities

FAS 126 makes the fair value disclosures of FAS 107 optional for entities meeting the following criteria (FAS 126, par. 2 and FAS 133, par. 537):

■ The entity is a nonpublic entity.
■ The entity has less than $100 million of total assets on the date of the financial statements.
■ The entity has no instrument that, in whole or in part, is accounted for as a derivative under FAS 133, other than commitments related to the origination of mortgage loans to be held for sale, during the reporting period.

> **OBSERVATION**
>
> Public accountants serving smaller nonpublic entities convinced the FASB that the practicability provisions of FAS 107 were useful in reducing the costs of compliance, but a cost is still incurred simply to document compliance, even if the fair value information is deemed to be not practicable.
>
> The FASB observed that smaller nonpublic entities are less likely than larger entities to engage in complex financial transactions. These smaller entities' financial assets tend to consist of traded securities, investments in other closely held entities, and balances with related parties. Their financial liabilities tend to be trade payables and variable-rate and fixed-rate loans. The FASB also observed that the types of financial instruments commonly held by smaller nonpublic entities, such as trade receivables and payables and variable-rate instruments, already are carried at amounts that approximate fair value, or that information about fair values already is required by other authoritative pronouncements, such as FAS 115, *Accounting for Certain Investments in Debt and Equity Securities,* and FAS 124, *Accounting for Certain Investments Held by Not-for-Profit Organizations.* Taken together, these mutually reinforcing observations led the FASB to conclude that the FAS 107 disclosure requirements should be optional for smaller nonpublic companies.

Estimating Fair Value

One of the greatest challenges in applying FAS 107 is estimating the fair value of financial instruments. FAS 107 provides examples of procedures for estimating the fair value of financial instruments. The examples are illustrative and are not meant to portray all possible ways of estimating the fair value of a financial instrument to comply with FAS 107.

Fair value information frequently is based on information from market sources. There are four types of markets (FAS 107, par. 19):

- **Exchange market**—Having an exchange provides high visibility and order to the trading of financial instruments. Closing prices and volume levels are typically available.
- **Dealer market**—Dealer readiness to trade—either buy or sell—provides liquidity to the market. Current bid and ask prices are more readily available than information about closing prices and volume levels. ("Over-the-counter" markets are considered dealer markets.)
- **Brokered market**—Brokers attempt to match buyers with sellers. Brokers know the prices bid and asked by the respective parties, but each party is typically unaware of the other party's price requirements. Prices of completed transactions may be available.
- **Principal-to-principal market**—Transactions are negotiated independently, with no intermediary. Little information typically is released publicly.

Financial Instruments with Quoted Prices. Quoted market prices are the best evidence of fair value of financial instruments. The price from the most active market is the best indicator of fair value (FAS 107, par. 20). In some cases, management may decide to provide further information about fair value of a financial instrument. For example, an entity may want to explain why the fair value of its long-term debt is less than the carrying amount and why it may not be possible or prudent to settle the debt (FAS 107, par. 21).

Financial Instruments with No Quoted Prices. The entity should provide its best estimate of fair value. Judgments about the methods and assumptions to be used must be made by those preparing and attesting to the entity's financial statements (FAS 107, par. 22). FAS 107 offers the following guidelines for making these judgments:

- For some short-term financial instruments, the carrying amount may approximate fair value because of the relatively short period of time between origination and expected realization. Likewise, for loans that reprice frequently at market rates, the carrying amount may be close enough to fair value to satisfy disclosure requirements, provided there has been no significant change in the credit risk of the loans (FAS 107, par. 23).
- Some financial instruments may be "custom tailored" and, thus, may not have a quoted market price. Examples include interest rate swaps

and foreign currency contracts. Fair value may be estimated based on the quoted market price of a similar instrument, adjusted for the effects of the tailoring. Alternatively, the estimate might be based on the estimated current replacement cost of the financial instrument (FAS 107, par. 24).

- Other financial instruments that are commonly "custom tailored" include options (e.g., put and call options on stock, foreign currency, or interest rate contracts). A variety of option-pricing models have been developed, such as the Black–Scholes model, and may be useful in estimating fair value (FAS 107, par. 25).

- An estimate of fair value of a loan or group of loans may be based on the discounted value of the future cash flows expected to be received from the loan or group of loans. A single discount rate could be used to estimate the fair value of a homogenous category of loans. A discount rate commensurate with the credit, interest rate, and prepayment risks involved, which could be the rate at which the same loans would be made under current conditions, may be appropriate. A discount rate that reflects the effects of interest rate changes and then makes adjustments to reflect the effects of changes in credit risk may be appropriate (FAS 107, par. 27).

- Fair value for financial liabilities for which quoted market prices are not available can generally be estimated using the same technique used for estimating the value of financial assets.

EXAMPLE

A loan payable to a bank can be valued at the discounted amount of future cash flows, using the entity's current incremental borrowing rate for a similar liability.

- Alternatively, the discount rate could be the rate that an entity would pay to a creditworthy third party to assume its obligation (FAS 107, par. 28).

- For deposit liabilities with defined maturities (e.g., certificates of deposit), an estimate of fair value may be based on the discounted value of the future cash flows expected to be paid on the deposits. The discount rate could be the current rate offered for similar deposits with the same remaining maturities. For deposit liabilities with no defined maturities, the fair value should be the amount payable on demand at the reporting date (FAS 107, par. 29).

OBSERVATION

An important dimension of FAS 107 is the latitude that entities have in deciding whether applying procedures such as those described above is "practicable." **Practicable** means that an entity can estimate fair value without incurring excessive costs. It is a dynamic concept—what is practicable in one year may not be in another. Cost considerations are important in judging practicability and may affect the precision of the estimate, leading to determination of fair value for a class of financial instruments, an entire portfolio (rather than individual instruments), or a subset of a portfolio. Whatever is practicable to determine must be disclosed. The burden of this decision rests on the reporting entity and its auditor; if the decision is made that determining fair value is not practicable, reasons for not disclosing the information must be given. The explanation will normally be found in notes to the financial statement (FAS 107, par. 15).

Current Developments in Fair Value Measurement. In 2003 the FASB began a project to improve the standards on fair value measurement. This project was exposed for public comment in late 2004 and has undergone revisions in 2005. At the date that this course went to press, the Board was targeting the fourth quarter of 2005 for issuance of a new statement, however, the effective date and transition provisions had not yet been announced. Although the provisions of FAS 107 will likely continue in effect well into 2006, readers should check with the FASB website at www.fasb.org for the most current developments on this proposed statement.

This project focuses on how to measure fair value. The question of what should be measured at fair value will be considered separately on a project-by-project basis.

The changes to current practice that are expected to result from implementation of the proposed statement center primarily on methods for fair value measurement, and expanded disclosure requirements. The most significant of those changes are:

- A revision of the definition of fair value to refer to "an estimate of the price that could be received for an asset or paid to settle a liability in a current transaction between marketplace participants that are both able and willing to transact in the reference market for the asset or liability."
- Addition of a requirement that the fair value of financial instruments traded in active dealer markets be estimated at bid price for assets (long positions) and asked price for liabilities (short positions) when bid and asked prices are more readily available than closing prices.
- Addition of a requirement that the fair value of restricted securities be estimated using quoted prices of identical unrestricted securities, adjusted for the effects of the restriction.

- Addition of a requirement that fair value be estimated using multiple valuation techniques consistent with the market approach, income approach, and cost approach, when quoted prices for similar assets or liabilities are absent.
- Clarification of existing guidance for using present value techniques to estimate fair value, and the elevation of that guidance to Level A GAAP.
- Expansion of disclosure requirements about the use of fair value to re-measure assets and liabilities.
- Establishment of a five-level fair value hierarchy.

STUDY QUESTIONS

14. Over-the-counter markets are considered to be which type of market?

  a. Principal-to-principal

  b. Brokered

  c. Dealer

  d. Exchange

15. Although determining the fair value of financial instruments having no quoted prices may prove difficult, for loans that reprice frequently at market interest rates, the _____ may be close enough to fair value to satisfy disclosure requirements of FAS 107, absent changes in the loans' credit risk.

  a. Estimated current replacement cost of the financial instrument

  b. Carrying amount

  c. Discounted value of future cash flows

  d. None of the above enables these loans to satisfy disclosure requirements for fair value under FAS 107

CONCLUSION

This chapter discussed the identification of derivative and other types of financial instruments, and the recognition and measurement principles and reporting requirements for derivatives and hedging. It has also dealt with the changing landscape of fair value measurement, including current standards for estimating the fair value of financial instruments, and the related disclosure requirements, along with a summary of the most significant of the proposed revisions that are under consideration in this area.

TOP ACCOUNTING ISSUES FOR 2006 CPE COURSE

Answers to Study Questions

MODULE 1 — CHAPTER 1

1. a. Correct. SAB 101 had a large impact on the revenue recognition policies of a number of companies, and many changed their revenue recognition policies as a result.
b. Incorrect. The bulletin had a positive impact on company revenue recognition policies.
c. Incorrect. Even companies whose policies did not change as a result of the bulletin have paid attention to the guidance it contains.
d. Incorrect. The bulletin was targeted at public companies. Private companies have also focused more on revenue recognition policies and procedures.

2. c. Correct. When an executive recruiter conducts a search, the mileposts for revenue recognition are less clear than for an immediate exchange of goods or services or a one-time transaction.
a. Incorrect. Revenue recognition is straightforward in this case: at the point of sale.
b. Incorrect. Revenue recognition in this instance is fairly straightforward, as are the timelines.
d. Incorrect. Lawn-mowing is a discrete service with a distinct beginning and end, making revenue recognition straightforward.

3. d. Correct. A deliverable can also be termed an element.
a. Incorrect. A pledge is not the same as a deliverable.
b. Incorrect. A promise may imply intent, but it is not synonymous with the term **deliverable.**
c. Incorrect. A stake is not synonymous with the definition given for deliverable.

4. b. Correct. FAS 13 provides guidance for determining the model to use for deliveries in lease transactions.
a. Incorrect. FAS 48 concerns revenue recognition when the right of return exists.
c. Incorrect. FAS 71 concerns accounting for the effects of certain types of regulation.
d. Incorrect. SOP 00-2 concerns accounting by producers or distributors of films.

5. d. Correct. An installation service is better suited to this model and is not as easily tracked using another one, such as the Proportional Performance model. The customer may not realize any value until the entire installation is completed.

a. Incorrect. The Proportional Performance model would be better for a monthly service contract because the customer receives value as each monthly mowing or fertilization is performed.

b. Incorrect. When a home health agency provides weekly services, the client receives value every week, and the Proportional Performance model is more appropriate.

c. Incorrect. Provision of online services and Internet access throughout the year is better suited to the Proportional Performance model because value is delivered to the customer on a regular, ongoing basis.

6. b. Correct. FAS 48 covers cancellation rights for product transactions but not cancellation rights in service transactions.

a. Incorrect. FAS 48 does not cover cancellation rights in service transactions.

c. Incorrect. Although service transactions are not specifically covered under FAS 48, the application of similar concepts may allow a service company to make reliable estimates of refunds or cancellations.

d. Incorrect. One of the three choices is correct regarding FAS 48.

7. d. Correct. Price protection and bonuses are areas that the seller can control.

a. Incorrect. Changes in the inflation rate are not under the seller's control.

b. Incorrect. Customer usage is under the customer's control.

c. Incorrect. The agent's fee is not under the seller's control but the control of a third party.

8. a. Correct. Third-party transactions are less predictable than customer actions.

b. Incorrect. It is generally appropriate to assume that a third party will take action to reduce a customer's revenue if it is able to do so.

c. Incorrect. Revenue should not be recognized if the fee is at risk and the customer still has cancellation rights.

d. Incorrect. Third-party actions are usually harder to predict than are customer actions.

9. b. Correct. FAS 109 prohibits this type of assumption until the items in question actually becomes a law.

a. Incorrect. FAS 66 deals specifically with accounting for sales of real estate.

c. Incorrect. FAS 133 deals specifically with accounting for derivative instruments and hedging activities.
d. Incorrect. FAS 5 involves accounting for contingencies.

10. c. Correct. These areas are not specifically covered in the contract; thus, they are called noncontractual terms.
a. Incorrect. These rights and obligations are not actually "assumed"—they are dictated by common business practice, local law, and custom.
b. Incorrect. These terms are not "customary"—they vary from location to location.
d. Incorrect. "Nondefinable terms" does not describe these terms. They may be "definable" but are not an official part of the contract.

MODULE 1 — CHAPTER 2

1. b. Correct. The plan should include the expected completion, not starting, date of all the actions.
a. Incorrect. Identification of these actions and activities is indicative of the existence of an exit plan.
c. Incorrect. Identifying the location of the activities is part of the exit plan.
d. Incorrect. Identifying the methods by which activities are to be disposed is part of the exit plan.

2. False. Correct. Neither company would have incurred an incremental cost before the acquisition, not just the acquirer.
True. Incorrect. An incremental cost is one that would not have been incurred by **either** company before the acquisition.

3. d. Correct. All three choices are required disclosures.
a. Incorrect. Such actions regarding employees are required disclosures.
b. Incorrect. The type and amount of liabilities assumed and included in the acquisition cost allocation for costs to exit an activity are required disclosures.
c. Incorrect. Disclosures must include both unresolved issues and the types of additional liabilities that may result in an adjustment of the allocation of the acquisition cost.

4. c. Correct. To recognize a loss under FAS 5, before the financial statements are issued it must be probable that an asset has been impaired or a liability has been incurred and that the amount of the loss is reasonably estimable.
a. Incorrect. Although FAS 88 is one source of guidance for loss recognition for curtailments and liabilities, it is not the primary guidance.

b. *Incorrect.* FAS 112 is not the primary guidance for loss accruals, although it describes costs related to the termination of employees under a postemployment benefit plan that may result in curtailment losses or accruals for contractual termination benefits.

d. *Incorrect.* FAS 106 provides guidance for postretirement curtailment losses but is not the primary guidance on loss accruals for curtailments and liabilities.

5. b. *Correct.* The write-off of in-process R&D occurs before deferred taxes are measured on the initial basis differences.

a. *Incorrect.* In-process R&D amounts are ineligible for deferred taxation; no deferred taxes are provided on the initial basis differences.

c. *Incorrect.* The amounts cannot be capitalized because they have no future use; in-process R&D by definition has no future use.

d. *Incorrect.* One of the choices reflects the EITF's consensus about in-process R&D amounts at the time of business combinations.

6. a. *Correct.* FAS 150, *Accounting for Certain Financial Instruments with Characteristics of Both Liabilities and Equity,* provides guidance to issuers concerning the classification and measurement of instruments with these characteristics.

b. *Incorrect.* FAS 133, *Accounting for Derivative Instruments and Hedging Activities,* does not address instruments with characteristics of liabilities and equity.

c. *Incorrect.* APB 16 has been superseded by FAS 141.

d. *Incorrect.* FAS 141 concerns accounting for contingency arrangements based on security prices.

7. c. *Correct.* Citing FAS 107, par. 40 and FAS 115, par. 40, the EITF argued that the basis of calculations should be future cash flows required to extinguish the debt.

a. *Incorrect.* This opinion does not resolve the apparent conflict between the positions in paragraphs 87 and 88.

b. *Incorrect.* This position reflects that of paragraph 87 but does not address how to value accounts payable, long-term debt, and other claims payable.

d. *Incorrect.* One of the choices was the EITF consensus that resolved the discrepancy in treatment of debt.

8. False. *Correct.* Paragraph 74, not 94, was the EITF consensus, in that the Task Force stated that the market price of securities over a reasonable period of time before and after the entities agree on the purchase price and announce the proposed transaction.

True. *Incorrect.* The EITF consensus was the use of paragraph 74 of APB 15 by using the market price of the securities over a reasonable period of time before and after the entities agree on the purchase price and announce the combination.

9. a. Correct. Although these effects are part of the EITF consensus, they are not included in estimating discounted and undiscounted cash flows used to determine the assets' impairment.
b. Incorrect. These are part of cash flows used in the determination of impairment of the mining assets.
c. Incorrect. These effects should be included in the estimate of discounted and undiscounted cash flows.
d. Incorrect. One of the three choices should not be included.

10. b. Correct. SEC registrants are required to adopt new-basis accounting only if virtually 100 percent of the stock has been acquired.
a. Incorrect. New-basis accounting is required if there is no outstanding preferred, not common, stock.
c. Incorrect. New-basis accounting is required if there is no outstanding publicly held debt, not less than 10 percent.
d. Incorrect. Only one of the choices mandates new-basis accounting.

11. c. Correct. In a roll-out, certain assets are placed into the limited partnership by the partnership's sponsor, and units representing the assets are distributed to shareholders.
a. Incorrect. In a roll-up, two or more legally separate limited partnerships are combined into one MLP.
b. Incorrect. In a drop-down, units of a limited partnership that was formed with a sponsor's assets (usually a corporate entity) are sold to the public, not to shareholders.
d. Incorrect. A reorganization involves liquidating an entity by transferring all of its assets to an MLP.

12. d. Correct. A shareholder having at least 20 percent of the total voting interests in Newco is automatically included in the control group.
a. Incorrect. The shareholder need not be a majority shareholder to be included automatically in the control group.
b. Incorrect. The threshold for automatic inclusion in the control group is not 30 percent.
c. Incorrect. For automatic inclusion of a shareholder in the control group of Newco, the voting interest must be a different percentage.

13. d. Correct. Securities from Oldco shareholders may be recognized at fair value if at least 80 percent of the consideration net of that used to acquire shares in Newco, consists of cash, debt, and debt-type instruments.
a. Incorrect. More than half of the securities must consist of cash, debt, and debt-type instruments.

b. Incorrect. Cash, debt, and debt-type instruments must compose a different percentage of Oldco's securities.

c. Incorrect. A different percentage is the baseline amount for recognition of the securities at fair value.

14. True. Correct. Newco equity securities issued to acquire an interest in Oldco should be valued at predecessor basis, because the portion of Newco's investment in Oldco recognized at fair value should not exceed the percentage of total monetary consideration.

False. Incorrect. The portion of Newco's investment in Oldco recognized at fair value should not exceed the percentage of total monetary consideration.

15. a. Correct. The proportion of fair value and predecessor basis is the same as the proportion used to determine the amount of Newco's investment in Oldco.

b. Incorrect. The proportion is the same.

c. Incorrect. The treatment is similar to the one used in consolidation.

d. Incorrect. One of the choices represents the way basis is allocated under the partial purchase method.

16. True. Correct. Fair value is used under the purchase method using an objective, reliable basis to value shares. This is true regardless of the method of payment.

False. Incorrect. The consensus of Issue 90-5 is that the acquiring subsidiary's consolidated financial statements should reflect the acquired subsidiary's assets and liabilities at their historical cost in the parent company's consolidated financial statements.

17. c. Correct. The consensus of the EITF was that the APB was referring to the parent company's basis in the subsidiary's assets and liabilities when the APB used the term.

a. Incorrect. Some practitioners believed this to be the APB's meaning, but that definition was not in the EITF's consensus about the term.

b. Incorrect. This was neither the view in the EITF's consensus nor the belief of other practitioners.

d. Incorrect. One of the choices is the consensus of the EITF about the meaning of **historical cost.**

18. c. Correct. The assumed liabilities are accounted for as part of the purchase price because an acquirer allocates cost of an acquiree to identifiable assets acquired and liabilities assumed based on their fair value.

a. Incorrect. An acquirer allocates cost of an acquiree to identifiable assets acquired and liabilities assumed based on their fair value.

b. *Incorrect.* Future value is not considered for the assumed liabilities.

d. *Incorrect.* The fair value of the assumed liability after the acquisition date may differ from the amount previously recognized on the acquiree's balance sheet as deferred revenue.

19. d. *Correct.* All of the choices are exceptions to the guarantees described in Topic D-54, according to FASB staff.

a. *Incorrect.* The FASB stated that the announcement does not apply to transactions outside the scope of APB 16.

b. *Incorrect.* Business combinations accounted for as poolings are not covered by the announcement.

c. *Incorrect.* IPOs are outside the scope of APB 16; thus, the announcement does not apply to such offerings.

20. True. *Correct.* The carrying amount of goodwill includes the carrying amount of intangible assets, but the implied fair value of goodwill does not include the fair value of the intangible assets.

False. *Incorrect.* The carrying amount of goodwill includes the carrying amount of intangible assets, but the fair value of goodwill does not include the fair value of the intangible assets.

MODULE 2 — CHAPTER 3

1. c. *Correct.* Pension plans are accounted for on the accrual basis.

a. *Incorrect.* Plans do not use the cash method.

b. *Incorrect.* Hybrid accounting does not apply to pension plan accounting.

d. *Incorrect.* One of the choices is the accounting method used for pension plans.

2. a. *Correct.* FAS 35, *Accounting and Reporting by Defined Benefit Pension Plans,* covers accounting and reporting for a defined benefit pension plan as a separate entity.

b. *Incorrect.* Although FAS 87 addresses defined benefit pension plans of single employers, it is not applicable to defined benefit plans as separate entities.

c. *Incorrect.* FAS 132, Employers' Disclosures about Pensions and Other Postretirement Benefits concerns disclosures about pensions.

d. *Incorrect.* FAS 132 (revised 2003) requires incremental disclosures to those required by FAS 132 but is not focused on defined benefit plans as separate entities.

3. d. Correct. All three choices are types of actuarial assumptions.
a. Incorrect. The date on which a benefit becomes fully vested is one of the actuarial assumptions.
b. Incorrect. The interest earned on plan assets is an actuarial assumption.
c. Incorrect. The employee's retirement age is an actuarial assumption.

4. b. Correct. The accumulated benefit obligation measure uses current or past levels of employee compensation unlike the projected benefit obligation, which uses future compensation levels.
a. Incorrect. Future compensation levels are not used to calculate benefits in the accumulated benefit obligation measure.
c. Incorrect. The projected benefit obligation, not the accumulated benefits obligation, uses the actuarial present value of all vested or unvested pension contributions.
d. Incorrect. One of the choices is the method of calculating benefits in the accumulated obligation measure.

5. a. Correct. The unrecognized net asset gain or loss is a component of net periodic pension cost that is either partially recognized or not recognized at all on the employer's books during the period in which it arises.
b. Incorrect. The discount rate on the projected benefit obligation is used in the estimate.
c. Incorrect. The average remaining service periods of active employees covered by the plan is used in calculating net periodic pension cost before the beginning of a period.
d. Incorrect. The expected long-term rate of return is used in the actuarial assumptions to estimate net periodic pension cost before a period begins.

6. d. Correct. All three of the choices are changes reflected in calculating the assumed compensation levels.
a. Incorrect. The general price levels are a change used in assumed compensation level calculations.
b. Incorrect. Seniority of employees is factored in the assumed compensation levels.
c. Incorrect. Productivity is a change considered in calculating assumed compensation levels.

7. c. Correct. Contributions to and distributions from the plan are adjustments to the difference in value of plan assets determining the actual return on assets.
a. Incorrect. Mortality rates of benefit recipients are not part of calculating return on assets.

b. Incorrect. Changes in interest rates are part of the difference during the period; they are not adjustments to that difference.

d. Incorrect. One of the choices represents the adjustment to the fair value of plan assets used to calculate the actual return on assets.

8. a. Correct. The future service periods of only active employees expected to receive benefits is used in calculating unrecognized prior service costs for retirees.

b. Incorrect. Past service periods of retirees are not used to determine the unrecognized prior service costs included in the net periodic pension cost.

c. Incorrect. Because retirees have no future service periods, such a factor does not exist for this calculation.

d. Incorrect. One of the choices is the method used to calculate unrecognized prior service costs for retiree benefits.

9. b. Correct. The expected long-term rate of return is an actuarial assumption that includes the current rate of return and likely reinvestment rate of return to reflect the average rate of earnings expected on plan investments.

a. Incorrect. The expected distribution levels are not factors in calculating the expected rate of return on assets.

c. Incorrect. Past rates of return are not included in calculating the expected future return.

d. Incorrect. One of the choices is a factor in calculating expected return on pension plan assets.

10. c. Correct. The only exceptions to this rule are when the amortization period is less than 15 years or if the plan is composed of a majority of inactive participants (retirees or former employees).

a. Incorrect. Retirees have no remaining service period and thus would not be included in calculations involving the remaining service period.

b. Incorrect. Obligations for inactive employees are not included in the calculation of the unrecognized net obligation or net assets.

d. Incorrect. One of the choices is the amortization approach used.

11. d. Correct. All three choices are conditions requiring recognition of an additional minimum liability.

a. Incorrect. If an accrued or prepaid pension cost has been recognized, as well as the other conditions, an additional minimum liability must be recognized.

b. Incorrect. Recognition of such a liability is one of the conditions requiring recognition of an additional minimum liability.

c. Incorrect. Recognition of an asset as a prepaid pension cost is one of the conditions requiring recognition of an additional minimum liability.

12. a. Correct. Comparable or similar investments' selling prices are used.
b. Incorrect. Amortized cost is the approach employed for assets that are used in the actual operation of a plan.
c. Incorrect. Historical cost less accumulated depreciation or amortization is the approach composing amortized cost for assets employed in the actual operation of a plan.
d. Incorrect. One of the choices is the approach used when there is no active market for an asset.

13. d. Correct. Companies must report expected benefits for the next five fiscal years and the aggregate for the five fiscal years thereafter, and the employer's best estimate of contributions to be paid to the plan during the next fiscal year.
a. Incorrect. These are not the number of years specified in FAS 132 (revised 2003).
b. Incorrect. The numbers of years are not the same for plan benefits paid as contributions received.
c. Incorrect. The number of years is not the same for reporting the future benefit payments as for contributions.

14. d. Correct. Public companies must show these effects on the aggregate of the service and interest cost components of net periodic postretirement healthcare benefit costs and the accumulated postretirement benefit obligation for healthcare benefits.
a. Incorrect. Two years is not the required length for projecting trends in the rates.
b. Incorrect. Private, not public, companies must describe the ultimate trend rates and expected date of achieving them.
c. Incorrect. Private, not public, companies give general, not specific, descriptions of the direction and pattern of changes.

15. c. Correct. Initial recognition is at an asset of the plan, and subsequent recognition is at fair value.
a. Incorrect. The cost of a participation right is never a liability.
b. Incorrect. The initial recognition is not at fair value, and subsequent recognition is not at its amortized cost.
d. Incorrect. One of the choices reflects the two ways the cost is recognized.

MODULE 2 — CHAPTER 4

1. b. *Correct.* The primary emphasis of the deferral method was matching revenues and expenses, focusing first on the income statement. Adjustments to balance sheet items were determined by the measurement of income tax expense.
a. *Incorrect.* In fact, the deferral method first addressed the income statement.
c. *Incorrect.* The liability method places primary emphasis on the valuation of current and deferred tax assets and liabilities.
d. *Incorrect.* One of the choices is the primary emphasis of the deferral method.

2. c. *Correct.* The amounts are remeasured when tax rates change to approximate more closely the amounts at which those assets and liabilities will be realized or settled.
a. *Incorrect.* Deferred tax asset and liability amounts are not remeasured annually.
b. *Incorrect.* Remeasurement occurs at other times than at the disposition of the asset or liability.
d. *Incorrect.* One of the choices reflects the circumstance under which tax assets and liabilities are remeasured.

3. c. *Correct.* The issue of preparing financial statements for foreign enterprises in accordance with U.S. GAAP is covered by FAS 109.
a. *Incorrect.* Accounting for income taxes during interim periods is discussed in APB 28, *Interim Financial Reporting,* and FIN 18, *Accounting for Income Taxes in Interim Periods.*
b. *Incorrect.* Discounting deferred income taxes is not covered in FAS 109 because it is beyond the scope of that pronouncement.
d. *Incorrect.* One of the choices is covered by FAS 109.

4. a. *Correct.* Deferred assets and liabilities represented as temporary differences are so reported when taxpayers assume those assets and liabilities will eventually be realized (assets) or settled (liabilities).
b. *Incorrect.* Transactions that are taxable versus those that are deductible are not temporary in nature.
c. *Incorrect.* Temporary differences do not arise from recognition versus nonrecognition of gains or losses but rather the timing of their recognition or nonrecognition.
d. *Incorrect.* One of the choices represents the source of the differences.

5. d. *Correct.* Deductible temporary differences result in deferred tax assets, whereas taxable temporary differences result in deferred tax liabilities, when the temporary differences reverse.

a. *Incorrect.* A taxable temporary difference is one that will result in the payment of income taxes in the future when the temporary difference reverses. Such a situation would not cause the taxable temporary difference to give rise to deferred assets.

b. *Incorrect.* Future tax liabilities are created by taxable, not deductible, temporary differences.

c. *Incorrect.* Deferred tax liabilities do not arise from deductible temporary differences.

6. b. *Correct.* The valuation allowance is required if it is more likely than not that some or all of the deferred tax assets will not be realized. **More likely than not** is defined as a likelihood of more than 50 percent.

a. *Incorrect.* The minimum requirement for a valuation allowance considering that it is more likely than not that some or all deferred tax assets will not be realized is more than 40 percent.

c. *Incorrect.* 60 percent is not the quantity **defining more likely than not.**

d. *Incorrect.* The quantity defining **more likely than not** is less than 75 percent.

7. c. *Correct.* Such an excess that is sufficient to realize the deferred tax asset is not an example of negative evidence but rather positive evidence.

a. *Incorrect.* Such a brief period is an example of negative evidence.

b. *Incorrect.* Expired, unused operating loss or tax credit carryforwards are examples of negative evidence.

d. *Incorrect.* One of the choices is not an example of negative evidence.

8. a. *Correct.* Such losses are an example of negative, not positive, evidence.

b. *Incorrect.* Such an aberration is an example of positive evidence.

c. *Incorrect.* Such conditions are examples of positive evidence.

d. *Incorrect.* One of the choices is not an example of positive evidence.

9. a. *Correct.* Income tax expense is reduced after the tax benefits for noncurrent intangible assets and goodwill related to the acquisition.

b. *Incorrect.* A different tax benefit is reduced last.

c. *Incorrect.* Goodwill related to the acquisition is reduced first.

d. *Incorrect.* One of the choices is the last tax benefit reduced.

10. d. *Correct.* All three choices are specialized applications of FAS 109.
a. *Incorrect.* Specialized applications of the Standard comprise business combinations that have temporary differences, operating losses, or tax credit carryforwards.
b. *Incorrect.* Regulated enterprises are not exempt from FAS 109's requirements regarding tax accounting and reporting, plus recognition and adjustments of liabilities.
c. *Incorrect.* FAS 109, par. 28, describes the elimination of a deferred tax liability or asset when an enterprise becomes nontaxable.

11. c. *Correct.* Reduction of income tax expense is the last in order for recognition of tax benefits.
a. *Incorrect.* Reduction of goodwill related to the acquisition is the first in order for recognition of tax benefits.
b. *Incorrect.* Reduction to zero of other noncurrent intangible assets is second in sequence of recognition of tax benefits after the acquisition date.
d. *Incorrect.* One of the choices is the last in the sequence of recognition for tax benefits in business combinations.

12. False. *Correct.* The deferred tax asset is recognized in this case only if the temporary difference will reverse in the foreseeable future.
True. *Incorrect.* The deferred tax asset is not recognized if the temporary difference will become a permanent difference.

13. False. *Correct.* All current deferred tax liabilities and assets for a particular taxpaying component of an enterprise within a particular tax jurisdiction are offset and presented as a single amount. The same procedure is followed for all noncurrent deferred tax liabilities and assets. This does not apply to different taxpaying components or to different taxpaying jurisdictions.
True. *Incorrect.* Deferred tax liabilities and assets that are attributable to different taxpaying components of the enterprise or to different tax jurisdictions are **not** offset.

14. b. *Correct.* The tax benefits of carryforwards are listed as a component of tax expense from continuing operations. The amounts and expiration dates of these carryforwards are, however, a disclosure requirement.
a. *Incorrect.* Government grants are listed as a component of continuing operations
c. *Incorrect.* Deferred tax expense or benefit is considered a significant component.
d. *Incorrect.* Adjustments to a deferred tax liability resulting from enacted changes in tax rates are considered a significant component.

15. c. Correct. Public companies are required to include such approximated tax effects, whereas nonpublic companies merely describe the types of temporary differences and carryforwards used.

a. Incorrect. These are not the required disclosure for public companies; private companies do have required disclosures under FAS 109.

b. Incorrect. These are not the requirements for either type of company.

d. Incorrect. One of the choices does reflect the major difference between disclosures required for public and nonpublic companies.

MODULE 2 — CHAPTER 5

1. d. Correct. All three of the choices are typical characteristics of derivative instruments.

a. Incorrect. Derivative instruments have one or more underlyings, such as a specified interest rate, security price, commodity price, foreign exchange rate, or index of prices.

b. Incorrect. Derivative instruments typically have one or more notional amounts, such as a number of currency units, shares, or other unit specified in their contract.

c. Incorrect. Derivative instruments typically specify payment provisions.

2. b. Correct. Mortgage-backed securities are not a specified scope exception to FAS 133.

a. Incorrect. Purchases and sales of when-issued securities are scope exceptions to FAS 133.

c. Incorrect. Regular-way security trades requiring delivery of existing securities within a regulated timeframe are scope exceptions to FAS 133.

d. Incorrect. One of the choices is not a type of security transaction considered a scope exception to FAS 133.

3. d. Correct. All three choices are scope exceptions.

a. Incorrect. Contracts issued as contingent consideration in business combinations are a type of scope exception.

b. Incorrect. Contracts issued by the entity in connection with stock-based compensation arrangements are a scope exception to FAS 133.

c. Incorrect. Forward purchase contracts for the reporting entity's shares that require physical settlement that are covered by paragraphs 21 and 22 of FAS 150 are a scope exception to FAS 133.

4. b. Correct. Derivatives are recognized in the statement of financial position measured at fair value.

a. Incorrect. Derivatives are recognized in a different statement.

c. Incorrect. Derivatives are not recognized in the income statement.

d. Incorrect. Derivatives are recognized in another financial statement.

5. c. Correct. Changes in the fair value of a foreign currency hedge are accounted for in the comprehensive income as part of the cumulative translation adjustment.
a. Incorrect. A different type of derivative instrument records changes in the current income.
b. Incorrect. Current net income is used for accounting of a different derivative instrument.
d. Incorrect. Changes in the fair value of a foreign currency hedge are accounted for in a different line item of the statement.

6. d. Correct. Changes in the fair value of a foreign currency hedge are accounted for in the other comprehensive income (outside net income) line item of the statement.
a. Incorrect. A different type of derivative instrument records changes in the current income.
b. Incorrect. Current net income is used for accounting of a different derivative instrument.
c. Incorrect. Changes in the fair value of a cash flow hedge are accounted for in a different line item.

7. a. Correct. In a fair value hedge, held-to-maturity debt securities are hedged against credit risk, foreign exchange risk, or both.
b. Incorrect. Interest rate risk is a designated risk being hedged for financial assets or liabilities, not debt securities.
c. Incorrect. This risk is associated with nonfinancial assets or liabilities other than a recognized loan servicing right or nonfinancial firm commitment with financial components.
d. Incorrect. Cash flow risk is a designated risk being hedged in cash flow hedges when the hedged transaction is the forecasted purchase or sale of a financial asset or liability.

8. c. Correct. In addition to simply describing the objectives of holding or issuing the instruments, FAS requires companies to explain the context needed to understand the objectives and companies' strategies for achieving them.
a. Incorrect. These considerations are not essential disclosures for hedging instruments under FAS 133.
b. Incorrect. Previous experience with hedging instruments is not a required disclosure under FAS 133.
d. Incorrect. Required disclosures under FAS 133 do not include any alternatives the issuer considered before entering the hedge.

9. d. Correct. All three choices represent required cash flow hedge disclosures under FAS 133, par. 45b.

a. Incorrect. The timeframe of the hedges' exposure is required.

b. Incorrect. Under FAS 133 the amounts of gains and losses that become reclassified into earnings when the cash flow hedges are discontinued are required disclosures.

c. Incorrect. Net gains or losses recognized during the reporting period resulting from the hedges' ineffectiveness are required disclosures.

10. c. Correct. A master netting agreement is an exception to FIN 39, not one of its criteria for net positions.

a. Incorrect. One of the criteria under FIN 39 is the intent of the reporting entity to net settle.

b. Incorrect. The right of setoff must be enforceable at law under FIN 39 requirements for net positions.

d. Incorrect. The liability of each party must be a determinable amount in order for the offset and display as a net position.

11. a. Correct. Core deposit intangibles are separate intangible assets, not financial instruments.

b. Incorrect. Quoted market markets are the best evidence of the fair value of financial instruments.

c. Incorrect. Management's best estimate of fair value of financial instruments is used when quoted market prices are not available.

d. Incorrect. One of the choices does not affect the fair value estimate.

12. d. Correct. FIN 39 describes permitted offsets related to contracts, and FIN 41 describes offsets of amounts related to repurchase and reverse repurchase agreements.

a. Incorrect. FAS 105 pertains to disclosures for off-balance-sheet risk and concentrations of credit risk.

b. Incorrect. FAS 52 is a pronouncement regarding translation of foreign currency, and FAS 65 pertains to loan commitments held for sale.

c. Incorrect. FAS 107 does concern disclosures of fair value information about financial instruments but does not change requirements for recognition, measurement, or classification of financial instruments in financial statements.

13. True. Correct. Warranty obligations presented issues that were unresolved at the time FAS 107 was issued and thus excluded from its scope, whereas leases are subject to disclosure requirements of other authoritative pronouncements and not changed by FAS 107.

False. Incorrect. This pronouncement excludes warranty obligations, which the FASB believed presented difficulties requiring further consideration, and leases are excluded from the scope of FAS 107 because they are subject to other disclosure pronouncements.

14. c. Correct. OTC markets are considered dealer markets.

a. Incorrect. Principal-to-principal markets have no intermediary such as dealers.

b. Incorrect. In brokered markets, brokers match buyers with sellers using bid and ask prices. They do not typically involve over-the-counter investments.

d. Incorrect. These markets involve investment exchanges such as NASDAQ and the New York Stock Exchange. Over-the-counter investments are managed without such exchanges.

15. b. Correct. FAS 107, par. 23, provides that for loans that reprice frequently at market rates, the carrying amount may be close enough to fair value to satisfy disclosure requirements, provided there has been no significant change in the credit risk of the loans.

a. Incorrect. Such estimates are used for custom-tailored financial instruments such as interest rate swaps and foreign currency contracts.

c. Incorrect. The discounted value of future cash flows relates to deposit liabilities with defined maturities, not loans that reprice at market rates.

d. Incorrect. One of the choices states the manner in which disclosure requirements are satisfied for loans that reprice frequently at market rates.

TOP ACCOUNTING ISSUES FOR 2006

Index

F

CPE Quizzer Instructions

The CPE quizzer is divided into two modules. There is a processing fee for each quizzer module submitted for grading. Successful completion of Module 1 is recommended for **6 CPE Credits.*** Successful completion of Module 2 is recommended for **9 CPE Credits.*** You can complete and submit one module at a time, or both modules at once for a total of **15 CPE Credits.***

To obtain CPE credit, return your completed answer sheet for each quizzer module to **CCH Tax and Accounting, Continuing Education Department, 4025 W. Peterson Ave., Chicago, IL 60646**, or fax it to (773) 866-3084. Each quizzer answer sheet will be graded and a CPE Certificate of Completion awarded for achieving a grade of 70 percent or greater. A quizzer answer sheet is located after each module's quizzer questions for this course.

Express Grading: Processing time for your answer sheet is generally 8-12 business days. If you are trying to meet a reporting deadline, our Express Grading Service is available for an additional $19 per module. To use this service, please check the "Express Grading" box on your answer sheet, and provide your CCH account or credit card number and your fax number. CCH will fax your results and a Certificate of Completion (upon achieving a passing grade) to you by 5:00 p.m. the business day following our receipt of your answer sheet. **If you mail your answer sheet for express grading, please write "ATTN: CPE OVERNIGHT" on the envelope.** NOTE: CCH will not Federal Express Quizzer results under any circumstances.

NEW ONLINE GRADING gives you immediate 24/7 grading with instant results and no Express Grading Fee.

The **CCH Testing Center** website gives you and others in your firm easy, free access to CCH print courses and allows you to complete your CPE exams online for immediate results. Plus, the **My Courses** feature provides convenient storage for your CPE course certificates and completed exams.

Go to **www.cchtestingcenter.com** to complete your exam online.

---

* Recommended CPE credit is based on a 50-minute hour. Participants earning credits for states that require self-study to be based on a 100-minute hour will receive ½ the CPE credits for successful completion of this course. Because CPE requirements vary from state to state and among different licensing agencies, please contact your CPE governing body for information on your CPE requirements and the applicability of a particular course for your requirements.

Date of Completion: The date of completion on your certificate will be the date that you put on your answer sheet. However, you must submit your answer sheet to CCH for grading within two weeks of completing it.

Expiration Date: December 31, 2006

Evaluation: To help us provide you with the best possible products, please take a moment to fill out the course evaluation located at the back of this course and return it with your quizzer answer sheets.

CCH INCORPORATED is registered with the National Association of State Boards of Accountancy (NASBA) as a sponsor of continuing professional education on the National Registry of CPE Sponsors. State boards of accountancy have final authority on the acceptance of individual courses for CPE credit. Complaints regarding registered sponsors may be addressed to the National Registry of CPE Sponsors, 150 Fourth Avenue North, Suite 700, Nashville, TN 37219-2417. Web site: www.nasba.org.

CCH INCORPORATED is registered with the National Association of State Boards of Accountancy (NASBA) as a Quality Assurance Service (QAS) sponsor of continuing professional education. State boards of accountancy have final authority on the acceptance of individual courses for CPE credit. Complaints regarding registered sponsors may be addressed to NASBA, 150 Fourth Avenue North, Suite 700, Nashville, TN 37219-2417. Web site: www.nasba.org.

Recommended CPE:	6 hours for Module 1
	9 hours for Module 2
	15 hours for both modules
Processing Fee:	$60.00 for Module 1
	$90.00 for Module 2
	$150.00 for both modules

One **complimentary copy** of this course is provided with certain CCH Accounting publications. Additional copies of this course may be ordered for $25.00 each by calling 1-800-248-3248 (ask for product 0-0903-200).

TOP ACCOUNTING ISSUES FOR 2006 CPE COURSE

Quizzer Questions: Module 1

1. All of the following statements are true **except:**

   a. The accounting literature on revenue recognition is not comprehensive or easy to follow.
   b. The SEC's Division of Corporate Finance frequently questioned revenue recognition policy disclosures.
   c. Revenue recognition is an area that has had minimal impact on Internet-based companies.
   d. Improper revenue recognition was the area in which the SEC brought the greatest number of enforcement actions between 1997 and 2002.

2. Which of the following is an example of a transaction in which revenue is earned and realized at different times?

   a. A customer purchases an airline ticket in advance of the trip.
   b. A plumber fixes a leak in a customer's sink.
   c. A restaurant provides a meal which is eaten and paid for by the customer via credit card.
   d. A customer makes a purchase at the cash register of a retail store.

3. Which of the following statements accurately summarizes persuasive evidence?

   a. Persuasive evidence of an arrangement requires a written contract.
   b. Revenue cannot be recognized until there is persuasive evidence of an arrangement.
   c. A restaurant check does not constitute persuasive evidence of an arrangement.
   d. A click on the Submit button on an Internet site does not constitute persuasive evidence of an arrangement.

4. The Proportional Performance model is:

   a. Sometimes referred to as the product model
   b. The preferred model to use with the delivery of products
   c. Frequently used in the delivery of a service
   d. Used for all service transactions

5. Which of the following statements does **not** describe the Completed Performance model?

    a. It coincides with the point in time at which the customer has realized value.

    b. It is used when a single point in time can be identified at which the vendor has completed its obligation.

    c. It is used when performance takes place over a period of time but value is not transferred to the customer until the final act is completed.

    d. When it is used, there is no need to specify the point in time when the performance is completed.

6. Which of the following is correct about a fixed and determinable fee?

    a. SOP 97-2, SOP 00-2, and SAB 101 provide clear definitions of what it means for a fee to be fixed and determinable.

    b. Whether a fee is fixed and determinable is always an "all-or-nothing" proposition.

    c. SOP 97-2, SOP 00-2, and SAB 101 use examples to illustrate various concepts regarding a fixed or determinable fee.

    d. The fact that information about past events must be gathered and analyzed precludes a conclusion that the fee is fixed or determinable.

7. Which of the following statements is correct for coupons or rebates?

    a. Newspaper coupon redemption rates are usually 50 percent or above.

    b. A long offer period does not impair a company's ability to make a reasonable estimate of coupon or rebate redemptions.

    c. The EITF concluded that revenue potentially subject to rebate or refund may be recognized in all cases regardless of the ability to make a reliable estimate of breakage.

    d. The EITF concluded that revenue potentially subject to rebate or refund may be recognized as long as a reliable estimate of breakage can be made.

8. For price-matching:

    a. If reliable estimates can be made, revenue may be recognized net of expected price-matching payments.

    b. A simple process is used to estimate the effects of a price-matching offer.

    c. Historical data and a stable competitive environment are of little use in estimating the effects of a price-matching policy.

    d. Even if reliable estimates cannot be made, revenue can be recognized before the price-matching period ends.

9. A document that amends a contract by granting the customer additional rights, altering payment terms, or requiring the seller to provide additional products or services is called a:

    a. Sidecar

    b. Sidebar

    c. Stretch letter

    d. Side letter

10. All of the following statements are correct *except*:

    a. It is rare that consideration of breakage results in immediate income recognition.

    b. In most situations, delivery of services should be evaluated under the assumption that the vendor will not have to fulfill all of its obligations if some of them are only to be performed if the customer requests them.

    c. There must be significant objective evidence available to support a conclusion that obligations will not have to be fulfilled.

    d. The SEC would generally question an accounting model that results in immediate income for breakage.

11. Which pronouncement eliminated the pooling-of-interests method of accounting for business combinations?

    a. FAS 72

    b. FAS 141

    c. FAS 147

    d. APB 16

12. Which Standard of the FASB supersedes APB 16?

    a. FAS 72
    b. FAS 109
    c. FAS 112
    d. FAS 141

13. Under APB 16, par. 76, costs to exit an acquiree's activity or to involuntarily terminate or relocate an acquiree's employees that do not meet the required conditions to exit an activity or involuntarily terminate or relocate the employees should be accounted for:

    a. As adjustments to the purchase price of the acquired entity
    b. By allocating the costs to the acquiree's other liabilities
    c. The same as indirect and general expenses of an acquisition
    d. None of the above

14. All of the following are considered to be contractual termination benefits considered in Issue 96-5 *except:*

    a. Postemployment plans requiring payments for involuntary terminations
    b. Union agreements requiring payment of termination benefits for involuntary terminations when a plant closes upon a business combination
    c. Golden parachute employment agreements that require payment if control changes in a business combination
    d. All of the above are contractual termination benefits

15. The guidance on contingent consideration in APB 16, pars. 78–83 was carried forward _____ to FAS 141, pars. 26–31.

    a. With no changes
    b. With minor changes in reporting rules
    c. With major revisions because of the method change to purchase business combinations
    d. The guidance was completely revised and was not carried forward

16. The EITF consensus in Issue 97-15 was that a purchaser that has given a stated or implied below-market value guarantee in a business combination should recognize the cost of the acquisition:

    a. At its fair value of the unconditional consideration at the date of the combination
    b. At its fair value with consideration of the contingency arrangement factored into the securities' price
    c. At its target value at a specified future date
    d. The below-market guarantee should be ignored because it is not substantive

17. In determining the measurement date to use for the market price of acquirer securities in a purchase business combination, the EITF consensus was that when a formula was used in which the consideration could change, the measurement date for valuation should be:

    a. Unchanged from a reasonable period before and after the date on which the acquisition terms are agreed to and announced
    b. The first date since the date of the agreement and announcement of acquisition terms become fixed
    c. The initial date on which the parties agreed to the terms of the purchase transaction
    d. None of the above

18. FAS 150 provides guidance to issuers on the classification and measurements of:

    a. Business combinations requiring employers' accounting for postemployment benefits
    b. Business combinations having contingency arrangements based on security prices
    c. Financial instruments with characteristics of both liabilities and equity
    d. Transactions in which all entities transfer net assets or transfer equity interests to a newly formed entity

19. In a drop-down method of creating a master limited partnership:

    a. An entity is liquidated by transferring all of its assets to an MLP.
    b. Units of a limited partnership that was formed with a sponsor's assets are sold to the public.
    c. A sponsor places certain assets into a limited partnership and distributes its units to shareholders.
    d. Two or more legally separate limited partnerships are combined into one MLP.

20. A new basis is appropriate to use in which of the following circumstances?

    a. The MLP's general partner in a roll-up was also the general partner of the predecessor limited partnership.
    b. The MLP is created as a reorganization.
    c. The MLP is created as a roll-out.
    d. None of the above is an appropriate circumstance.

21. Which of the following is *not* a condition under which control of voting interest changes?

    a. A shareholder who did not control the old company gains control of the new company by owning a majority voting interest.
    b. The control group of the new company has no subset of members that had control of the old company.
    c. A group of new shareholders that does not comprise shareholders in the old company gains control of the new company and meets the criteria for inclusion in the control group.
    d. All of the above are conditions prompting a change of control.

22. Issue 88-16 dictates requirements for a change of control in LBOs that _____ of the new company is obtained by an individual or group that did not control the old company and the change in control must be _____.

    a. Majority interest; permanent
    b. Unilateral control; temporary
    c. Majority interest; temporary
    d. Unilateral control; not temporary

23. The predecessor basis measures:

   a. A shareholder's proportionate share of the equity of a business after redemption of equity securities with liquidation features
   b. The basis of an investment in a business measured as the original cost plus or minus the shareholder's share of the change in business equity
   c. A shareholder's proportionate share of all securities that gives the shareholder voting rights
   d. None of the above

24. Historical cost should be used to record all of the following *except*:

   a. A transfer of net assets or an exchange of shares between companies under common control
   b. Long-lived assets transferred between a parent and subsidiary
   c. A cost-method investment in a company considered to be the acquiree
   d. Historical cost should be used for all of the above

25. The *underlying* question in Issue 91-5, *Nonmonetary Exchange of Cost-Method Investments,* is whether:

   a. The investor's exchange of shares of one entity for shares in the combined entity is an event that culminates the earnings process
   b. The investor should continue carrying the investment at its historical cost
   c. The investor is required to report realized gains or losses in comprehensive income
   d. None of the above

26. The FASB staff announced through Topic D-87 that the measurement date for securities other than those issued by the acquirer in a business combination should be:

   a. The date that a purchase business combination transaction is consummated
   b. The date on which the shareholders ratify the transaction
   c. The date the terms of the combination are agreed to and announced
   d. None of the above is the measurement date

27. Under APB 16, the decision whether to recognize contingent consideration based on earnings in a business combination as an adjustment of the acquisition cost versus compensation for services, use of property or profit sharing is subject to judgment that should be based on the relevant facts and circumstances. *True or False?*

28. The cash flows associated with VBPP estimates of future discounted and undiscounted cash flows should **not** be included in the evaluation of mining assets for impairment under FAS 144. *True or False?*

29. The SEC will not object to the use of new-basis accounting in a drop-down MLP if at least four-fifths of the MLP is sold to the public and its limited partners can replace the general partner through a reasonable vote. *True or False?*

30. In a leveraged buyout transaction accounted for under the EITF consensus in Issue 88-16, when part of the investment is valued at the predecessor basis, the allocation of fair value to each asset and liability will be equal to the new company's investment in the old company. *True or False?*

TOP ACCOUNTING ISSUES FOR 2006 CPE COURSE
Quizzer Questions: Module 2

31. Pension plan assets may include all of the following **except:**

   a. Freely transferable securities of the employer
   b. Stocks and bonds
   c. Real estate, furniture, and fixtures
   d. All of the above are includible assets

32. For purposes of the employer's plan accounting under FAS-87, the funded status of the plan is the difference between the _____ _____ and the fair value of plan assets as of a given date.

   a. Prior service cost
   b. Projected benefit obligation
   c. Unrecognized net obligation at the date of initial application of FAS-87
   d. Net periodic pension cost

33. All of the following are components of the net periodic pension cost **except:**

   a. Amortization of unrecognized prior service cost
   b. Actual return on plan assets
   c. Average remaining service periods of active employees
   d. Service cost

34. If pension benefits in excess of those reflected in an existing benefit formula are indicated by an employer's substantive commitment, FAS-87 requires that the pension plan be accounted for:

   a. Based on the employer's substantive commitment and the appropriate disclosure be made in the financial statements
   b. After reducing the excess benefit level
   c. By amending the plan to bring the contribution level in line with the benefit obligations
   d. None of the above reflects the proper accounting

35. If a pension plan benefit formula attributes a disproportionate portion of total pension benefits to later years, _____ is used as the basis for assigning total pension plan benefits.

    a. Accumulated benefit obligation
    b. Funded status of plan
    c. Total projected benefit
    d. Best estimate of contributions to be paid to the plan

36. A significantly high return on pension plan assets during a period can result in:

    a. Plan amendment requirements to increase benefit levels
    b. Net periodic pension income
    c. Amortization of income over the overall expected long-term rate of return on the assets
    d. None of the above is a result

37. When is an alternative amortization approach permitted under FAS-87 for prior service costs?

    a. Whenever the approach more slowly reduces the amount of unrecognized prior service cost
    b. If the prior service cost is immaterial to the financial statements' accuracy
    c. If the majority of participants is inactive (retired)
    d. If the alternative method is used consistently and disclosed in the financial statements

38. Any decrease in the amount of the projected benefit obligation due to a plan amendment:

    a. Shall increase the rate of amortization applied to the balance of the unrecognized prior service cost
    b. Shall reduce the balance of existing unrecognized prior service cost
    c. Shall increase retroactive benefits for retirees over their remaining service periods
    d. None of the above shall occur

39. The gains and losses component of net periodic pension cost consists of any required amortization of unrecognized gain or loss from previous periods as well as:

    a. The difference between the value including the expected long-term rate of return and current market-related value of plan assets

    b. The difference between fair value of plan assets at the beginning and end of a period

    c. The difference between expected and actual returns on plan assets

    d. Short- and long-term capital gains (losses) from disposition of plan assets during the reporting period

40. When there is no accrued or prepaid pension cost on the employer's statement of financial position as of the transition date to FAS-87:

    a. The funded status of the pension plan and the unrecognized net obligation or net asset are exactly equal.

    b. The unrecognized net obligation (asset) exceeds the funded status of the plan.

    c. The amortization rate of the unrecognized net obligation adjusts accordingly.

    d. None of the above occurs.

41. For interim financial statements, the amount of additional minimum liability:

    a. Does not reflect changes in values for plan assets and obligations since the date of last full set of statements

    b. Is not a required disclosure

    c. Is zero, because the minimum liability remains unchanged in the interim

    d. Is reported reflecting adjustments for subsequent accruals and contributions but otherwise is the same as reported in the previous year-end statement of financial position

42. The employer's best estimate of contributions expected to be paid during the next fiscal year is a required disclosure for every set of financial statements **except:**

    a. Those of public companies

    b. Those of nonpublic companies

    c. Interim statements

    d. The estimate of contributions to be paid is required for all of the above

43. When the purchaser recognizes a new asset or liability, all of the following are eliminated at the date of a business combination accounted for by the purchase method *except*:

   a. Projected benefit obligation
   b. Unrecognized net obligations or assets existing at the date of initial application of FAS-87
   c. Unrecognized prior service cost
   d. All of the above are eliminated

44. Actuarial assumptions used to calculate the previous year's net periodic pension cost are used to calculate that cost in subsequent interim financial statements unless more current valuations of plan assets and obligations are available or a significant event has occurred. *True or False?*

45. FAS-132 (revised 2003) requires an employer to recognize the interest cost on the projected benefit obligation as a component of net periodic pension cost. *True or False?*

46. FAS 109 applies to all of the following *except*:

   a. Domestic and foreign operations that use the equity method
   b. Foreign enterprises whose financial statements are prepared in accordance with U.S. GAAP
   c. Deferred income taxes that are discounted
   d. Foreign, state, and local taxes based on income

47. Following the basic principles of the liability method under FAS 109:

   a. Current as well as deferred tax assets and liabilities are measured based on enacted tax law provisions
   b. Deferred tax liabilities are reduced by a valuation allowance
   c. Deferred tax assets rather than liabilities are recognized for their estimated future tax effects of temporary differences
   d. Deferred tax liabilities are recognized for the estimated future tax effects of carryforwards rather than temporary differences

48. Under FAS 109, the balance sheet recognition of deferred tax assets and liabilities reflects the assumption that assets and liabilities will eventually be realized at their:

   a. Net present value
   b. Recorded amounts
   c. Discounted value
   d. None of the above

49. A warranty liability is a temporary difference with all of the following features **except:**

    a. Expense is recognized on the accrual method for financial accounting but the cash basis for tax purposes

    b. Treatment as an asset to be recovered when its deduction is recognized for tax purposes

    c. A basis of zero for tax purposes

    d. All of the above are features of the warranty liability

50. A valuation allowance is used to reduce tax assets if:

    a. The assets are current

    b. It is more likely than not that the deferred tax assets will not be realized

    c. They are offset by deferred liabilities

    d. All of the above are instances in which a valuation allowance is used

51. When does an entity use the average graduated tax rate applicable to the amount of estimated annual taxable income in valuation allowance calculations?

    a. When the entity is subject to the highest corporate tax rate

    b. When the temporary difference becomes a permanent one

    c. When deferred taxes are insignificant

    d. When the entity's taxable income is small enough to make graduated tax rates a significant factor

52. All of the following result in adjustments to the measure of deferred tax assets and liabilities **except:**

    a. Changes in the applicable income tax rate

    b. Changes in the amounts of cumulative temporary differences

    c. Changes in the tax law

    d. All of the above result in adjustments

53. The tax benefit of an operating loss carryforward or carryback generally is reported in the same manner as:

    a. The source of the operating loss carryforward or taxes paid in a prior year

    b. The source of expected future income that will result in realization of deferred tax assets for an operating loss carryforward from the current year

    c. The source of the income or loss in the current year

    d. None of the above

54. If an entity quasi-reorganization was limited to the elimination of a deficit in retained earnings by a noncurrent reduction in contributed capital before the entity adopted FAS 109, subsequent recognition of the tax benefit of prior deductible temporary differences and carryforwards is:

   a. Offset by subsequent temporary differences and carryforwards

   b. Included in income, then reclassified from retained earnings to contributed capital

   c. Included in estimated future earnings

   d. Discounted

55. For consolidated tax returns of a group of entities, all of the following are methods that are inconsistent with the principles of FAS 109 *except:*

   a. Allocation of taxes to members of the group by applying FAS 109 to each member as if it were a separate taxpayer

   b. Allocation of no current or deferred tax expense to a member of the group that has taxable income because the consolidated group has no current or deferred tax expense

   c. Allocation of deferred taxes to a member of the group using a method different from the liability method

   d. All of the above methods are inconsistent with the broad principles of FAS 109

56. Separately issued financial statements for entities that are members of a group filing consolidated tax returns must disclose all of the following *except:*

   a. Adjustments to deferred tax liabilities or assets by affiliated members

   b. The amount of any tax-related balances due to or from affiliates

   c. The principal provisions of the allocation method for current and deferred tax expense

   d. Members must disclose all of the above

57. Whenever a deferred tax liability is not recognized because of exceptions under APB 23, which of the following information is *not* required to be disclosed (FAS 109, par. 44)?

    a. A description of the types of temporary differences for which a deferred tax liability has not been recognized and the types of events that would cause those temporary differences to become taxable
    b. The cumulative amount of each type of temporary difference
    c. The amount of the deferred tax liability for temporary differences other than those in the previous item above that is not recognized based on exceptions granted by APB 23
    d. All of the above are required disclosures

58. Identifying temporary differences may require significant professional judgment because similar items may be temporary differences in one instance but not in another. *True or False?*

59. FAS 109 requires that regulated enterprises recognize a deferred tax liability for tax benefits that flow through to customers when temporary differences originate. *True or False?*

60. If the temporary difference creating the deferred tax asset of liability is reflected in a balance sheet asset or liability, the deferred tax is classified by that related asset or liability. *True or False?*

61. Which of the following is (are) characteristic of a derivative financial instrument?

    a. A specified interest rate, security or commodity price, or other variable including the occurrence or nonoccurrence of a specified event
    b. Terms that require or permit net settlement
    c. A notional amount
    d. All of the above are characteristics of a derivative financial instrument

62. Normal purchases and normal sales contracts:

    a. Are a scope exception to FAS 133
    b. Are contracts that concern the purchase or sale of financial instruments over a long term course of business
    c. Are not subject to GAAP accounting
    d. All of the above pertain to normal purchases and normal sales contracts

63. Under FAS 133 rules for fair value hedges, a hedged item may **not** be any of the following **except:**

    a. An equity instrument issued by the entity and classified in the statement of financial position as stockholders' equity

    b. A portfolio of similar assets or a portfolio of similar liabilities

    c. An equity investment in a consolidated subsidiary

    d. All of the above represent features prohibited for hedged items in fair value hedges

64. Changes in the fair value of derivative instruments that qualify as fair value hedges are recognized currently in:

    a. Cumulative translation adjustments

    b. Other comprehensive income

    c. Earnings

    d. None of the above is the proper place for recognition of the changes in fair value

65. Changes in the fair value of derivative instruments that qualify as cash flow hedges are recognized in:

    a. Current income

    b. Other comprehensive income

    c. Earnings

    d. None of the above is the proper place for recognition of the changes in fair value

66. Changes in the fair value of derivative instruments that qualify as foreign currency hedges are recognized in:

    a. Current income

    b. Other comprehensive income

    c. Earnings

    d. Comprehensive income as part of the cumulative translation adjustment

67. Which of the following is **not** a required disclosure for accumulated other comprehensive income in accordance with FAS 130?

    a. Related net change associated with current period hedging transactions

    b. Net amount of any reclassification into earnings

    c. Beginning and ending accumulated derivative gain or loss

    d. All of the above are required disclosures

68. Fair value is defined as the amount at which the financial instrument could be exchanged:

   a. Between related parties
   b. Between willing parties
   c. In a forced sale
   d. None of the above is the circumstance that determines fair value

69. What type of risk concentration exists if a number of counterparties are engaged in similar activities and have similar economic characteristics that would affect their ability to meet contractual obligations in a similar way as economic conditions change?

   a. Credit risk
   b. Market risk
   c. Interest rate risk
   d. Currency conversion risk

70. FAS 107 disclosures apply only to:

   a. Financial assets and liabilities
   b. Minority interests in consolidated subsidiaries
   c. Company equity instruments included in stockholders' equity
   d. All of the above are subject to disclosures under FAS 107

71. All of the following are criteria for making the fair value disclosures of FAS 107 optional for certain entities *except:*

   a. Their assets on the date of their financial statements total less than $100 million.
   b. The entities must be nonpublic.
   c. None of the entity's instruments is accounted for as a derivative under FAS 133 (except for mortgage loan origination commitments).
   d. They must have no investments in other closely held entities.

72. The type of market in which transactions are negotiated independently with no intermediary is:

   a. Exchange market
   b. Dealer market
   c. Brokered market
   d. None of the above is the market type in which no intermediary is involved

73. An embedded derivative instrument should be separated from its host contract and accounted for as a derivative instrument if the hybrid instrument is not remeasured at fair value under otherwise applicable GAAP. *True or False?*

74. If a written option is designated as hedging the variability in cash flows for a recognized asset or liability in a cash flow hedge, the combination of the hedged item and the written option must provide more potential for favorable cash flows than it does the exposure to unfavorable cash flows. *True or False?*

75. The exception to the offset rules for derivative contracts with the same counterparty under a master netting agreement according to FIN 39 is an election, not a requirement, that must be applied consistently. *True or False?*

TOP ACCOUNTING ISSUES FOR 2006 CPE COURSE   (0723-2)

Module 1: Answer Sheet

NAME _____

COMPANY NAME _____

STREET _____

CITY, STATE, & ZIP CODE _____

BUSINESS PHONE NUMBER _____

DATE OF COMPLETION _____

On the next page, please answer the Multiple Choice questions by indicating the appropriate letter next to the corresponding number. Please answer the True/False questions by marking "T" or "F" next to the corresponding number.

You will be charged a $60.00 processing fee for each submission of Module 1.

Please remove both pages of this Answer Sheet from this booklet and return it with your completed Evaluation Form to CCH at the address below. You may also fax your Answer Sheet to CCH at 773-866-3084.

You may also go to **www.cchtestingcenter.com** to complete your exam online.

METHOD OF PAYMENT:

☐ Check Enclosed   ☐ Visa   ☐ Master Card   ☐ AmEx

☐ Discover   ☐ CCH Account* _____

Card No. _____ Exp. Date _____

Signature _____

* Must provide CCH account number for this payment option

EXPRESS GRADING: Please fax my Course results to me by 5:00 p.m. the business day following your receipt of this answer sheet. By checking this box I authorize CCH to charge $19.00 for this service.

☐ Express Grading $19.00   Fax No. _____

SEND TO:

CCH Tax and Accounting
Continuing Education Department
4025 W. Peterson Ave.
Chicago, IL 60646-6085
1-800-248-3248

TOP ACCOUNTING ISSUES FOR 2006 CPE COURSE   (0723-2)

Module 1: Answer Sheet

Please answer the Multiple Choice questions by indicating the appropriate letter next to the corresponding number. Please answer the True/False questions by marking "T" or "F" next to the corresponding number.

1. ___	11. ___	21. ___
2. ___	12. ___	22. ___
3. ___	13. ___	23. ___
4. ___	14. ___	24. ___
5. ___	15. ___	25. ___
6. ___	16. ___	26. ___
7. ___	17. ___	27. ___
8. ___	18. ___	28. ___
9. ___	19. ___	29. ___
10. ___	20. ___	30. ___

Please complete the Evaluation Form (located after the Module 2 Answer Sheet) and return it with this Quizzer Answer Sheet to CCH at the address on the previous page. Thank you.

TOP ACCOUNTING ISSUES FOR 2006 CPE COURSE (0724-2)

Module 2: Answer Sheet

NAME _____

COMPANY NAME _____

STREET _____

CITY, STATE, & ZIP CODE _____

BUSINESS PHONE NUMBER _____

DATE OF COMPLETION _____

On the next page, please answer the Multiple Choice questions by indicating the appropriate letter next to the corresponding number. Please answer the True/False questions by marking "T" or "F" next to the corresponding number.

You will be charged a $90.00 processing fee for each submission of Module 2.

Please remove both pages of this Answer Sheet from this booklet and return it with your completed Evaluation Form to CCH at the address below. You may also fax your Answer Sheet to CCH at 773-866-3084.

You may also go to **www.cchtestingcenter.com** to complete your exam online.

METHOD OF PAYMENT:

☐ Check Enclosed   ☐ Visa   ☐ Master Card   ☐ AmEx

☐ Discover   ☐ CCH Account* _____

Card No. _____ Exp. Date _____

Signature _____

* Must provide CCH account number for this payment option

EXPRESS GRADING: Please fax my Course results to me by 5:00 p.m. the business day following your receipt of this answer sheet. By checking this box I authorize CCH to charge $19.00 for this service.

☐ Express Grading $19.00   Fax No. _____

SEND TO:

CCH Tax and Accounting
Continuing Education Department
4025 W. Peterson Ave.
Chicago, IL 60646-6085
1-800-248-3248

TOP ACCOUNTING ISSUES FOR 2006 CPE COURSE   (0724-2)

Module 2: Answer Sheet

Please answer the Multiple Choice questions by indicating the appropriate letter next to the corresponding number. Please answer the True/False questions by marking "T" or "F" next to the corresponding number.

31. ___	43. ___	54. ___	65. ___
32. ___	44. ___	55. ___	66. ___
33. ___	45. ___	56. ___	67. ___
34. ___	46. ___	57. ___	68. ___
35. ___	47. ___	58. ___	69. ___
36. ___	48. ___	59. ___	70. ___
37. ___	49. ___	60. ___	71. ___
38. ___	50. ___	61. ___	72. ___
39. ___	51. ___	62. ___	73. ___
40. ___	52. ___	63. ___	74. ___
41. ___	53. ___	64. ___	75. ___
42. ___			

Please complete the Evaluation Form (located after the Module 2 Answer Sheet) and return it with this Quizzer Answer Sheet to CCH at the address on the previous page. Thank you.

TOP ACCOUNTING ISSUES FOR 2006 CPE COURSE   (0903-2)

Evaluation Form

Please take a few moments to fill out and mail or fax this evaluation to CCH so that we can better provide you with the type of self-study programs you want and need. Thank you.

About This Program

1. Please circle the number that best reflects the extent of your agreement with the following statements:

	Strongly Agree				Strongly Disagree
a. The course objectives were met.	5	4	3	2	1
b. This course was comprehensive and organized.	5	4	3	2	1
c. The content was current and technically accurate.	5	4	3	2	1
d. This course was timely and relevant.	5	4	3	2	1
e. The prerequisite requirements were appropriate.	5	4	3	2	1
f. This course was a valuable learning experience.	5	4	3	2	1
g. The course completion time was appropriate.	5	4	3	2	1

2. This course was most valuable to me because of:

_____ Continuing Education credit   _____ Convenience of format

_____ Relevance to my practice/   _____ Timeliness of subject matter
      employment   _____ Reputation of author

                                         _____ Price

_____ Other (please specify)

3. How long did it take to complete this course? (Please include the total time spent reading or studying reference materials, and completing CPE quizzer).

   Module 1 _____   Module 2 _____

4. What do you consider to be the strong points of this course?

5. What improvements can we make to this program?

Evaluation Form *cont'd*

General Interests

1. Preferred method of self-study instruction:

    ____ Text   ____ Audio   ____ Computer-based/Multimedia   ____ Video

2. What specific topics would you like CCH to develop as self-study programs? (Select more than one if appropriate.)

    ____ Accounting Standards   ____ Auditing
    ____ Compilation and Review   ____ Financial Reporting
    ____ Fraud   ____ Government Standards

3. Please list other topics of interest to you _____

    _____

    _____

About You

1. Your profession:

    ____ Accountant   ____ Auditor
    ____ Controller   ____ CPA
    ____ Enrolled Agent   ____ Risk Manager
    ____ Other (please specify) _____

2. Your employment:

    ____ Self-employed   ____ Public Accounting Firm
    ____ Service Industry   ____ Non-Service Industry
    ____ Banking/Finance   ____ Government
    ____ Education   ____ Other _____

3. Size of firm/corporation:

    ____ 1   ____ 2-5   ____ 6-10   ____ 11-20   ____ 21-50   ____ 51+

4. Your Name _____

    Firm/Company Name _____

    Address _____

    City, State, Zip Code _____

5. I would like to be informed of new CCH Continuing Education products by electronic message. My e-mail address is: _____.
    If you prefer, send your e-mail address to CCH.CPE@cch.com.

THANK YOU FOR TAKING THE TIME TO COMPLETE THIS SURVEY!

NOTES

NOTES